D1015438

*f*P

ALSO BY DUSKO DODER AND LOUISE BRANSON

*Gorbachev: Heretic in the Kremlin*

ALSO BY DUSKO DODER

*Shadows and Whispers: Power Politics Inside the Kremlin from Brezhnev to Gorbachev*

*The Yugoslavs*

# MILOSEVIC

## Portrait of a Tyrant

DUSKO DODER AND
LOUISE BRANSON

THE FREE PRESS

THE FREE PRESS
A Division of Simon & Schuster, Inc.
1230 Avenue of the Americas
New York, NY 10020



Designed by Ellen R. Sasahara

Manufactured in the United States of America

10 9 8 7 6 5 4 3 2 1

Library of Congress Cataloging-in-Publication Data

Doder, Dusko.
Milosevic : portrait of a tyrant / Dusko Doder and Louise Branson.
p. cm.
Includes bibliographical references and index.
1. Milošević, Slobodan, 1941– . 2. Presidents—Yugoslavia—Serbia Biography. 3. Serbia—Politics and government—1945– . 4. Yugoslavia—Politics and government—1980–1992. 5. Yugoslavia—Ethnic relations. I. Branson, Louise. II. Title.
DR2047.M55D63 1999 99-41729 CIP
949.7103'092—dc21
[B]

ISBN 0-684-84308-0

for Thomas and Nicholas

# Contents

# Acknowledgments

Most of the information for this book was gathered while we lived in Belgrade on journalistic assignments from 1990 to 1996. So many people have helped us in various ways that it would be invidious to try to list them—even if there were no risk in acknowledging those who still live under Milosevic's dictatorship. We are indebted to them, and we hope that this book will prove useful once they are permitted to publicly examine the misdeeds committed in their name by this singularly malevolent dictator.

First and foremost, we want to thank our superb editor, Paul Golob, for his discernment, imagination, and unstinting support; this is also his book.

Our gratitude goes to the U.S. Institute of Peace; its president, Richard H. Solomon; and Joseph Klaits, director of the Jennings Randolph Program for International Peace. Thanks also to Andrew Neil, the former editor in chief of the Sunday *Times*.

We also want to thank colleagues and friends who read parts of the manuscript or provided valuable suggestions and other help: Robert J. Lieber, Dennis Snider, Dan Morgan, Mihajlo Mihajlov,

Arkady Lvov, Blaine Harden, William Booth, Alys Yablon, Darren Christensen, Nancy Porterfield, and Predrag Paul of the Library of Congress. However, we alone bear responsibility for the facts and judgments in this book.

Finally, we wish to acknowledge special gratitude to our sons, Thomas and Nicholas, who bore with us as we wrote this book, which is dedicated to them.

SWITZERLAND
AUSTRIA
N
ITALY
SLOVENIA
Ljubljana
Sava R.
Trieste
Zagreb
CROATIA
Kms.
0
75
Miles
75
BRIONI I.
Rakovica
Bihac
KRAJINA
Zadar
Vukovar
Novi Sad
CROATIA
VOJVODINA
ROMANIA
Sava R.
Danube R.
Brcko
Bijeljina
Sabac
Belgrade
Pancevo
Bubanj Potok
Danube R.
Umka
Pozarevac
Tuzla
SUMADIJA
Brezane
Celopek
Zvornik
BOSNIA-HERZEGOVINA
Velika Plana
Bratunac
Valjevo
SERBIA
Han Pijesak
Srebrenica
Sarajevo
Pale
Visegrad
Paracin
Cacak
Jahorina Mtn.
Gorazde
Drina R.
Ivanjice
Krusevac
Black Peak
Aleksandrovac
Nis
Raska
Mt. Durmitor
Banjska
Podujevo
Leskovac
ITALY
MONTENEGRO
Kosovska Mitrovica
Gornje Oberinje
LIJEVA RIJEKA
Uvac
Pec
Pristina
Drenica
Kosovo Polje
Herceg-Novi
Podgorica
Malisevo
Gnjilane
Cetinje
Račak
Stimle
KOSOVO
DJENERAL JANKOVIC
Kukes
Kms.
25
0
25
Miles
ALBANIA
Skopje
MACEDONIA

HUNGARY
ROMANIA
Danube R.
Horgos
Karadjordjevo
Yugoslavia prior to 1991
Present-day Yugoslavia
WESTERN SLAVONIA
EASTERN SLAVONIA
VOJVODINA
Novi Sad
Area of detail
Sava R.
Bosanski Brod
Omarska
Banja Luka
Keraterm
Manjaca
BOSNIA-HERZEGOVINA
Belgrade
Danube R.
SERBIA
Jajce
Travnik
Kakanj
Kupres
Sarajevo
Drina R.
BULGARIA
HERZEGOVINA
DALMATIA
Mostar
MONTENEGRO
Pristina
Sofia
Dubrovnik
Podgorica
KOSOVO
Skopje
ADRIATIC SEA
MACEDONIA
Tirana
Lake Ohrid
ALBANIA
GREECE
Ioannina
Corfu
© A·Karl/J·Kemp, 1999

# Authors' Note

In an effort to make this book more accessible to the general reader, we have adopted some journalistic conventions, especially with respect to the spelling of names and the often complex historical details. We have, for example, usually referred to "Bosnia" rather than the full "Bosnia and Herzegovina." And we have avoided using the accents that occur on many letters.

In the use of the words "Serb" and "Serbian," "Croat" and "Croatian," we have followed the system of the historian Ivo Banac. When used as an adjective, "Serb" refers to people. "Serbian" refers to the language and the attributes of the state. The Serbs live in many parts of the former Yugoslavia: Serbia, Montenegro, Bosnia-Herzegovina, Croatia, and Macedonia. Those living in Serbia are referred to as the Serbians. The Serbs who live in Montenegro are Montenegrins; those living in Bosnia-Herzegovina, we refer to as Bosnian Serbs, and the Serbs living in Croatia's region of Krajina we refer to as Krajina Serbs. Serb nationalists regarded Slobodan Milosevic as the leader of all Serbs the moment he became the president of Serbia.

We have not anglicized any names except those known in the

English-speaking world, such as Prince Alexander or Belgrade, not Beograd. Also, the Croat Fascists during World War II are referred to as the Ustashe, and the Serb royalists as the Chetniks.

We use Serbian names of places in Kosovo, because the majority of world atlases have always used them. For the most part we use Albanian family names as they were spelled by the Albanians in the former Yugoslavia when Serbo-Croatian was the official language. We have also simplified various lengthy and confusing Communist Party titles; for example, we refer to Milosevic as the Communist leader of Belgrade when he assumed the control of the Communist Party organization in the capital, even though his formal title was Secretary of the Belgrade City Committee of the League of Communists of Yugoslavia. For the same reason we refer to the League of Communists by its original name, the Yugoslav Communist Party.

# MILOSEVIC

# Introduction

The scene inside Belgrade's White Palace, home of Serbian kings, had a distinct quality of irrationality.

The special American envoy, Richard Holbrooke, had flown to Belgrade to deliver an ultimatum to Serb leader Slobodan Milosevic. But Milosevic was in no mood to compromise. He would defy the North Atlantic Treaty Organization, the mightiest military alliance in the world. He would not sign a proposed NATO peace treaty for the war-torn Serb province of Kosovo that would mean accepting foreign soldiers on Serbian soil.

"Look, are you absolutely clear in your own mind what will happen when I get up and walk out of this palace that we're now sitting in?" Holbrooke asked.

"You are going to bomb us," replied the president with a coldness on his broad face.

"That's right," said Holbrooke.

Only Milosevic knows for sure what was going on in his mind as he took that fateful decision. Did he think the United States and its NATO allies were bluffing? Was he worried about being deposed if he permitted foreign troops on his soil? Was he concerned about his place in history? Or did he succumb to the demons in his soul to risk a national suicide for the sake of his pride and his power?

Whatever the truth, there was something symbolic about his defiance, something very Serbian in inviting a great tragedy without making a last-ditch attempt to reach the compromise needed to avert ruin. In the historical myth seen as defining the Serb character, the Serb medieval prince, Lazar, similarly decides to accept defeat by the Turks. In return, in songs and stories recounted in Serbia to this day, he gains the glory of the everlasting kingdom of heaven, having allowed no compromise of his nation's honor.

A few hours after Holbrooke shook hands and departed the palace, Milosevic's prime minister went on national television to declare a "state of immediate threat of war." The British Embassy lowered its flag, and other Western embassies, including that of the United States, announced they were closing down. Only Italy and Greece kept their embassies open. A strange feeling of dizziness hung in the air, as if the whole country had been awakened from a deep sleep to find itself poised above an abyss.

As war panic swept the city the next day, the Serb parliament held a day-long televised session of patriotic oratory in support of Milosevic's self-destructive course. As was his habit, the president kept silent.

Two days later, on March 24, 1999, the first bombs fell on Yugoslavia.

Over the next three months, as the air strikes intensified, Kosovo escalated from an ethnic conflict into the most serious crisis of the NATO alliance, which threatened its very future. Milosevic achieved a sort of negative apotheosis as he was vaulted onto the world stage by some malignant destiny.

Enraged world leaders referred to him in the starkest terms—"the heart of darkness," "an evil dictator," "Europe's new Hitler." Yet he remained resolutely in the shadows, allowing no one, not even his own people, a glimpse into his soul and purposes, drawing a veil around his persona.

* * *

The world might never have heard of Slobodan Milosevic, then a gray Communist apparatchik, if he had not been sent in 1987 to the southern Serbian province of Kosovo to mediate what was considered a minor incident in a dispute between the ethnic Albanian majority and minority Serbs. Television footage makes it clear that he was uncertain and apprehensive; fear was evident on his face as he tried to calm a mob of Serbs complaining that Albanian police were mistreating them. But when he uttered the words "No one will ever dare beat you again!" his course was set.

The crowd rewarded him as a hero. It did not matter that his little speech was almost embarrassing in its coldness, with not a breath of spontaneous feeling in the words. What mattered was that he had broken the taboo of the late Communist dictator, Marshal Tito, against invoking nationalism—a taboo credited with submerging ethnic hatreds and holding Yugoslavia together for more than forty years. He had legitimized the venting of Serb ethnic grievances against the Albanian majority.

This might have been the end of him, for he was promptly criticized by his colleagues in the Communist leadership of Serbia, the largest of Yugoslavia's six republics. But the upsurge in his personal popularity was sensational; with that one speech, Milosevic discovered the intoxication, hitherto unknown to any of the Communists, of genuine popularity, and he was shrewd and cunning enough to exploit that popularity to gain power. By the end of 1987, he was the ruler of Serbia.

It was not an auspicious beginning to the reign of a man who foresaw ruling Yugoslavia—not just Serbia—into the twenty-first century. The initial impact was catastrophic: rabid ethnic nationalism swept all regions of Yugoslavia like a disease.

Two years after becoming Serb leader, Milosevic set off the disintegration of the former Yugoslavia in earnest—fittingly enough—at Kosovo Polje, a scene of ancient bloodshed. The date was auspicious: June 28, 1989, the six hundredth anniversary of St. Vitus Day, when the Serb nation—and their prince, Lazar—was defeated by the Muslim Turks on the Field of Blackbirds. After the defeat, the Serbs were ruled by the Turks for five centuries. During that time the battle acquired a mystical significance for the Serbs.

On that sun-drenched day in 1989, on the wide rolling field, almost 2 million people chanted: "Slobo-dan, Slobo-dan" as a freedom mantra. (The name "Slobodan" is derived from "freedom" in Serbo-Croatian.) It was the greatest gathering of Serbs ever; they came from all parts of Yugoslavia, from Europe, North America, and Australia. Milosevic descended from heaven in a battle-green helicopter to rouse the crowd to new heights of nationalist delirium as he paid homage to the dead of six centuries earlier.

Surrounded by black-robed, bearded Orthodox bishops atop an elaborate stage erected for the occasion, he presided at his own coronation, replacing communism with nationalism. Whirling maidens in national costumes danced as he was hailed as the reincarnation of Prince Lazar, who died at that very spot six hundred years earlier while resisting a superior Ottoman army. Never again, Milosevic told them. Nobody would ever enslave the Serb nation, vowed the new prince, who seemed a strong and forceful figure, a man who understood power and possessed the capacity to command.

At this point, he could have afforded to be generous and cast himself and Serbia in a new light. But instead he rattled his saber on that day, Serbia's most sacred, as he identified himself with a holy cause and invoked the spirit of violence.

Only when the cause was won could the saber be sheathed. "After six centuries we are again waging struggle and confronting battles," Milosevic said unflinchingly, staring straight ahead as if reviewing the troops. "These are not armed struggles, though that cannot yet be excluded."

The speech was repeatedly interrupted by the crowd, chanting verses adapted from epic poetry that conferred instant historic greatness on him:

*Oh Tsar Lazar, you didn't have the fortune*
*To walk shoulder to shoulder with Slobo.*

The setting and the occasion had been carefully chosen by the new Serb leader. Kosovo has provided the Serbs with their defining myths of nationalism, pain, and endurance in their songs and ballads. Serb children through the centuries have been taught the words of the long-forgotten bards who transformed the 1389 defeat into an entire moral universe in which Lazar's options are limited: on the eve of the battle, the prophet Elijah appears in the form of a gray falcon to bring Lazar a message from the Mother of God. He is offered the choice of a heavenly or an earthly empire. If he wants the first, he should prepare himself and the Serb Army for destruction. If he desires the second, he should defeat the Turks, or reach an accommodation with them.

Lazar weighs the choice in one of the ballads:

*Kind God, what shall I do, how shall I do it?*
*What is the empire of my choice.*
*Is it the Empire of Heaven?*
*Or is it the empire of earth?*
*And if I shall choose the empire*
*And I choose the empire of earth,*
*The empire of earth is fleeting*
*Heaven is lasting and everlasting*
*And the Tsar chose the Empire of Heaven*
*Above the empire of earth.*

Lazar opts for the kingdom of heaven, which is to say, truth and justice. The Serbs lose. The myth tries to explain their plight by insisting that Lazar made the morally correct decision; dealmaking, maneuvering, flexibility are to be spurned. At the same time, it calls on them to avenge the injustice of Kosovo. No sacrifice is too great for the ultimate good: to free the homeland from foreign rule.

In private conversations with foreign visitors, Milosevic was prone to dismiss Serbia's ancient obsession as "bullshit," yet he cleverly molded it to his political purposes. His propaganda cultivated a popular sense of victimization at the hands of foreigners.

That was the source of his strength, apart from his consummate capacity for lying, intrigue, and secrecy.

But already by 1990, men of talent and substance began issuing warnings that Milosevic was leading the whole of Yugoslavia into disaster. His popularity had plunged; a huge crowd of demonstrators burned a large photograph of Milosevic in central Belgrade on June 13, 1990, shouting: "Red Bandits" and "Out with the Communists." And the man who had promised the Serbs three years earlier that "No one will ever dare beat you again!" now sent thousands of police with truncheons and tear gas against them. Among the injured was the novelist Borislav Pekic; he prophetically noted that the new despot would do anything to maintain himself in power.

By 1991, Milosevic could no longer take a walk in the streets of Belgrade: he was a hated dictator always surrounded by bodyguards in blue suits and dark glasses. When he was seen, a glimmer of a smile would flicker over his habitual scowl. In March 1991, he had to call in tanks, riot police, and tear gas to put down mass demonstrations against his rule.

When the neighboring republics of Croatia in 1991 and Bosnia in 1992 disintegrated into open ethnic warfare, Milosevic used intermediaries to foment and spread the violence, even as he presented the face of total non-involvement to the world. Relying on organized lying, his secret police and rogue proxies pushed the disintegration into a long bloodbath. The U.S. ambassador to Belgrade, Warren Zimmermann, saw in him the cool ruthlessness of evil. "Like most evil men he doesn't seem evil," he reported. "He could be charming, I have seen him charm American visitors."

But things didn't work out according to plan. By mid-1992, after a series of setbacks, Milosevic came close to being toppled from power. His policies and wars had turned Serbia into an economic disaster zone and a global pariah. A floodtide of war refugees was creating serious repercussions throughout Western Europe; the term "ethnic cleansing" had entered the vocabulary as a euphemism for barbaric intolerance, even genocide; the effect of UN sanctions on Serbia was hurting. Secretary of State Lawrence Eagleburger publicly accused Milosevic of war crimes for his role in the

Bosnian war, and indeed there was substantial evidence to justify bringing Milosevic before the International War Crimes Tribunal in the Hague.

Had that happened, the world could have been spared Kosovo. But Milosevic managed to convince the world—with assistance from various international diplomats—that he had converted from warmonger to peacemaker. He was even made the "guarantor" of Bosnia's peace worked out under the agreement at Dayton, Ohio, in November 1995. When the accords were signed, he shared the stage with President Bill Clinton and other high officials.

Ironically, the Dayton accords touched off growing unrest in Kosovo, which had been under police occupation since 1989. Dayton had addressed ethnic conflict in Bosnia but not in Serbia itself, and this failure to bring the plight of Kosovo to the international stage led younger Albanian leaders onto the path of military struggle for independence. By 1997, the newly formed Kosovo Liberation Army had started the struggle which, for the most part, meant warfare in the shadows, ambush, assassination, murder, and torture, leaving in its wake a trail of destroyed towns, burned villages, and wrecked families. A year later, the guerrilla activities had reached significant proportions and elicited brutal Serb countermeasures.

Invoking the threat of air strikes, the Clinton administration pressured Milosevic to restore Kosovo's autonomy. U.S. negotiator Richard Holbrooke, the architect of Dayton, was dispatched to Belgrade to broker a cease-fire. This was followed by "negotiations" at Rambouillet, outside Paris. The warring parties were required to accept a U.S.-drafted peace plan within two weeks, subject only to minor modifications.

It was a doomed enterprise. Despite the threat of NATO air strikes, Milosevic refused to bend.

The American initiative was based on Secretary of State Madeleine K. Albright's belief that Milosevic was likely to back down after an initial wave of air strikes, that he was a "schoolyard bully" who would cave in after a few punches. That was a serious misreading of both the man and the conditions in the region. Military and intelligence officials expressed doubts that airpower alone could bend Milosevic's will.

In their calculations, American strategists were guided by the Dayton experience, believing that Milosevic could be counted on to opt for an earthly empire and an accommodation in order to keep himself in power. But whereas Milosevic gave in on most of the demands of the Bosnian Serbs at Dayton, this time, he could not relinquish Kosovo—which Serbs regarded as the heart of Serbia itself—and hope to survive. He dismissed his generals when they confronted him with the sobering technicalities of the military balance. Milosevic was fatalism itself: war had been the way for him to hang on to his earthly empire—war in Slovenia, in Croatia, in Bosnia, and again in Kosovo—and he chose this path despite warnings that it would mean the physical destruction of Serbia.

The NATO ultimatum, with its uncanny echoes of the mythical message brought to Lazar by the gray falcon, presented Milosevic with an agonizing choice: he could accept a plan giving Kosovo Albanians home rule with a NATO force on the ground to supervise it (and virtually ensuring their secession after three years). Or he could stand up to a mighty foe and risk annihilation.

When NATO air strikes finally came in March 1999, Milosevic responded with the ethnic cleansing of Kosovo that brought his true nature to the surface. Whatever his past misdeeds—the sowing of racial hatred that consumed Yugoslavia, waging wars against Croatia and Bosnia, his colonial subjugation of Albanians—Milosevic's move to denude Kosovo of its Albanian population was one of the most cynical acts in Europe in the second half of a bloody century. In scenes that evoked images from the Holocaust, tens of thousands of Albanian refugees were herded out of Kosovo into neighboring countries while the United States and its NATO allies, with all their military power, watched impotently.

The NATO missile strikes and air bombardments were met with Serb defiance. Faced with a foreign assault, the people rallied around Milosevic and mocked Western claims that NATO had no quarrel with the Serbian people but only with their leaders.

Milosevic calculated—correctly as it turned out, at least in the short run—that the spectacle of a leader uncompromisingly rejecting a foreign ultimatum fitted the nation's psyche, much as Lazar had refused to accommodate to the Turks in 1389. There arose a wave of patriotic euphoria which projected Milosevic as the leader of a united people embarked on a holy cause. The nation's top military commander, speaking in the language of the myth, told his troops to "prepare for martyrdom."

But the air war began to grind down Serbia's will to resist. And Milosevic was undercut by his indictment by the International War Crimes Tribunal in the Hague on May 27 on charges of crimes against humanity. Thinking about his political survival, he concluded that months of additional bombing might utterly devastate Serbia and destroy the remnants of his support. On June 3, he capitulated, accepting a Western peace plan supported by Russia that was only a slight improvement on Rambouillet. The NATO air strikes continued until June 10, when a detailed agreement was reached on complete Serb withdrawal from Kosovo, which became in effect an international protectorate under NATO control.

Milosevic addressed the nation that evening from the ornate state room in the White Palace, saying, "we never lost Kosovo," and listing cosmetic provisions of the agreement to prove his assertion that "we have survived and we defended the country." His speech again tapped into the Serb mythology which casts heroic resistance as something like a victory. His party claimed he had inspired a small nation to a noble struggle against the world's mightiest military alliance.

At bottom, however, Milosevic was guided as much by Serb mythology as by some dark spirit inside his soul. Some forensic psychologists have speculated that Milosevic is a depressive, scarred by a family history of suicide and abandonment. With respect to NATO and perhaps his own people, he may be playing out a syndrome known as "suicide by cop" in which individuals provoke others to kill them. Certainly, he has instigated mighty forces—external and internal—against himself. If he leaves his country, he risks arrest and transportation to the Hague to face war crimes charges. A $5 million bounty, offered by the U.S. government to anyone providing information "leading to the arrest or conviction" of Milosevic "in any country," was bound to heighten his sense of isolation and danger. In Serbia, with the patriotic fever subsiding, his grip on power could weaken once the population grasps the full scope of the economic ruin. More than ever, his only support came from a large police force and an army that had withstood NATO's air assaults without cracking.

Milosevic's history in more than ten years as Serbia's ruler reveals a man whose only pleasure lies in controlling others. The psychologists surmise that he lives in a narcissistic, self-centered place where he is the sun and everything revolves around him. He does not think about what he will be doing five years from now, for he does not expect to live that long. Indeed, he seems not to care what happens after he is gone—not about his legacy or his children, and certainly not his people. But he takes great pleasure in the attention he receives on the world stage.

One thing is for certain. He is not a man to go quietly. Slobodan Milosevic is the Saddam Hussein of Europe, doomed to wreak havoc and go to war—as he has done repeatedly already—in order to preserve his own power and distract his people's attention from repression and poverty. As long as he remains in power, he will be an impediment to stability in the Balkans. In little more than a decade, he has brought post–cold war Europe back to the matter that dominated the beginning of the twentieth century and led to World War I: the matter of Serbia—the definition of the Serb nation, its borders, its destiny, and its leadership. In the process he has reawakened atavistic nationalist demons, bringing uncertainty to Europe at the dawn of the twenty-first century. To understand how that matter manifests itself, we must first understand the man who embodies it.

# I

# Cold Narcissus

Montenegro is a small region of majestic mountain ranges that rise above the Adriatic Sea. After the collapse of the medieval Serb kingdom in 1389, Serb tribes withdrew into these inaccessible mountains, refused to acknowledge Turkish authority, and established their own state. The land was poor; it was cultivated by women. The men practiced only one occupation—they were warriors. Deeply ingrained in their consciousness were the ideas of independence, honor, and physical courage. The principality, whose total population at the end of the nineteenth century was about seventy thousand, was ruled by the prince-bishop, giving the state a religious component that reinforced its anti-Turkish politics. Montenegrins' love of freedom, their ferociousness in battle, and their reckless bravery were largely a response to a beleaguered form of life. The Montenegrins' motto was coined by their most famous poet: "Die gloriously, when you must die."

The roots of Montenegro's independence lay in an oral tradition. The people preserved the legend of Kosovo, adding to it the exploits of their ancestors, which were passed down through generations as richly embroidered stories and legends. Against their primitive existence and excruciating poverty, the tales of ancestral valor provided the highlanders with an immense sense of pride in their family and clan traditions. They were known for their single-mindedness of purpose, quick temper, and bravery.

Montenegrin researchers cite genealogical evidence showing that Slobodan Milosevic's family can be traced to the legendary 1389 Kosovo battle and the Strahinic clan of Banjska, near the town of Kosovska Mitrovica. Milosevic is also a descendant of Milos, the son of Marko (at that time the Montenegrins had no family names), the Montenegrin chieftain renowned for his military campaigns against the Turks in the first decades of the eighteenth century. Milosevic's grandfather Simeun was a senior officer in the Royal Montenegrin Army, with the rank of captain first class, and had distinguished himself in several battles against the Turks.

There is a thin line between the heroic and the bizarre. For some, as for Lord Tennyson, Montenegro was a "rough rock-throne of Freedom." Others viewed the Montenegrins as curious savages. In her brilliant book *Black Lamb and Grey Falcon* (1941), Rebecca West quotes Sir Gardner Wilkinson, an English visitor to Montenegro in the 1840s. Expecting an encounter with ignorant and superstitious natives, Sir Gardner was immensely impressed by his host, the prince, who spoke a number of foreign languages and seemed a serious student of philosophy. But one thing scandalized and distressed the Englishman: he saw Turkish heads displayed as trophies on stakes in the capital of Cetinje. The Englishman remonstrated with the prince, who replied that he could do nothing about it. If the Serbs stopped paying out the Ottomans in their own coin, the prince said, the Turks would interpret this as a sign of weakness.

Deeply shocked, Sir Gardner traveled to the Ottoman-held province of Herzegovina and called on its Turkish governor, the vizier of Mostar. The Englishman was "still more shocked" by the sight of Montenegrin heads fixed on stakes around the vizier's office. The practice would not be proscribed by the prince until 1876, in response to news stories in the European press that described the Montenegrins as "head-hunters." Even so, the highlanders during the next thirty years would return from battles with ears and noses cut from their Turkish victims to prove their valor.

Throughout the Ottoman centuries in the Balkans, only tiny Montenegro managed to live in freedom until, following a rebellion in the early nineteenth century, Serbia won political autonomy and then independence. Other South Slavs gained freedom in 1918 after the collapse of the Ottoman and Austro-Hungarian Empires in World War I. They voluntarily joined Serbia and Montenegro in forming a new state; but the Serbs always believed that they were the heart of Yugoslavia, which they had created with their own blood from the ruins of the Ottoman and Austrian Empires.

Hitler and Mussolini conquered Yugoslavia in 1941, but faced a strong guerrilla resistance. By 1944, Marshal Josip Broz Tito's Communist Partisans emerged as the masters of the country, which they re-created as a federation of six South Slav republics. One of them was Montenegro, which once again became a political entity, joined by Serbia, Croatia, Slovenia, Bosnia-Herzegovina, and Macedonia.

Tito not only made Montenegro a republic, but also decreed its people a separate nationality. Tito's senior deputy at the time, Milovan Djilas, admitted after his fall from power that Tito's goal was to dilute the dominance of the Serbs, the largest tribe in Yugoslavia, and Djilas himself was "particularly involved in advancing untenable theoretical explanations concerning the Montenegrin nation."

Djilas, a Montenegrin Serb, defined in one of his novels the relationship between the Serbs and the Montenegrins: "I am not a Montenegrin because I am a Serb, but I am a Serb because I am a Montenegrin. We Montenegrins are the salt of the Serbs. All the strength of the Serbs is not here [in Montenegro], but their soul is."

A generation later, Slobodan Milosevic eagerly accepted this definition. The Serbs and the Montenegrins, he declared, "are like two eyes in the head."

Explaining a man in terms of supposed ethnic traits is a perilous enterprise. Milosevic's father and mother grew up in a Montenegro in which the clan structure was dissolving to make way for a modern political system. They moved to Serbia the year Milosevic was born, which meant that he never lived in Montenegro. Yet his roots may account for his self-confidence and a profound, rich arrogance that set him apart from other Serb politicians; he was so sure of himself that he felt no need to flaunt his authority and indeed preferred others to take the limelight that goes with pomp and ceremony. To the end he remained, at least in spirit, a mountain man.

When Ivor Roberts, the British ambassador, asked him in 1997 whether his family had lived in the mountains or along Montenegro's sea coast—an important distinction—Milosevic replied: "The mountains, of course. The only true Montenegrin people are mountain people."

Slobodan Milosevic's origins were humble and inauspicious. He was born on August 22, 1941, in the small town of Pozarevac, a drab, provincial backwater about an hour's drive east of Belgrade, the capital of both Serbia and Yugoslavia. The town's reputation, to the extent it had one, was based on a large nineteenth-century prison with which its name had become synonymous.

His parents, Svetozar and Stanislava Milosevic, moved to Pozarevac from Montenegro earlier that year with their three-year-old son, Borislav. It was the year of Nazi Germany's attack on Yugoslavia. Waves of Luftwaffe planes destroyed a good portion of central Belgrade in a single day. The black Gestapo flags and swastikas were soon fluttering in the central square of Pozarevac and throughout Serbia. The resistance movement immediately mounted a campaign of diversion and terror, and the subsequent merciless German retribution has lived in popular memory ever since. When a handful of German soldiers lost their lives in a battle with the Partisans, the Nazis went into a high school in a town not far from Pozarevac and machine-gunned all the students and their teachers in the schoolyard.

Slobodan spent the war years barely aware of the privations and uncertain times he was living through. He was four when the war ended and Tito's Partisans seized control of Yugoslavia.

It is difficult to imagine how devastated, poor, and hungry Yugoslavians were after the war. Milk, lard, cheese, and other foodstuffs were rationed; the main source of protein came in the shape of powdered eggs—dubbed "Truman eggs"—a novelty supplied by the United States through the UN relief agencies. Children were without shoes. They studied in cold classrooms where books were as scarce as sacred scrolls. The women of Pozarevac made their own soap and washed clothes on a wooden board. Refrigerators were unknown. There were no cars, except a few hundred for the use of top officials and generals. No gas stations. No central heating.

Communism and Communist fervor were in the air—including in the modest Milosevic home in Pozarevac. His mother, a schoolteacher, became a party member, something perhaps natural for the sister of General Milislav Koljensic, a Partisan war hero and a senior general in Tito's military intelligence. But Slobodan's father, Svetozar, a defrocked Orthodox priest, did not join the party.

The Yugoslav Communists infused the country with fanaticism, optimism, and hope in the early years—which were also the early years of Milosevic's life. The victorious Partisans were a people of extremes. They were more Communist, more fanatical, more hardline than anyone, and their imaginations were fired by the heroes of oral tradition. Communism, to them, was meant to be Utopia. The wartime Partisan struggle under Tito was mythologized out of any resemblance to the truth: each written word, each broadcast had to further the progress of communism, and the party was represented as the purest of humankind's hopes for the future.

But while the Yugoslav Communist revolution and Milosevic were still young, the country was thrown into turmoil in 1948 when Tito refused to take orders from Moscow and took his country out of the Soviet bloc. Since the whole of the Soviet bloc had until then been portrayed as paradise, with Stalin in Moscow as the sun, an unimaginable thing had occurred. It posed a traumatic choice for many party members, including Milosevic's beloved uncle Milislav, who had been taught to love Stalin and who identified communism with Soviet Russia with a mysticism akin to religious rural youth daydreaming about paradise.

Uncle Milislav, the Partisan hero, shot himself through the

head. He left no note. There was no investigation of the incident. But conventional wisdom held that Tito's break with Moscow may have been too traumatic for someone who believed that the Soviet Union was the shining way of the future. The suicide was a stigma for the family in the context of the times, smacking of betrayal of his country.

It was the first trauma for young Slobodan. His mother's brother had been a major figure and hero in his life to that point.

Two years later, Slobodan suffered another blow. His father abandoned his wife and two sons and returned to Montenegro to teach Russian. Slobodan and Borislav remained with their mother in Pozarevac. Just what caused the breakup of the marriage is uncertain, but failed marriages, rare at the time, were regarded with utmost disapproval in provincial Serbia. Old Pozarevac ladies still gossip about his parents as last-ditch depressives whose vision of life was bleak.

Stanislava insisted that her boys not show their poverty as she struggled alone to bring them up. Women in Pozarevac remember her as an austere and industrious person whose life revolved around her sons; she instilled faith in communism into them.

This sequence of traumatic events served primarily to harden Slobodan's character. His survival instinct was reinforced and for the rest of his life he would always be on guard. And a loner. His relatives in their ancestral village of Uvac, high in the mountains in the Lijeva Rijeka region of northern Montenegro, remember the two boys' visits during school holidays. "I remember them playing together, seeing who could throw rocks the furthest," recalled a cousin, Mitar Milosevic, years later. "His brother always used to win. I could never have imagined either of the boys would become president of Yugoslavia, but if one had to be, I would have said Borislav. He was taller, more handsome, he spoke several languages."

On the surface, Slobodan was uninspiring and conformist. He was a good student, serious and disciplined, though he was not interested in sports. A stocky boy, with typical Serb features of rounded face and high forehead, he did not strike his classmates as anyone who would make a mark in life. "I thought he would make a good pedantic bureaucrat, perhaps the railway stationmaster," said one. Slobodan completed high school at the top of his class.

It was at school that he met Mirjana Markovic, his first—and his friends believe his only—girlfriend, who would exert a powerful influence over him and Yugoslavia's future. Though she was already a member of the Communist elite when they met, Mirjana had been traumatized by its treatment of her mother, Vera Miletic.

Miletic had forsaken the privileges of her wealthy family to become a Communist while studying French at Belgrade University. She met and had an affair with a young Partisan named Moma Markovic, who was already a senior member of the Communist Party. Shortly after the Nazis attacked Belgrade in the spring of 1941, Markovic fled into the mountains to organize Partisan resistance while Vera remained in Belgrade and joined the underground resistance; she was appointed secretary of the Belgrade Communist organization. The couple's daughter, Mirjana, was born on July 10, 1942, in the village of Brezane, as her mother hid in the house of a wealthy farmer who was a Communist supporter. The baby was almost immediately dispatched to her grandparents in Pozarevac; her mother returned to the dangerous work of organizing disruptive actions against the Germans in Belgrade.

Mira claims that the first thing she remembers was being hidden in a storage cupboard amid firewood at her grandparents' home, as soldiers searched for her renowned Partisan mother. That may be true, but it was more likely a story her grandparents told her, since she was only a baby at the time.

Vera Miletic's luck ran out in March 1943, when she was captured by the Gestapo. Soon afterward, scores of leading Communists were arrested, destroying the underground network. This wave of arrests prompted suspicions that Miletic had betrayed her comrades, including an undercover agent. The party's official history refers to her "cowardly behavior," language reserved for traitors.

There are two versions of Vera Miletic's execution later that year. They both agree on one point: that she was subjected to severe torture. Communist propaganda at that time asserted that she died at the hands of the Gestapo. But that version could have been invented to shield her lover, Moma Markovic. In the course of the Partisan resistance he had distinguished himself as a guerrilla general and was formally proclaimed a people's hero, as was his brother, Draza Markovic, who became one of Tito's top lieutenants and the Communist leader of Serbia. It is more likely that Vera was killed by the Communists themselves, who captured Belgrade in 1944 and gained access to police files. Moma Markovic, in his memoirs, *War and Revolution,* condemned Vera as a traitor. She and another imprisoned Communist, he wrote, had "revealed everything about the work of the party in a detailed report they wrote for the police. Both were executed in 1944." However, all documents about the case disappeared when Slobodan Milosevic rose to the top of the Serbian state.

Mira's father, like Slobodan's, abandoned her immediately after the war when he formed a new family. Mira stayed in Pozarevac to be raised by her grandparents. She saw her father only during summer holidays on Brioni, Tito's private Adriatic island off the northern coast of Croatia. The Yugoslav leader owned a sumptuous mansion and vineyards on the island and built several other villas for his top associates, whom he invited to vacation there as a mark of special favor. He would also entertain world leaders on Brioni.

Mira should have felt favored, too, among the Communist elite. But she hated these visits. She felt unwanted, an outsider. She looked at her father, she said later in an interview, "but saw before me a man who did not feel he was my father." Having been rejected by him and his family, she fiercely clung to the memory of her late mother, whom she viewed as a victim of "unscrupulous colleagues."

Items her mother knitted for her in prison became holy relics: a needlework red Communist star, woolen booties, and a heart with her name on it. Her favorite literary work was *Antigone,* the Greek tragedy in which a young woman struggles to rehabilitate the memory and reputation of her beloved brother, who has been killed for defying the tyrant Creon. She was reading *Antigone* in the school library in 1958, seeking solace after getting a C in history, when Slobodan walked in and began talking to her. He was seventeen, she sixteen.

"Her sorrow attracted her to him," wrote her friend Liljana Habjanovic-Djurovic. "He felt the need to relieve her pain, to protect and cherish her."

From that point on, the two emotionally bruised teenagers were inseparable. Mira abandoned her girlfriends. She told Habjanovic-Djurovic that Slobodan made her "no longer afraid of the winter, nor darkness, nor mosquitoes, nor the beginning of the school year, nor a possible C in math." He was always on her side, whether she was right or wrong. "We nicknamed them Romeo and Juliet," recalled Radomir Mladenovic, an old friend who now operates the Café Godfather on the outskirts of town, "because from about the age of sixteen they were never apart. She always dressed like a middle-aged woman.

"At the *korzo* [promenade] they wouldn't talk to the rest of us kids. They were always in the third row with the older people, talking to schoolteachers." Mladenovic remembered hanging out with Slobodan in the yard of the church behind the school, but only if a teacher had failed to turn up. "He was always very conscientious and always attended classes. He used to brush his hair back and tried to look older, more serious. He was a modest guy, really."

Mira and Slobodan were always together at the *korzo,* a ritual in provincial towns where young people would parade in the evenings down the one Pozarevac street that retained a mix of elegant nineteenth-century stucco homes and even older single-story shops with tile roofs dating back to Ottoman times. Slobodan must have walked countless times past the statue to Prince Milos Obrenovic, a fighter against the Turks, with the inscription so sacred to the Serbs: "Life in freedom or death." But that inscription seemed to belong to a different, bygone era.

Mira was the one with the more obvious bitterness, a trait that may well over time have fed the darker side of her husband's nature. Many Serbs feel it was Mira who pushed her husband toward the apex of power, partly in an effort to rehabilitate her mother, as well as to prove herself to her prominent Communist family, which she felt had rejected her.

Even at that early stage in their relationship, according to her memoirs, Mira saw herself as the more ambitious, romantic, and sophisticated partner, who shaped her future husband. "He was a simple and pragmatic boy," she wrote, "who never showed any inclination for long coffee bar conversations and meditations aloud." She, by contrast, was someone with sophisticated and refined tastes—from Sartre novels to Resnais's *Last Year in Marienbad*—who always wore black.

On quiet evenings, Mira would recite her favorite lines, which Slobo remembered. Her ideas influenced him so much, according to Habjanovic-Djurovic, that he would begin to "utter her thoughts and assessments as his own, unaware of where she ends and he begins."

She adhered fiercely to the Communist ideology her mother had fought for. "Communism is in my genes," she is fond of saying, even today. Apart from her father and her uncle, both of them Communist leaders of Serbia under Tito, she had a claim to the Communist elite through her aunt, Davorjanka Paunovic, a frail but beautiful college student who had been Tito's wartime secretary and mistress. Tito was deeply in love with her and they lived together in the White Palace after the Communists seized Belgrade in 1944. Tito was heartbroken when she died of tuberculosis two years later; he had her body buried in the White Palace garden outside his bedroom window.

Mira's dedication to her mother's memory was total. Although her full name is Mirjana, she insisted that she be called Mira, which was her mother's Communist nom de guerre. Despite being a Communist, she started marking the religious day of her mother's patron saint, St. Nicholas. She wanted everyone to believe that her mother had not been a traitor. She told her friends that even if her mother had betrayed her comrades, she must have succumbed only when the torture had gone beyond the realm of human endurance. For Mira, her mother was pure as the driven snow—in contrast, she wrote later, "to party intriguers who have thrown mud at her."

Slobodan and Mira, both good students, went on together to study at Belgrade University. She majored in sociology; he took up law. In later years, she would publicly blame him for pushing her into that subject—considered more practical in the Communist era—rather than letting her follow her dreams and study literature, her true love, and become a writer.

There were few signs marking the couple as future partners in power who would shape the tragic destiny of Yugoslavia. They embraced the Communist ideology with enthusiasm and joined the Communist Party, which, as in all other Communist states, was the single road to success. Slobodan had joined first, on January 15, 1959, while he was still in high school. Mira followed a year later.

The route to power led first to Belgrade. At university, they threw themselves into party activism. It was perhaps the first hint of Slobodan's ambition to exercise power over others. He became such a true Bolshevik that he was known as "Little Lenin." One of his classmates, Nebojsa Popov, who is today a leading democratic opposition leader, likes to say that he launched Milosevic on his political career by promoting him to be his deputy in the powerful Communist Party organization of the law school. "The other candidate was much smarter, but he was born in the same region as I," Popov explained. "So I had to avoid the impression of favoring my friends and chose Milosevic instead."

It was here, too, that the young Slobodan first demonstrated his talent for manipulation and political survival. Popov recalled that Milosevic was a master apparatchik—"he was a genius of the party apparat, and when we had to get something done, he was certainly the most efficient person around." It was this experience—organizing rallies, mobilizing students for "volunteer" work, patiently networking—that gave him an understanding of the importance of party organization and that would later enable him to maintain an iron grip on the power structure even without the support of Marxist ideology.

In his third year, Milosevic was put on the party payroll as an activist in charge of ideology.

One public manifestation of Milosevic's Bolshevik spirit—and of his growing ambition—occurred in 1963, during a constitutional debate at Belgrade University's Law School, with a number of top Communist officials in attendance. Tito had decided to drop the Stalinist phrase "People's Republic" from the official name of the country; the new official name was to be: the Federal Socialist Republic of Yugoslavia. During the debate, Milosevic raised his hand to propose a change in the word order to put the emphasis on the word "Socialist." The proposal was endorsed and the amendment drafted. For the next three decades, the country's official name would bear Milosevic's stamp: the Socialist Federal Republic of Yugoslavia.

Milosevic had come to understand that to rise in the party one must gain power over others, but that one must do so patiently and unobtrusively, without exposing oneself to attacks. He had seen how talented men and women who exposed their ambitions were promptly sidelined by the party. He had to work within the party. His colleague Jagos Djuretic recalled an incident during a seminar for the political leadership of Belgrade University. "Milosevic and I were the two representatives of the Law School and we were together virtually round the clock throughout the four-day-long seminar. I remember our long discussions. Our views were absolutely identical when we criticized student careerists who shamelessly tried to ingratiate themselves to 'top comrades.' And this was one of the reasons that I decided to remove my name from the list of candidates for the next university party committee. I told Slobo my decision was irrevocable. And you know, he was surprised. He could not understand it. And I thought, even then, that he was more realistic about the phenomenon of politics."

And yet Djuretic never suspected that his young Bolshevik friend—always considerate, cooperative, helpful—harbored high ambitions of his own. "We saw him as an energetic young Bolshevik," Djuretic recalled, a skilled operative who possessed "a clear understanding of what is politically essential" as well as a high degree of self-confidence. "Only later I began to think these very qualities breed lack of tolerance and the belief that almost anything can be resolved by the use of force."

Only Mira knew of Slobo's secret ambitions. The journalist Slava Djukic, in his book *He, She and We,* quotes a conversation between Mira and her cousin during a family holiday in the Adriatic city of Zadar in the fall of 1968. While walking in the town square, the two women stopped by a shop window in which Tito's photograph was prominently displayed.

"One day Slobo's photograph will also be there," Mira said in a whisper.

"What do you mean? You think Slobo will be president of Serbia?"

"Slobo's picture, like Tito's, will be displayed in shop windows," Mira replied.

At the university, the promising young Bolshevik met Ivan Stambolic, an engaging man five years older who became his best friend and mentor, and who was to play the most important role in Milosevic's life.

Stambolic, a gangly young man with blue eyes and a winning smile, came from a patriarchal family of farmers in a village near Ivanjice who were Communist supporters during the war. He was one of three brothers. As was the custom in such families at the time, children's future careers were determined by their parents. In Ivan's case, one brother was sent to school to obtain a higher education, one was to be a farmer, and Ivan was to become an industrial worker.

Ivan indeed followed the path set for him. After high school, he was employed first at a machine tool factory in Cacak, then moved to the Rakovica motor factory outside Belgrade. Although his uncle, Petar Stambolic, was among the ten top Communist officials in Yugoslavia, Ivan lived the life of an ordinary worker. But Ivan, while anxious to please his parents, was also ambitious. He wanted to follow his brothers and make something of himself. So he began working the night shift at Rakovica and enrolled at the Belgrade University Law School the same year as Milosevic. The two awkward provincials met in the corridors and instantly took a fancy to each other. Soon they became fast friends. Like Milosevic, Stambolic was a party member too, but one whose famous name and family connections were bound to put him on the fast track.

In 1962, while Milosevic was studying in Belgrade, getting his first taste of a wider world, news came from Montenegro that his father had committed suicide. An investigation revealed that he had suffered from depression. The trigger may have been the suicide of one of his students whom he had flunked.

None of Slobodan's former classmates could recall his reaction when he received the news after some delay—he was visiting Russia at the time with a student group and did not attend the funeral. His father had been a distant figure for most of his life, and the only time Milosevic mentioned the incident was to deny that it ever took place.

Milosevic finished Law School in 1964 near the top of his class, with an average of 8.90 out of 10. The mark would have been higher had it not been for the consistently low grades he got in "premilitary education," a mandatory subject for all students (something akin to the ROTC program on American campuses). Indeed, he had always had problems when it came to demonstrating physical agility and prowess.

Upon graduation, he decided to stay in Belgrade, the center of federal power and the capital city of Serbia. He even declared himself a Serb on his Yugoslav passport, forsaking the Montenegrin identity of his parents. He and Mira were married on March 14, 1965. She was already pregnant with their first child, Marija.

Over the course of the 1960s, Milosevic held a number of party positions in the Belgrade city government. He was economic adviser for the city mayor for three years before he did his obligatory military service in 1968. During the separation from Mira, they wrote letters to each other once or twice a day (she still keeps them all in bags with a floral design). She said she dreamed about his having the more romantic occupation of architect and she would still have liked to have been a writer. But Milosevic was finding a place on the lower rungs of power, and he was gaining lessons in how power was exercised. At the end of 1968, he was appointed chief of the information department of the city government. In this job he acquired his propaganda skills, particularly the understanding of the power of media and the way to control them.

In Tito's system, censorship and media management were based on direct links between the party's ideological and propaganda department and the top officers of media outlets. Top Communist politicians were placed in charge of all outlets to ensure that instructions were carried out to maintain the faith of the masses by controlling the flow of information. For example, the director of the daily newspaper *Politika* was invariably a senior Communist politician, while its managing editor was a professional journalist, usually one of the most distinguished professionals. The party relied primarily on these two men; but senior politicians regularly attended the meetings of the Communist Party organizations within media outlets to explain party policies and ensure compliance.

Mira continued her graduate studies at the less prestigious University of Nis, about 170 miles south of Belgrade, and successfully defended her doctoral dissertation. She combined teaching Marxist sociology at Belgrade University and raising Marija. A second child, Marko, was born much later, in 1976.

Milosevic's mentor Ivan Stambolic rapidly moved up the ladder of the party hierarchy with the help of his uncle. After serving as director general of Technogas, a state energy company, he was appointed director of the Belgrade Chamber of Commerce in 1970, then secretary of the Serbian Central Committee, and finally prime minister of Serbia in 1975. Stambolic in turn helped Milosevic advance. Milosevic replaced Stambolic as director general of Technogas in 1970. Five years later, in one of his first actions as prime minister, Stambolic appointed Milosevic president of Beobanka, the largest state-run bank.

In 1972, Milosevic suffered another emotional blow when he was informed by telephone call from his hometown of Pozarevac that his mother Stanislava had hanged herself from a living-room light fitting. In the town, the gossip was that she was broken-hearted because after her sons' success—for which she had struggled ceaselessly—they and their wives rarely visited her. She and Mira actively disliked each other: a friend quoted Milosevic shortly after his mother's death as saying, "She never forgave me for Mira." There was no official investigation of the incident, but critics of Milosevic who knew his tragic family history would later comment that it was no wonder that "it's hard to spook Slobo."

Milosevic also began learning another skill which he would later use with success on a series of powerful people, including Western leaders. He discovered that he had the power to charm and flatter, to disguise his true intentions and ambitions. Orthodox Marxists in the party hierarchy regarded him as a staunch Bolshevik. At the same time, Western diplomats saw him as a young and energetic bank president who was pragmatic, reasonable, and pro-Western. He played his roles well: he talked liberal economics to one audience while he emphasized the need to maintain Marxist orthodoxy to another. He became friends with Lawrence Eagleburger, the U.S. ambassador to Belgrade from 1977 to 1981, and with a number of other American diplomats and bankers, including David Rockefeller of Chase Manhattan. They saw in him a new breed of liberal Communist. He was a frequent guest at Eagleburger's dinner table and their friendship continued after Eagleburger's tour of duty in Belgrade was over.

Milosevic's most important constituency, though, was Ivan Stambolic. He cultivated the relationship: the two families met regularly for barbecues, spent holidays together. Milosevic always brought gifts to Stambolic's wife, Katja, from his frequent trips to New York—he made about sixty trips there during his years as bank president. "I love him like a brother," Stambolic frequently told his friends. Milosevic played to his vanity, without falling into sycophancy. Stambolic saw him, in retrospect, as "a good servant, but a bad master."

In 1980, Tito's death at age eighty-eight changed all the rules of politics in Yugoslavia. But not immediately. At first, fear forced the ruling Communist oligarchy to close ranks and maintain the same course. Milosevic remained in his bank job, but became more active in his volunteer party work in the Old Town district of Belgrade.

The country was now ruled by a hopelessly inefficient collective presidency that Tito had devised, an eight-man presidency with representatives from each of the six republics—Slovenia, Croatia, Bosnia, Serbia, Montenegro, and Macedonia—and Serbia's two autonomous regions, Kosovo and Vojvodina. The titular head of state was a position that rotated annually. Yugoslavia had a federal parliament, six republican and two provincial assemblies, and a federal government. But while Tito was alive there was no doubt who held the reins of power.

Now Yugoslavia was turning into a country of eight regional Communist parties and eight regional governments. The fragmentation proceeded rapidly, which was a somewhat unsettling experience for a one-party country accustomed to one man's control. But this was not immediately apparent as the regional oligarchs maintained the appearance of cohesion to protect their power.

The only Yugoslav institution not directly affected by the fragmentation was the army. It decayed for a different reason: it no longer had a universally accepted and respected commander in chief.

Already a year after Tito's death, in the fall of 1981, ethnic Albanians took to the streets of Pristina, the capital of Kosovo, demanding independence from Serbia and that Kosovo become the seventh republic of Yugoslavia. The protests were crushed by the federal army and police. The incident ushered in a period of political uncertainty, with Kosovo becoming the focal point for Serbia's disaffection with the Yugoslav federation. The reasons were obvious to the Serbs. They were the biggest nation, twice as populous as the second largest, the Croats. The Yugoslav constitution was designed to weaken Serbia. In theory, Serbia had three seats on the collective presidency—Kosovo and Vojvodina being parts of Serbia—but in practice the two autonomous provinces were often hostile to Belgrade's interests. Moreover, Kosovo's huge Albanian majority demanded independence from Serbia.

In Belgrade, the Kosovo problem was soon placed on the back burner as one of those intractable matters that are better left alone. In Kosovo, however, the rift between the two communities began to widen steadily. Significantly, Kosovo's Serb minority began to organize. They resolutely opposed changes in Kosovo's status; as an autonomous region, Kosovo did not have the right to secede, which republics arguably enjoyed.

There are no indications that Milosevic held any strong views on the problem at that time. But the climate of political uncertainty in the capital produced demands for a generational change that finally brought Milosevic onto the path to real power. In 1982, Ivan Stambolic was named the Communist Party leader of Belgrade, the third highest position in the Serbian Communist establishment. Stambolic, in turn, plucked Milosevic from his bank job and placed him on the executive committee of the Serbian party.

It was Milosevic's first step into the inner circles of the leadership.

Milosevic was a largely unknown figure in those years. He rarely addressed public meetings or did anything to attract public attention. On one occasion in the spring of 1983, he appeared at the Communist Party meeting of *Politika,* the leading daily newspaper, which even in the darkest days of Tito's dictatorship had managed to preserve professional standards that made it a unique institution in Yugoslavia. Tito himself had a soft spot for the paper and allowed it more latitude than any other: its prewar owner, millionaire Vladimir Ribnikar, had been a closet Communist who offered refuge to Tito in his Belgrade villa while the Communist leader was being hounded by the royalist police.

Even when control of the media was strict, *Politika* was always something of an exception, its journalists frequently thumbing their noses at an indulgent old leader whose personal prestige was so formidable that he ignored such infractions. It was not only the nation's oldest newspaper; it was also the only true quality daily that traditionally exercised influence in Yugoslavia the way *The New York Times* or *Le Monde* do in the United States and France. *Politika* did toe the Communist line by doing the minimum required from it, but never stooping to the vulgar agitations that marked the rest of the Yugoslav media. Most of its journalists were party members, of course, but they constantly resisted party discipline and outside interference. Senior politicians regularly attended the meetings of the paper's party organization to coax, pressure, and persuade the journalists into compliance. But nobody lectured to *Politika,* which, within a strong hierarchy of the system, jealously guarded its privileges.

By 1983, of course, Tito was dead. A generational change was underway. Nobody could recall later what precisely Milosevic had told the meetings—those in attendance said he was talking in general terms as to what was expected from them—but as soon as he had finished, one of the paper's star journalists, Miro Radojcic, exploded: "Who are these people who come to our meetings and lecture to us? What right do you have to interfere in journalistic business?"

Milosevic was stunned, not quite grasping what was happening, and his face went white, according to those present. But he did not respond. The meeting was quickly ended; only a couple of years later, when Milosevic seized control of *Politika,* did its journalists begin to speculate that that must have been the fateful beginning of his effort to bring the whole of the media under his personal control.

Another thing happened in the fall of 1983 that signaled the reemergence of Serb nationalism and that left a deep imprint on the Communist establishment. A long-forgotten Serb Communist leader, Alexander Rankovic, died. He had once been one of the most powerful figures in the land, the founder and chief of the dreaded secret police. He was also the top Serb representative in Tito's inner circle. Though an orthodox Communist, Rankovic was a fierce Serb nationalist and saw himself as the defender of Serb interests in the ruling council. In Kosovo, his name was synonymous with a reign of terror: prominent Albanian nationalists and separatists were simply murdered by his police with the official explanation that they had been shot while trying to flee across the border to Albania. In Macedonia, Rankovic insisted that the local Orthodox church remain under the control of the Serb patriarch, thereby in effect denying the existence of a Macedonian nation, whom the Serbs regarded as "southern Serbs." This may seem a trivial matter to Western readers, especially since all of Yugoslavia was under Communist rule, but in the Eastern Orthodox world one of the essential symbols of national existence is the unbreakable unity of church and nation. (In fact, three months after the fall of Rankovic, and at the initiative of the Macedonian Communist leaders, the Macedonian Church formally separated itself from the Serbian Orthodox Church.) Rankovic saw Belgrade as the center of a centralized country. This concept, in its practical aspects, had been identical with Tito's initial idea. But by the onset of the 1960s, as Tito began experimenting with economic reforms and decentralization, Rankovic resisted. He knew that once begun in earnest, Tito's course would have a degree of inevitability to it. Tito, on the other hand, thought in terms of a real federation—a mini-USA—as a way to keep different ethnic groups together. In 1966, he unexpectedly removed Rankovic from power and proceeded with reforms. He conferred nation status on the Bosnian Muslims for the first time; he also gave Kosovo's Albanians autonomy—which meant they ran their own schools, promoted their own language and culture, and had their own university and parliament. Tito's overriding taboo remained in place: no nationalism, just "Brotherhood and Unity."

Serb nationalists—many of them Communist Party members—grumbled that Tito's national policy was designed to fragment Yugoslavia, dilute the Serb dominance, and make it easier for Tito to rule unchallenged. This was also Rankovic's view; but having been declared a non-person in 1966, he was never heard from again. His name vanished from the press. It came up in conversations during periodic outbursts of Albanian nationalism in Kosovo, when the Serbs would say, "What we need is another Rankovic." Yet about 100,000 Serbs turned up at the private funeral services for a man who had been a political corpse for seventeen years, chanting his name and turning the event into a nationalist demonstration. Jagos Djuretic, Milosevic's college friend who is now director of a major publishing house, recalled years later that the Rankovic funeral was discussed privately among the Serb Communist elite. Milosevic was "baffled" by the sheer magnitude of the nationalist outpouring, recalled Djuretic, but it was clear that the demonstration made a deep impression on him.

When Ivan Stambolic became the Communist Party leader of Serbia in 1984, it was quite natural for him to ease his best friend, "Little Lenin," once more into the job he was vacating. Stambolic had moved up through a system that relied upon trust and loyalty. This was the way he operated, too.

He had been essentially anointed himself, brought to Tito's attention, and put on the fast track to power by his uncle. That was when Tito had carried out a purge of members of the leadership pressing for change. For Tito, Stambolic was a member of the new, postwar generation who could be trusted to carry out his policies and be loyal to him.

Though many Serbs described Stambolic as ruthless in carrying out party policy, friends saw him as generous and fiercely loyal to those around him. Much as Tito, he understood by instinct which individuals he could trust and rely on to protect him and carry out his policies. He had two advisers he trusted completely. One of them was Slobodan Milosevic.

Given this trust, he picked Milosevic for the sensitive job of Communist leader of the city of Belgrade. It was a unique position in the establishment: as Communist chief of the capital of both Serbia and Yugoslavia, part of his job was to maintain the lines of communication with the top officials and the Serbian establishment. In terms of day-to-day responsibilities, running the cosmopolitan capital city was a particularly important job. The Communists had always regarded Belgrade as the center of opposition, an "enemy lair" crowded with liberals, Trotskyites, bourgeois college professors, restive students, militant nationalists, and unruly intellectuals. The job of the Communist chief of Belgrade was normally given to energetic, ideologically strong, thoroughly reliable officials who could be counted on to ride roughshod over oppositionists. Stambolic felt that Milosevic was just such a man.

Indeed, he proved to be a staunch Communist. His first public pronouncement in his new job was a blazing attack on dissidents, political liberals, and writers. "What do some two [to] three hundred writers represent when compared to the 20,000 workers of Rakovica [the Belgrade suburb]," he said in one of his first speeches. In particular, "Little Lenin" insisted on enforcing rigorous Marxist norms in the media. When a Belgrade publisher, after obtaining tacit support of the top leadership, announced plans to publish some work by Slobodan Jovanovic, the distinguished Serb writer who had been living in exile in London since 1941, Milosevic mounted a furious campaign that stopped the publisher in his tracks. "Slobodan Jovanovic is a war criminal, and as such he will never be present in Belgrade," he declared at an open session of the party leadership. "You all can be sure of that." Five years later, Milosevic would sing a different tune as Serbia's leader, hailing the publication of the complete works of Jovanovic as a great cultural event and according the author the regime's highest award.

Using his power in Belgrade, Milosevic began to reshape the relationship between the regime and the media. By all accounts this was his personal priority. According to his friend Jagos Djuretic, Milosevic was among the first to realize that, in the conditions of general weakening of the Communist ideology, the role of the media would become ever more important, and particularly that of television. He had concluded that the old system of media management was inefficient and cumbersome. He gradually decreased the party's direct role in guiding the media in favor of more stringent controls carried out by a group of loyal friends and obedient journalists who were prepared unreservedly to do his bidding. These people were assembled around the Commission for Information, which was accorded full authority to determine staffing positions in the state media. In the course of less than two years, these men devastated the Serb media and brought it to the lowest professional level ever. Dusan Mitevic, one of Milosevic's college friends, took over Belgrade Radio and Television; Zivorad Minovic, a thoroughly unscrupulous and malevolent hack, became the editor in chief at *Politika;* and Slobodan Jovanovic (no relation to the famous writer), a discredited journalist who had been fired from a student newspaper for incompetence and stealing, was placed in charge of the evening *Ekspres.*

Another mainstay of Milosevic's drive to power were the numerous Marxist professors whose careers were advanced by the party. Milosevic's ideological slogan was the need to "return to Marxism." His wife, Mira, was instrumental in assembling the professors into a coherent bloc opposing the educational reforms that were being advanced by more liberal party voices around Stambolic, who was about to become the next president of Serbia. The orthodox Marxist faction succeeded in preventing the removal of obligatory Marxist education in colleges during a July 17, 1985, session of the Serbian party's Central Committee. It was at that session that Milosevic's name was first proposed—among others—as Stambolic's successor as the Communist Party leader of Serbia.

Emboldened by the changes underway in the Russia of Mikhail Gorbachev, the liberals within the Serbian Communist Party vigorously opposed Milosevic's nomination. There were eight candidates for the job, among them Mira's uncle, Draza Markovic, who had consistently resisted Milosevic's steady advancement within the party—as did Mira's father.

But on January 25, 1986, after months of factional struggle, Milosevic was named Communist Party chief, largely due to the influence of Stambolic, who was elevated to the presidency of Serbia without opposition. Stambolic now stood alone at the peak of power in Serbia; the old Communists were fading away and he had no competitor among the new generation. Stambolic wanted to have his trusted friend by his side and maneuvered the Central Committee into avoiding a divisive vote. "We did not start off with one candidate," he declared from the rostrum, "but have come to the one" he wanted—Slobodan Milosevic. He appeared to be a man after Stambolic's heart. Stambolic valued his friend's loyalty and his personal modesty, which must have appeared to him to be the mark of a man who did not harbor personal ambitions. There was never a whiff of corruption or impropriety about him, nor any greed for the trappings of power. He and Mira lived in a modest two-bedroom apartment in the middle-class Vracar district of Belgrade. They used the house where Mira grew up in Pozarevac as the family's weekend retreat. The Stambolics and the Milosevics were so close that the two Milosevic children, Marija and Marko, then aged twenty and nine, both thought of Ivan Stambolic as their godfather.

The delegates approved Stambolic's choice.

The next day, among the guests dining in the crowded restaurant Kod Ere were the new leaders of Serbia, Stambolic and Milosevic. Stambolic would later recall that evening as one of the most pleasant occasions during a quarter century of their friendship. They celebrated their victory with a bottle of Dingac, a mellow Croatian wine, and talked about the old days and old dreams.

Milosevic must now have sensed that the goal he and Mira had coveted for so long was within his grasp. But he kept any ambitions well hidden. Over the next months he seemed a man at ease with himself, remaining in his Vracar apartment as if nothing had changed in his life.

# 2

# Faustian Bargain

A short, white-haired, bespectacled novelist named Dobrica Cosic gave Slobodan Milosevic the intellectual underpinnings for the crude nationalist assault upon which he was about to embark. "He has a lot to answer for," said U.S. ambassador Warren Zimmermann. The relationship was characterized by Milosevic's former classmate Nebojsa Popov as that of Faust and Mephistopheles.

On a rare occasion when the two men were seen talking together in public—at a diplomatic reception—their cryptic parting was interpreted as symbolic.

"Hope to see you again," Milosevic said.

"We are neighbors, only the fence separates us," replied Cosic.

"I hope this fence is not too high," Milosevic responded jokingly.

Cosic was a hero to the Serbs, as the writer of a tetralogy of novels of historical fiction about Serbian agony and heroism in World War I. As a young man he had joined Tito's Partisans, become a dogmatic Marxist, and risen in the ranks of the Communist hierarchy to be a member of the ruling Central Committee.

He became disenchanted with communism at the time of the 1968 Soviet invasion of Czechoslovakia. He quietly abandoned politics and began writing the novels that became so popular they were translated into several languages. By the mid-1970s, he was a millionaire.

Cosic was a serious man, an ascetic type who stood out in the bohemian atmosphere of Belgrade's intellectual café society. He worked hard, enjoyed serious conversations, and seemed imbued with a clear sense of purpose.

He lived in a comfortable villa in the exclusive Belgrade suburb of Dedinje, his neighbors being the ambassadors of Britain, China, and the United States.

Despite this cosmopolitan neighborhood, Cosic was surprisingly unfamiliar with the West. "Cosic once asked me in all seriousness why it was objectionable to aim for a Great Serbia when we had our own Great Britain," said Ivor Roberts, who was the British ambassador in the 1990s. "My attempts to persuade him that Great Britain was no more than a distinction between us and Brittany were met with incredulity."

Under Tito, in 1975, Cosic became an open political dissident by publishing an article calling for greater intellectual freedom. He denounced the Communist elite as "a group of spiritual nihilists," who were responsible for "the poverty and spiritual misery of the ordinary people," and he forcefully endorsed the demands of political dissidents:

> In the history of the world and of this country, the greatest misuse of freedom has always been perpetrated by those in power and by political passions. Thus, today, the frequent and fatal misuse of freedom for socialist ends is the fault of those in power rather than those working in science, the arts and philosophy. It must be emphasized again that deprivation of freedom is the worst crime.

Other artists who publicly voiced such ideas risked ostracism, reprimand, even punishment. But Cosic was the country's most popular living novelist.

His overt anti-communism combined with his uncritical celebration of Serb nationalism made him even more popular—and politically influential—in the years following Tito's death in 1980. By the time Milosevic rode the wave of Serb nationalism to political power in 1987–88, Belgrade had been whipped into a frenzy of nationalist hysteria, presided over by Cosic and his allies. Milosevic's media—television, radio, newspapers, magazines—created a buzz around Cosic, calling him the "Father of the Nation."

Only later, after Serb nationalism had hardened into chauvinism, would he understand that he had been used by Milosevic, who squeezed him like a lemon and then discarded him.

The exact time when Milosevic the Bolshevik began transforming himself into Milosevic the nationalist was the fall of 1986, a few months after his appointment as head of the Serbian Communist Party. Cosic and his friends at the Serbian Academy of Sciences and Arts circulated a "Memorandum" that caused an uproar when it was published on September 24 in the Belgrade evening newspaper *Vecernje Novosti*. Its main argument was that the Serbs in general and Serbia proper in particular had been shortchanged by the Communists and exploited by Tito's Yugoslav federation. The fulcrum of the argument was Kosovo, where "the physical, political, legal and cultural genocide of the Serbian people" is worse than ever before. Such language from a prestigious institution had never been heard before in Communist Yugoslavia:

> A nation which after a long and bloody struggle regained its own state, which fought for and achieved a civil democracy, and which in the last two wars lost 2.5 million of its members, has lived to see the day when a Party committee of apparatchiks decrees that after four decades in the new

Yugoslavia it alone is not allowed to have its own state. A worse historical defeat in peacetime cannot be imagined.

More to the point, the Memorandum singled out a reported incident involving a fifty-six-year-old Serb farmer in Kosovo who claimed he had been abused by two Albanians, who allegedly tied him down and forced a bottle into his rectum, bottom first. The farmer, Djordje Martinovic, was left unconscious and bleeding. After he came to his senses, he said, he crawled to a nearby hospital.

The original news stories reported the incident as factually correct. The local Albanian authorities initially condemned what they termed a "despicable crime." But three days later they issued a different statement, saying that "the internal injuries of Djordje Martinovic are accidental consequences of a self-indulged practice." Kosovo Albanian police also reported that the farmer's wounds were self-inflicted and that he had confessed while still in Pristina Hospital. In a written statement they concluded that "it appears that the wounded performed an act of 'self-satisfaction' in his field, that he put a beer bottle on a wooden stick and stuck it in the ground . . . then sat on the bottle." An Albanian physician who examined the farmer said the wound was self-inflicted; he also confirmed that the farmer had "confessed."

But the Serbian authorities formed a special commission of inquiry to look into the matter. The farmer was brought to Belgrade for a medical examination; Serbian doctors concluded his wound could not have been self-inflicted. Martinovic also claimed to have been forced into making a false confession; his family felt compelled to testify that he had "no deviant sexual tendencies."

Shortly afterward, while interrogated jointly by Albanian and Serb police officials, he stated for the record that he had not been attacked but had injured himself.

The gruesome dispute dragged on for several months. Finally, an investigating judge announced on November 15, 1985, that a new team of experts had concluded that the wound could have been either self-inflicted or inflicted by others.

Most of the Serbian media concluded at the time that Martinovic's injuries had been self-inflicted. Inter-ethnic violence in Kosovo was rare; in the period between 1981 and 1987 there were five inter-ethnic murders (the Kosovo crime rate was the lowest in Yugoslavia). The entire incident would probably have been forgotten had not the Serbian Academy decided that the farmer had been impaled by a beer bottle and announced that to the public. The Martinovic incident, the Memorandum bluntly asserted, "was reminiscent of the darkest days of the Turkish practice of impalement."

This had an enormous impact on the Serb consciousness. Every Serb knows about the gruesome form of punishment used by the Turks. Nobel laureate Ivo Andric in *The Bridge on the Drina* described graphically how a victim would be impaled on a stake, run from rectum to neck, then hoisted upright in a public place for everybody to witness the slow and horrible death. The Memorandum, in effect, kept the Martinovic case alive for several years as a symbol of Serb victimization. The impalement metaphor was used by Milosevic's staunchest supporters in the weeks before the outbreak of the Croatian war in 1991; also in 1991, a Belgrade court awarded Martinovic compensation from the state for the injuries inflicted by "Shiptar terrorists."

The Memorandum gave Milosevic the idea that he could have a real base among the intellectuals for a nationalist assault on the Communist Party leadership, and the Kosovo Serbs could become an instrument to attain power. And while other Communists launched an attack on the controversial document, Milosevic kept silent. But there was no doubt that he understood that he now had the rationalization for his ambitions and the underpinnings for his vault to power.

Kosovo is an area of rich farmlands, roughly half the size of Maryland, surrounded by snow-capped mountain ranges to the west, south, and east. By the 1980s, Kosovo was being gradually overwhelmed by its ethnic Albanian population, largely due to their high birth rate. The Serbs were almost paranoid on this score. Their protests became loud and vehement once the Memorandum began circulating, touching off an anti-Albanian campaign that quickly escalated into accusations of "demographic genocide" against the fast-breeding Kosovars.

Cosic led the chorus of chauvinist lamentations by warning that "Albanians are decomposing the ethnic and social structure of Yugoslavia." The poet Matija Beckovic, who was president of the Serbian Writers Union at the time, insisted that Serbia's manifest destiny was in Kosovo and that it would "remain Serbian forever even if not one Serb lived there."

In order to reduce the high Albanian birth rate, the Serb nationalist novelist Vuk Draskovic suggested legislative steps to limit child benefits to a maximum of four children. "If you want to have five children," he proposed, "you will lose all benefits on the first four, and you will be taxed for the fifth. You will pay double tax for the sixth, a quadruple tax for the seventh, and so on. If Allah orders Albanians to have twenty children each so that they can take over the Serbian state, then Allah must find the money for them."

Scores of other writers contributed to the polyphony of crazed ideas with their hate-filled, warmongering rhetoric, hurling frenzied indictments against an entire people and accusing them of raping Serb women, though the statistics have never borne this out. But Cosic's preeminence in this ghastly enterprise remains undisputed. On the level of psychology, the subtext of his message was that the Serbs were more sinned against than sinning, that evil deeds may be necessary to eliminate evil, and that the legacy of Kosovo imposes that course on the nation to achieve its resurrection. Cosic's neighbor and frequent visitor, Warren Zimmermann, said later that the novelist "gave Milosevic the intellectual foundation, the political framework, the ideology for a totally atrocious, savage behavior."

Cosic and the others who wrote the Memorandum did not have their nationalist anger fixed only on Kosovo. They also were deeply convinced that other large swatches of territory had been detached from Serbia by malevolent foreign powers and by Tito's Communists: the whole of the neighboring republic of Bosnia; a Serb-inhabited region of Croatia known as the Krajina; as well as parts of the Dalmation coast.

Cosic was also the first important intellectual to revive the doctrine that all Serbs should live in one country—the "Greater Serbia" concept first advanced by Ilija Garasanin, Serbia's foreign and interior minister in 1844, and the underpinning of much of the nationalist turmoil in the region in the early part of the twentieth century.

Serbia, which rid itself of Turkish rule following an 1804 insurrection, had always sought to unite all the Serbs who lived scattered and ruled by other nations. Belgrade fomented unrest in Bosnia-Herzegovina in the second part of the nineteenth century, which led to a series of Christian rebellions against the Ottoman rulers and the 1878 Congress of Berlin, which awarded the territory to the Habsburgs. The great powers of the day also explicitly prohibited the construction of communication links between the two weak Serb states—Serbia and Montenegro—and left a sliver of territory dividing them in the joint hands of Austria-Hungary and Turkey. Serbia enlarged its territory in two Balkan wars in 1912 and 1913; unrest in Bosnia culminated in the assassination in 1914 of the Austrian archduke Franz Ferdinand and the start of World War I.

In recognition of Serbia's mighty struggle on the side of the Allies, a new country was created in 1918 out of the destruction of Ottoman Turkey and Austria-Hungary; the Serbian royal house was given hereditary rule over the Kingdom of the Serbs, Croats, and Slovenes (soon renamed Yugoslavia), which united all Serbs (though they enjoyed numerical plurality—about 40 percent—not a majority). The country survived separatism and slaughter during World War II to emerge as a relatively happy halfway house between East and West in a divided Europe. But Cosic and many other nationalists were deeply convinced that throughout this sequence of events the Serb nation had been sold down the Danube by the great powers and in particular by Tito. In Cosic's novels, which focus on the terrible Serb struggle in the two Balkan wars and World War I, the underlying theme is one of an enormous sacrifice in blood that bore little fruit. It was this resentment that became the theme of the Memorandum.

Ivan Stambolic roundly denounced the Memorandum, calling it a requiem for Yugoslavia. Liberals and hard-line Communists followed suit.

Only Milosevic was silent. The new Communist Party leader saw no advantage in taking a firm position. The Communist system, he knew, tended to seek scapegoats for its own shortcomings, and so he let others fight this battle. In closed party meetings, he criticized the Memorandum as a manifestation of "black nationalism"—"the poison injected by domestic and foreign enemies to destroy Yugoslavia."

His remarks to a police college audience in early 1987 showed that he knew exactly what the document was about; it was proposing, he said, "the liquidation of the present political system in our country." It was also setting a political objective which he took as his own—the quest for a Greater Serbia.

Both the nationalists and the Communists were convinced that Milosevic was on their side. General Nikola Ljubicic, Tito's longtime defense minister and perhaps the most influential member of the old generation of Yugoslav Communists, publicly endorsed him: "Slobodan has been valiantly struggling against nationalism, liberalism and all other forms of counterrevolution in Belgrade. He has passed the exam. I see Slobodan Milosevic as a fighter against counterrevolution and I wish he would continue this activity with even greater persistence."

At the same time, Milosevic's refusal to express his views publicly was interpreted by Cosic and other nationalist intellectuals as an indication of support.

When Stambolic showed some concern about Milosevic's public silence, he was quickly reassured by Dusan Mitevic, Milosevic's old college friend. "Milosevic thinks that there was already too much discussion about it and he does not want to add to the confusion,"

Mitevic said. "He is like a football player who usually plays a supporting role but then scores the goals."

In early 1987, Stambolic called on Milosevic to deal with growing unrest in Kosovo, where the Serbs were threatening a new major exodus. They claimed they were discriminated against by the Kosovo Albanian provincial government. "Calm them down," Stambolic told him. Indeed, Milosevic prepared a speech designed to stimulate a conciliatory spirit in the province. He never delivered it. Before the meeting was to start at the Hall of Culture in Pristina, thousands of angry Serbs appeared in front of the building throwing rocks and shouting, "Thieves, thieves!" "Murderers, murderers!" The local police were unprepared for a large demonstration of people who demanded to talk to Milosevic. They used nightsticks to stop the crowd; the demonstrators began breaking the windows.

Milosevic was confused and uncertain. Never before had he been forced to meet an angry crowd, to address them without a prepared speech. When he began speaking, with the standard line that "The party is going to solve this problem," he merely provoked a new wave of anger.

"They are beating us," angry protesters shouted.

"No one will ever dare beat you again!" Milosevic blurted out, with the Kosovo Albanian leader Asem Vlassi standing next to him. The camera has captured the moment: Milosevic's facial expression and demeanor are those of a man uncomfortable with his task, and someone unaware that the populist phrase he uttered would not merely calm the restive crowd but set in motion a dramatic series of events that would transform his life.

It was exactly what the crowd wanted to hear. The mood changed dramatically. "Slobo, Slobo," they shouted enthusiastically.

Buoyed by the shouts, Milosevic continued:

> You must stay here. Your land is here. Here are your houses, your fields and gardens, your memories. You are not going to leave them, are you, because life is hard and because you are subjected to injustice and humiliation? It was never in

> the spirit of the Serb and the Montenegrin peoples to succumb before obstacles, to quit when one has to fight, to be demoralized in the face of hardship.

He promised changes. "Yugoslavia does not exist without Kosovo! Yugoslavia will disintegrate without Kosovo! Yugoslavia and Serbia will not give up Kosovo!"

"He instantly became the leader of all Serbs," said Slavko Curuvija, a Serbian journalist who stood not far from Milosevic at that moment and who understood the potency of the message.

It would not take long for Milosevic to see his chance.

Ivan Stambolic was stunned when he heard that Milosevic had publicly sided with the Serb minority.

Stambolic was an old-fashioned, almost romantic Communist. Nationalism was contrary to Tito's legacy, which he saw himself continuing. What was worse, Milosevic's outburst could destabilize the party establishment, which was already riddled with intrigues and plots.

The Serbian media used Milosevic's speech as the fulcrum for a national awakening. Belgrade Television repeatedly transmitted the "No one will ever dare beat you again!" statement. The newspaper headlines screamed, "We will win this battle too!" The literary weekly *Knjizevne Novine,* which had only the previous week criticized Milosevic's anti-democratic style of operating, published a front-page ode to Milosevic:

> *. . . but a handsome young speaker arrived*
> *the setting sun falling on his brushed hair,*
> *I will speak with my people in open spaces, he says,*
> *In schoolyards and in fields.*

The Yugoslav Communist leaders were upset. So were the police: he had openly condemned police violence before the whole world. To rectify things, Milosevic called in person on the minister of the interior, Dobroslav Culafic, to assure him that his speech in Kosovo was a matter of political expediency.

But Milosevic had had his first taste of the demonic pleasures of power and fame. By now, he took the problem of Kosovo personally, tracing his family tree back to the battle of 1389. He was also ready to cut off his closest friend, who over the years had pulled Milosevic on his coattails into the power structure.

Throughout the spring and summer of 1987, Milosevic kept building alliances within the leadership, playing his cards very close to the chest. Only Mira and a few close friends knew that he was preparing for war against Stambolic. The conviction in this inner circle, Dusan Mitevic later recalled, was that Milosevic could not reach the top by means of force—he did not control the army or the police—and that his only tools were propaganda and mass mobilization. Publicly Milosevic only hinted at his intentions. During a dinner in late August at the elegant Adriatic summer home of one of Mira's close associates, Marxist professor Milos Aleksic, Milosevic raised a glass to toast his closest friends and allies. "Eat and drink tonight," Dusan Mitevic quoted him as saying. "Starting with next month you'll have no time for it."

Indeed, upon his return to Belgrade, Milosevic mounted an orchestrated press attack on Stambolic which culminated in a special session of the Communist Party Central Committee that—in the interests of glasnost—would be televised live and end up in Stambolic's political demise.

An incident on September 3 provided the pretext.

On that day, an ethnic Albanian conscript, Aziz Keljmendi, went berserk and opened fire on other soldiers in the Yugoslav Army barracks in the Serbian town of Paracin, killing four and wounding six others. Among the ten victims only one was Serb; the other conscripts included five Muslims, two Croats, and one Slovene.

*Politika* devoted its entire front page to the incident, which it cast as an act of hard-core Albanian separatism against Yugoslavia (even though medical experts had ruled that the young Albanian was mentally disturbed). *Politika* staffers were immediately alerted that their coverage was tendentious and would generate anti-Albanian sentiments.

One journalist wrote the following memorandum:

> I was working on the desk that day and the editor of the local section, Petar Jankovic, informed me about the tragedy. Shortly afterward, I was urgently summoned to the office of Zivorad Minovic [the new editor in chief]. I found there an unusual scene: Minovic was happily excited as he told us—I don't remember all those who were there but I am sure that Petar Jankovic and Miroslav Cosic were among us—that four Serbian soldiers had been killed in Paracin, and that in this situation this is God-sent! He said the journalist Radivoje Petrovic should immediately go to Paracin.
>
> I was shocked by the euphoric atmosphere and depressed to witness such a tragedy being experienced in our office in this fashion. A few minutes later I got another shock. We were summoned back to Minovic's office where he told us, with visible disappointment, that although not all four dead soldiers were Serbs, we had to give top prominence to this incident. I rushed out of his office as if I was fleeing from hell.

When the first copies were available early in the evening of September 3, the veteran *Politika* journalist Slava Djukic phoned the night editor to warn him that "political emphasis" and the tone of the coverage could create turmoil in Serbia. "He told me he would talk to Minovic about it," Djukic later recalled. "The next morning he phoned me and said that Minovic would not permit any changes in the tone. 'Don't change a thing, it's going as is.'"

*Politika,* followed by *Ekspres* and Radio Television Belgrade—all in the hands of Milosevic's men—created an atmosphere of nationalist hysteria. *Politika* immediately assumed a conspiracy: "Mindless rounds of the murderer Keljmendi, who, everything indicates, did not pull the trigger alone, will not and cannot shake our trust in our army." The murders, committed "perfidiously and slyly," were presented as an additional proof of the Albanian menace.

The stridently anti-Albanian reports provoked acts of revenge. Albanian shops were destroyed throughout Serbia, but *Politika* and the rest of the media described these actions as peaceful protests "against the sickening crime." The press also focused on the Keljmendi family, whose home, it said, contained "subversive Albanian nationalist and separatist propaganda." When the Albanian rector of the University of Pristina publicly condemned the crime, *Politika* shrilled: "Would the rector have condemned the heedless deed had Keljmendi not been their student?" It proceeded with the condemnation of the entire Kosovo school system by insisting that "all the teachers that lectured to Aziz Keljmendi bear on their souls a part of his crime."

The potent cocktail of Serb nationalism and electronic communication was intoxicating. More than ten thousand people attended the funeral of the slain Serb soldier amid shouts of "Kosovo is Serbia!" "Down with traitors!" and "Azem Vlassi—kick him out of Yugoslavia!"

At the graveside, rabid nationalist rhetoric and calls for revenge at one point angered the father of the dead soldier, who demanded: "Stop these carryings-on over the coffin of my son."

Stambolic and his allies tried to block the rapidly growing climate of ethnic intolerance. A third-ranking member of the leadership, Dragisa Pavlovic, called a news conference on September 11 after consultations with Stambolic. Pavlovic was one of the two men—Milosevic being the other—in whom Stambolic had complete trust. Pavlovic assailed the media for generating "anti-Albanian" sentiments, "intolerance and hatred toward ethnic Albanians." Milosevic was not told in advance about the press conference, which he watched on the evening news with Dusan Mitevic. "This is it! There's nothing more to wait for," Milosevic told Mitevic.

Two days later, Milosevic summoned his top journalistic allies to his weekend home in Pozarevac. In addition to Mira, the meeting was attended by Dusan Mitevic, head of Belgrade Television; Zivorad Minovic, editor in chief of *Politika;* and Slobodan Jovanovic, editor of *Ekspres*. The strategy they decided on was for Milosevic to stay in the shadows, while the media would escalate attacks on Pavlovic and indirectly on Stambolic. Mira had prepared an article explaining that the attacks on the press in fact represented a struggle between two factions within the Communist Party. But since it was impossible for such a diatribe to be signed by the wife of the Communist Party leader of Serbia, the decision was taken to place it under the byline of Dragoljub Milanovic, a provincial journalist from Kosovo whom the new *Politika* editor in chief had brought to Belgrade for precisely that reason. Milanovic, who walked around the newsroom with a gun strapped on his belt, became overnight a leading figure in the Serb media. The Milosevic group would use him and his byline in the crucial phases of their struggle for power, and he eagerly played along.

A furious nationalist attack in the media focused on Dragisa Pavlovic, but most people understood that the real target was Ivan Stambolic himself. Pavlovic's press conference was presented as having "shaken the confidence in the ability of the Central Committee to open up new possibilities, especially with respect to Kosovo."

When Milosevic announced that he was calling a meeting of the Central Committee on September 23 to deal with the problem, Stambolic felt sufficiently alarmed and personally threatened by the proposed agenda to phone Milosevic directly.

"He told me not to worry," Stambolic recalled. "He said there was no problem in it for me."

The rest was something of an anticlimax. Milosevic knew he would win, for by now he had secured the crucial support of military and party chiefs. It was a coup from within, seemingly conducted in the open on live television, and Pavlovic was dismissed for straying from Tito's course even though precisely the opposite was true. Stambolic, who defended Pavlovic, emerged as a tragic victim; everyone knew it was only a matter of days before he too would be ousted. Until the very end, he seemed a desperate figure unaware of his own imminent demise and hoping to prevent Pavlovic's ouster. In his speech, Stambolic still believed that was possible:

> I would propose one other thing: let's not be angry, because it is not so important. It would be good for Slobo and Dragisa [Pavlovic] to meet for coffee every day for half an hour. Or they may drink lemonade. But they should meet to overcome their differences; I know them and I will not accept that they cannot find human solutions. I will not accept that.

Milosevic's rebuff was immediate:

> This question cannot be minimized by describing it as a personal conflict, as two kids having a squabble.

Then Stambolic appealed directly to his old friend: "I am certain that Comrade Milosevic will show greater abilities and sense in bringing people together and that he will prevent the danger of divisions [in the party leadership]."

Milosevic coldly ignored him. "The next speaker, please," he promptly announced.

The victory was cemented by a dirty trick dreamed up by Dusan Mitevic during a strategy session at the Milosevics' apartment on the night of September 23. Mitevic had contacted four close friends on the local party committee whom he summoned to an urgent meeting at the Café Fontana. The conspirators immediately agreed to sign a letter saying that Ivan Stambolic had attempted to pressure them into supporting Pavlovic.

Armed with the letter, Milosevic the next morning staged what his former mentor came to think of as an Oscar-winning performance. "When I saw Milosevic's face," Stambolic recalled later, "I thought the Russians had invaded or the Third World War had begun."

Holding a piece of paper in his hand, Milosevic said he had "hesitated for the last hour or two" whether to broach the subject. "We have received a letter. First I asked that its authenticity be checked, that there wasn't some mistake. Then I doubted whether one could really read out this letter . . . "

He proceeded to do so. The letter implicated Stambolic in a conspiracy against the party's ruling bodies. Stambolic was destroyed. "Milosevic implied that we were not with Tito; it was a public lynching," Stambolic said later.

At the end of the session, the triumphant Milosevic—his preeminence now established—offered words of cold comfort to his old friend: "I sincerely hope, I believe in it firmly, that Comrade Stambolic was manipulated and is not guilty."

Stambolic was officially dismissed on December 14, 1987.

A few weeks later, Stambolic's twenty-four-year-old daughter, Bojana, died in a car accident. Milosevic showed up at the funeral, entered the chapel, and embraced his old friend. But Ivan's wife, Katja, stared expressionless into the distance, refusing to accept Milosevic's hand or expression of condolences.

A few days after the funeral, the two former friends had their last conversation. An editorial in *Ekspres* had brought the vilification campaign against Stambolic to new heights by asserting that even "his seed in its roots must be crushed." Stambolic phoned Milosevic to complain about the tasteless and insensitive choice of words.

"I have nothing to do with that. This is done by others," Milosevic said. "We have freedom of the press."

Milosevic was forty-six and had served a mere five years in high party posts. But he had for some time known what he wanted. Kosovo was the launching pad; the goal was Yugoslavia.

Stambolic said later that one of the reasons he had misjudged Milosevic was the latter's tendency to eschew face-to-face disagreements. "Face to face he was always cooperative," Stambolic said. "He never had any political ideas of his own. The attack against me was a conjugal undertaking.

"Many people warned me about him but I didn't take them seriously. We were emotionally close, I thought. But I guess when somebody looks at your back for twenty years, it is understandable that he gets the urge to put a knife in it at some point."

A friend of Stambolic, the historian Ljubinka Trgovcevic, remarked that Stambolic was completely incapable of grasping what

Milosevic had done. "Stambolic comes from a patriarchal environment where you don't hit your best friend and where you never betray your party. He told me that he loved Milosevic more than his own brothers and that he had spent more time with him than with them."

In the course of the final power struggle, there were a few segments of the Serbian Communist Party that refused to line up behind Milosevic. The ethnic Albanian Communists, for example, controlled a large bloc of votes. As he was ceaselessly lobbying to make sure that he had a majority of votes in the committee, Milosevic approached Azem Vlassi, the Communist leader of the Kosovo Albanians.

"This is now or never," Milosevic told Vlassi. "Vote for me and tell the members of your delegation to do so, too. I'm going to pay you back later."

Vlassi was unimpressed. "You have never helped me in the past," he replied, "and I cannot help you now."

Milosevic was livid. "I always knew you were a cunt!" he hissed.

"And you are a liar and a cheat," was Vlassi's response.

The other source of resistance to Milosevic were the old-line Communist politicians led by Mira's father, Moma Markovic, and his brother, Draza. Mira was furious when she learned that they had cast their votes against her husband; she completely severed relations with her father and saw him only once again, in a hospital, shortly before his death in 1992.

Milosevic chose Kosovo as his launching pad because of its mystical importance to the Serbs. For them, it has parallels with Jerusalem for the Jews. A flourishing Serb medieval kingdom had left exquisite churches and other artifacts in Kosovo, even though many of them had fallen into disrepair or were severely damaged after the 1389 Turkish victory on the Field of Blackbirds. The memories of vanished glories had been kept alive in legends and folk songs on which every Serb child—including Milosevic—has been reared for the past six centuries.

Though the Serb nationalism which Milosevic cleverly exploited had not sprung from a vacuum, he fanned the long-dying embers into a modern inferno rather than letting them recede like the ancient legends of so many other aggrieved peoples.

Milosevic's father, like most Montenegrins of his generation, could recite the most evocative poem—*The Mountain Wreath,* rooted in Kosovo mythology—in its entirety. Most Serbs quote from it in daily conversations. The poems and folk songs belong to a world where people swung—from cradle to grave—in a hammock of family and clan ties. It is not hard to understand how the old ballads with their soothing lyrics explained enslavement but also fostered extremism and moralism, an insular, self-righteous attitude rooted in devotion to a heroic past. They filled their listeners with the illusion of order.

The invincible Prince Marko, for example, was the medieval equivalent of Superman; his horse had wings and talked in a human voice to his master. Marko killed dragons and Turks. He seemed to understand the people's needs so well and did everything to help them. In such ballads one would hear not only the clanging of sabers but also the precepts of a moral code.

Mythological heroes gave flesh as well to philosophical questions by recounting the deeds of the ancestors and passing judgment on their actions. Enslavement was ascribed to the moral flaws of a few. There is no historical evidence whatsoever to substantiate the claims that a Serb noble, Vuk Brankovic, had betrayed Lazar at Kosovo. On the contrary, the historical Brankovic resisted the Turks for two decades after the 1389 battle before he was defeated. But that did not matter; oral tradition had branded him a traitor.

This mythology has shaped the character of the Serb people—their messianic bent, their belief in the meaninglessness of loss and the promise of inevitable restoration. It holds that the Serbs are a chosen people with a special covenant with God, but who remained mired in self-obsession and a sense of victimization at the hands of foreigners. The mythology calls on the Serbs to avenge the injustice of Kosovo. No sacrifice is too great for the ultimate good.

After Serbia regained its independence in the nineteenth century, the obsession with Kosovo's past provided compensation for a deep sense of inferiority that came with the realization that the Serbs—like all other peoples in the Balkans—were a marginal people and lagged far behind the rest of Europe.

It would be hard to overestimate the grip of *The Mountain Wreath* on the Serb national psyche. The long poem was written in 1847 by the prince-bishop of Montenegro, Peter II Petrovic-Njegos. It deals with a 1702 massacre of "renegade" converts to Islam by their fathers and brothers who remained faithful to their Christian faith. This fratricidal incident provides the drama for the reaffirmation of the Serbian commitment to the legacy of the battle of Kosovo. The battle is not over, Njegos says, and the Serbs must heed Prince Lazar's warning:

*Of Serbians by nation and by birth,*
*and by their blood and their ancestry,*
*whoever does not fight at Kosovo,*
*may he have no dear children born to him,*
*may neither boy nor girl be born to him!*
*May nothing bear fruit that his hand sows,*
*neither the white wheat nor the red wine!*
*His blight rot all his brood while it endures!*

As a Christian bishop, Njegos agonizes over the conflict between duty to one's kin and duty to one's nation and faith. But as a prince, he comes down firmly justifying a man killing his own renegade brothers if they could not be persuaded to return to the true Christian faith.

While the Montenegrin elders hold a council to weigh their options, the poet argues that the fratricide is a necessary evil to prevent evil's triumph. There is no room for compromise. A compromise would amount to betrayal and reminds them that the "despicable" Brankovic is the source of Serbia's plight:

*Our Serbian chiefs, most miserable cowards,*
*The Serbian stock did heinously betray.*

But here is the rub: how does one try to talk the renegades into returning to true faith without exposing the entire plan? The Christian Serbs could not take that chance. Hence the converts, who are called "Turks," are taken by surprise in the middle of the night. After an orgy of mass murder, a Serb warrior recounts to his prince the outcome of the ghastly pogrom:

*No single seeing eye, no tongue of Turk*
*Escaped to tell his tale another day!*
*We put them all unto the sword,*
*All those who would not be baptized.*

Their houses were burned down and the mosques destroyed, the warrior concludes. The prince rejoices:

*Great gladness this for me, my falcons,*
*Great joy! Heroic liberty*
*Has resurrection morn today,*
*from every tomb of our ancestors dear!*

On one level, the poem perpetuates the medieval values of honor, which must be defended without compromise, and a certain self-sacrifice which justifies Lazar's choice at Kosovo. But underlying this is a belief in the eternal Serb illusions which were never extinguished but which never attained realization. The massacre, in Njegos's mind, has become a sacrificial offering on the altar of higher values:

*Everything doth perish saving honor*
*This lives on through everlasting ages*
*Life eternal marks the honored grave*
*A life of shame leads to eternal death.*

Rebecca West, who in her *Black Lamb and Grey Falcon* highlights the exotica, the anecdotal and partial, including the medieval moral code, likens Njegos's moral conflict to the world of classical Greek tragedies. Njegos's characters in *The Mountain Wreath* retain freedom at the price of fratricide. "It is certain that they were justified in their crime," she writes. "A man is not a man if he will not save his seed."

The extent to which the martial ethos of *The Mountain Wreath* had become an integral part of the Serb psyche could be seen in the nationalist flowering of the 1980s and 1990s, and Milosevic exploited the bruised collective ego in his rise to power. The Serb nationalists became ecstatic when the Communist chieftain suddenly assumed the mantle of protector of Kosovo. "Kosovo is not a part of Serbia," Milosevic declared. "It is the very heart of Serbia."

Dusan Mitevic was a crucial player in Milosevic's rise to power. The dandified and unscrupulous spin doctor, who was in charge of Radio Television Belgrade, had been at university with Milosevic and his wife and was one of a handful of persons admitted to Milosevic's home. He was perhaps the most detested figure in the regime, for he directed the campaign of public vilification of Serbia's rivals—ethnic Albanians, Bosnian Muslims, and Croats—with exceptional skills and zest.

Mitevic's orchestrated lying was grounded in a skillful exploitation of the Serb mythology to generate a mass sense of grievance at real and imagined conspiracies against the Serb nation—with Kosovo as their crowning affront. Mitevic's success was consummate, in large part because the intellectuals, always inclined to histrionics where Kosovo was concerned, lent credibility to the campaign.

It was a curious but formidable confluence of forces. State-run Radio Television Belgrade, which reached all parts of Yugoslavia, spread alarm throughout the neighboring republics of Bosnia and Croatia. The prophets of pan-Serbism could count on the support of patriotic Serbs—who had no dreams of aggrandizement but believed that it was time for the Serb nation to assert itself and prevent the breakup of a country they regarded as their own. The other Yugoslav nationalities—the Croats and the Slovenes in particular—were even more alarmed. The Yugoslav Communist Party, the glue that had kept Tito's multinational federation together, disintegrated in a matter of weeks under Milosevic's public onslaught on the Shiptars (a pejorative term used for the ethnic Albanians in Kosovo) and other nationalities.

The reconquest of Kosovo, the cradle of Serbia's identity and the mainspring of its ancient culture, was Milosevic's first priority. The Serbian Orthodox Church gingerly extended a supportive hand to the new convert. It sponsored the macabre undertaking of having the six-hundred-year-old bones of Prince Lazar dragged with pomp and ceremony throughout Yugoslavia for an entire year to promote Milosevic's concept of "All Serbs in one country." Submerged Serb nationalism suddenly bubbled up everywhere to sweep away the accumulated reserves of ethnic goodwill; and where reason had gone astray, a tide of emotion surged through the Serb population.

The homogenizing rhetoric was intoxicating. Cosic, now in his seventies, was once again a political activist and, according to the polls, the most popular figure in Serbia. He gave interviews, acting as if he carried the full weight of Serbian history on his shoulders and piously exhorting Serbs to become involved in politics. He explained Serbia's problems.

Rational arguments were dismissed. Historical arguments were fuzzy at best; those who invoked them did so because they believed that history—or their version of it—supported their aspirations.

For the Serbs, the numerous Orthodox shrines in Kosovo testified to their "historical right" to the territory. The fact that the Albanians accounted for 90 percent of Kosovo's 2.1 million population was of no importance. The Albanians were immigrants, and unwelcome immigrants at that.

Had the Albanians been able to put their own case—something out of the question as Milosevic had silenced their voice through relentless public vilification—they could have made an equally strong, if not stronger, claim to Kosovo.

Quite apart from the fact that the Albanians had lived in the Balkans long before the arrival of the Slavs, Kosovo's ethnic composition has been predominantly Albanian for several centuries.

After the fateful battle of 1389, the Serbs had begun leaving Kosovo. The largest single population shift took place in 1689, when 37,000 Serb families picked up their cradles, their emblems, and their icons, and left Kosovo to settle in Austria at the invitation of the emperor Leopold I. Leopold, bent on territorial expansion, had pushed deep into Ottoman territory before his forces were checked and defeated. He offered to settle the Kosovo Serbs along his borders as a way to check Turkey's expansion northward. The throng, almost 100,000 strong, led by Patriarch Arsenije III, the archbishop of the Kosovo town of Pec, walked across the Balkans and crossed the Danube into the Austrian Empire and the protection of a Christian (albeit Roman Catholic) prince.

A somewhat smaller migration occurred in 1737, this time induced by the Ottomans. The Turks also decided to downgrade the Serbian Orthodox Church by having the Pec archbishopric placed under the administrative control of the Greek patriarch in Constantinople.

The influx of Albanians over the centuries into the depopulated areas of Kosovo, Macedonia, and northern Greece was steady. Indeed, the capital of the southern Albanian region was Ioannina, now a Greek port. And the Muslim Albanians were considered socially superior to the Christian population in the eyes of their Ottoman overlords because they had accepted Islam. There is also a good deal of literature about the so-called Eastern Question which indicates that the Christians had been subjected to severe persecutions at the hands of the Muslims.

The British author Edith Durham, traveling through Kosovo in the first decade of the twentieth century, recorded in her book *The Burden of the Balkans* the raging Albanian hostility toward Serbs. Speaking in Serbian, she approached an Albanian Kosovar. When he failed to respond, she asked if he understood Serbian. After a long silence he replied:

> "I understand it, but I will not soil my mouth by repeating their dirty words!"
> "Why do you hate them so?"
> "Because we are born like that. It is in our blood."

When, after more than five centuries, the Serbs finally recaptured Kosovo in 1912, they burned countless villages and massacred thousands of men, women, and children. Leon Trotsky, who observed the terrible retribution as a foreign correspondent in the conflict, quotes in his book *The Balkan Wars* an account by a Serb officer:

> The horrors actually began as soon as we crossed into Kosovo. Entire Albanian villages were turned into pillars of fire. The picture was repeated the whole way to Skopje [capital of Macedonia]. There the Serbs broke into Turkish and Albanian houses and performed the same task in every case: plundering and killing.

The Serbs from the north and the Greeks from the south carried out a brutal "ethnic cleansing"—their aim being "the entire transformation of the ethnic character of regions inhabited exclusively by Albanians," in the words of a Carnegie International Commission inquiry in 1913.

Serbia's seizure of Kosovo was shortlived. As World War I unfolded, Austria-Hungary and Germany defeated the Serb Army in 1915, forcing it to retreat to Greece. The army had to retreat through Kosovo and Albania to reach sanctuary on Corfu, the Greek island just off Albania's coast; it lost an estimated 100,000 men during the retreat. Just how many of these casualties could be ascribed to a culture of revenge is debatable. The Serb Army's recapture of Kosovo a month before the war's end produced predictably horrific results for the Albanian population.

Kosovo was given to the Serbs by the great powers at the Paris Peace Conference after World War I, which also established the Kingdom of Yugoslavia. According to a 1921 Yugoslav census, 64 percent of Kosovo's inhabitants were Albanians. That percentage dropped to almost 50 percent during the period between World Wars I and II as the Serbian government encouraged Serbs to settle in Kosovo in an effort to redress the ethnic balance.

But an equally appalling retribution followed in 1941, when Nazi Germany dismembered Yugoslavia. The Albanians—now fighting on the side of Nazi Germany—massacred thousands of Kosovo Serbs, burned down Serb villages, and forced some ten thousand Serb families to flee to Serbia.

Ethnic peace in Kosovo was enforced by Tito's Communists after they seized control of Yugoslavia at the end of the war. Some small-scale score settling did take place during the postwar years, but that depended on who controlled the Kosovo police. The Serb domination during the first fifteen years of peace was particularly harsh. In response, and to tamp down Serb nationalism, Tito granted autonomy to the Kosovo Albanians in 1974, along with a seat on the ruling presidential council. Once the Kosovars were granted home rule and the police force was in their hands, they could not resist temptations to even the score. And yet, Tito's Yugoslavia did push the traditional enmity underground, and with considerable success, for there were people on both sides of the ethnic divide committed to peaceful coexistence, with local Communist Party committees brokering disputes and seeking to forge compromises. Kosovo's unfortunate history precluded more democratic healing processes.

Milosevic's reconquest policy began in late 1988 with a massive propaganda campaign. Then, in February 1989, he purged the whole of Kosovo's Albanian leadership and ordered the arrest of Azem Vlassi, the local Communist leader who had refused to support him two years earlier and had sided instead with the unfortunate Stambolic.

It seemed at the time to be an amazingly ill-considered decision. But, in retrospect, it was undoubtedly calculated by Milosevic to stir up trouble, to make his predictions a self-fulfilling prophecy and to exact a measure of personal revenge against Vlassi. Some of the men in his inner circle cautiously pointed out that Belgrade's objective should be to divide the Kosovars, not unite them. It was essential to keep relations with the old Titoist party establishment, which had a vested interest in Yugoslavia; the wholesale assault on them would turn the entire Albanian population toward secession.

The same point was made by a dismayed John Scanlan, the U.S. ambassador to Yugoslavia at the time, who called on Milosevic to warn him that he was making a fatal mistake. "You have got to have somebody down there in Kosovo who has the respect of the population and who can do it for you, who can keep things under control," Scanlan told Milosevic. "I think that is Vlassi. He can do it."

Scanlan noted a harsh look in Milosevic's eyes. "No, no," the Serbian leader said.

"Why does he have to go, Slobo?"

"Because he let the security situation get out of control!"

"The art of statesmanship is to employ people to your fullest advantage. Past is not what is important here, it's the future."

"No, no, there'll be others. He's got to go," Milosevic said with the air of finality.

Before Vlassi's arrest on trumped-up charges of counterrevolution, Milosevic met with the Communist chiefs of the other Yugoslav republics and made it clear that he intended to revoke Kosovo's autonomy. "Serbia will do what it wants, using any means it deems necessary, be it in accordance with the law or not."

Slovenia's Communist leader Milan Kucan replied, "Then this is the end of Yugoslavia."

Vlassi's arrest was the beginning of the end of all contacts between Kosovo's ruling establishment and Serbia. Despite the difficult and often violent history of Serb-Albanian relations, there had always been a segment of the ethnic Albanian elite that favored cooperation with Serbia. Now all such links would be severed.

Perhaps Milosevic had calculated that this was inevitable and sought to provoke an immediate confrontation. The mood of Kosovo had been gradually changing ever since the death in 1985 of Enver Hoxha, the Communist leader of Albania proper, which borders Kosovo, for the previous forty-one years. Under Hoxha's savage rule, Albania had been the last Stalinist kingdom. Aware of the appalling brutality and malevolence of Hoxha's savage dictatorship, most Albanians had considered themselves fortunate to be in Yugoslavia. On Hoxha's death, radicals voiced demands for a "Unification of all Albanian lands"—the old dream shared by all Albanians—but these demonstrations were quickly suppressed by the mainly ethnic Albanian police. A majority of Kosovars followed the local leaders, who were cautious and pragmatic. Most of them, though not all, were members of Tito's party, and many had deep personal and professional links to Belgrade.

What the Albanians wanted was to upgrade the status of Kosovo; it was conspicuously obvious to them that with 2.1 million people, Kosovo should be accorded the status of a republic within Yugoslavia. The neighboring republic of Montenegro, after all, had a population of only 600,000.

But instead of the start of militancy, as Milosevic may have expected, the man who emerged as Kosovo's leader after Vlassi's arrest was a literary historian and writer, Ibrahim Rugova, who counted Mahatma Gandhi and Dr. Martin Luther King Jr. as his heroes.

Rugova was a mild, professorial man who always wore a woolen scarf, no matter what the weather; it was, he said, his signature piece, ensuring that he would be recognized. He preached passive resistance. In the summer of 1989, he founded the Democratic League of Kosovo, an organization that turned into something between a mass movement and a political party. With Rugova as president, the League wanted gradually to move the Kosovars toward independence, but without violence.

The Kosovo Albanians went underground. They attended schools in each other's homes, ran their own makeshift clinics, subsisted largely on savings and money sent home from relatives and friends in Switzerland, America, and across Europe. And they lobbied every ambassador, diplomat, and dignitary they could, putting their case for independence, or at least republic status. To all outward appearances, Kosovo had turned into a surreal, tense state. It was under direct Serb police rule; but apart from reports of sporadic brutality, it was tranquil.

Having subdued Kosovo, Milosevic quickly seized control of Serbia's other autonomous region: Vojvodina, an area north of the Danube with a large ethnic Hungarian population. This populist operation—using nationalist crowds to wrest control from the existing institutions—went much more smoothly because the Serbs were a majority in Vojvodina. On October 7, 1989, hot on the heels of his successful conquest of Vojvodina, Milosevic engineered a coup in Montenegro and brought to power a group of young Communists led by thirty-four-year-old Momir Bulatovic. Having accomplished this, Milosevic turned his attentions to the rest of Yugoslavia.

# 3

# In Tito's Long Shadow

When he began trying to impose his persona on the rest of Yugoslavia in 1989, Milosevic modeled himself on his hero, Marshal Tito.

Milosevic started wearing the white summer suits that the debonair Tito favored and exchanged his cigarillos for Tito-style Havana cigars. When addressing select groups, he adopted Tito's standard ending: "I wish you success in your future work." He also moved from his apartment in the middle-class part of Belgrade to an elegant house in the posh suburb of Dedinje, next door to the novelist Dobrica Cosic and the ambassadors of Britain, China, the United States, and the Netherlands. He had the walls in his new residence reinforced and heightened.

What was lacking, however, was the intelligence and experience that would tell Milosevic what must be done. His goal was plain: initially he wanted to take over Tito's creation, but when that appeared impossible he decided to break up Yugoslavia and win most of it for himself.

The overriding impression, as one contemplates the quite remarkable vagaries of this policy over a decade, is that Milosevic himself never made up his mind exactly how to reach his goal. And being too proud and exceedingly uncomfortable with subordinates with good brains, he invariably turned to methods he understood: conspiracy, deception, and force.

His character was etched on his face, which was immobile, expressionless, devoid of emotional coloration; it was the mask of someone who is focused on a single idea and whose mind is so rigid that it is incapable of registering ideas that are outside that basic framework. He was a despot in his soul and the few known remarks about his desire to restore Serbia to the glory of its medieval empire reveal the grip of mythology and folklore on his psyche.

The irony is that a man devoted to a morbid past while seeking a grandiose future may have left a deeper imprint on history than Tito, who although born into the nineteenth century had been a thoroughly modern man. Whereas Tito rebuilt a country and forced upon it the spirit of tolerance, Milosevic destroyed Yugoslavia by his ethnic chauvinism.

Like Tito, Milosevic was a man of enormous self-confidence, charm, and determination. But the differences between them were vast and fundamental.

All his life Milosevic had turned toward the East—Moscow, Orthodoxy, despotism—and his entire career was spent in the offices of state-owned enterprises or the ruling Communist Party. His first foreign trip was to Russia, the citadel of Orthodoxy as well as communism. In later years, while he was president of the Belgrade bank, he did make numerous trips to the United States, but these were in the nature of shopping sprees that high Communist bureaucrats saw as their right. He was interested in gadgetry and luxury goods; he showed no natural curiosity in America's cultural or political life.

"Except for business meetings," recalled Zoran Kojic, an official in the Yugoslav trade office in New York who was assigned to escort Milosevic during a number of his visits, "he would spend most of his time at Macy's, Bloomingdale's, and Saks Fifth Avenue."

Tito, by contrast, was an essentially Western man. One of fifteen children of a Croat father and a Slovene mother (both Roman Catholics), he left his native village in 1907, at the age of fifteen, to work as a waiter and a locksmith apprentice near Zagreb, the capital of the Austrian province of Croatia.

Though he had only four years of primary education, Tito possessed a shrewd intellect, natural curiosity, and a passion for travel. While still a teenager he moved to Trieste, Italy, then to a series of German cities ranging from Mannheim to Munich; he settled down as a mechanic at the Daimler-Benz Works near Vienna. Drafted into the Austro-Hungarian Army during World War I, he became a sergeant major and was captured on the Russian front.

When the Russian Revolution broke out in 1917, he escaped and joined Lenin's Red Guards and the Bolshevik Party. At that time, Tito would say later, revealing his instinctive audacity, he had seriously considered emigrating to the United States, adding: "And you know, had I done it, I would have become a millionaire!"

He opted for politics instead.

In 1920, he returned to Croatia, now part of the new Kingdom of the Serbs, Croats, and Slovenes, joined the local Communist Party, and worked his way up the ladder. Having seen a huge empire crumble before the onslaught of a few determined men, he felt confident that he too would succeed one day. He served five years in a royalist jail; afterward the party sent him to Moscow, where he had a front-row seat during Stalin's murderous purges of the 1930s. He became Yugoslavia's Communist leader almost by default—Stalin had executed the Yugoslav party's entire leadership in 1937.

When Hitler dismembered Yugoslavia in 1941, he established the "Independent Croatian State" and made it a carbon copy of Nazi Germany. The Croatian Fascists, known as the Ustashe, committed unspeakable atrocities against Serbs, Jews, and Gypsies in Bosnia and Croatia, established detention centers for racial and political undesirables, and proselytized ruthlessly by forcing the conversion of non-Catholics to Catholicism. Their leader, Ante Pavelic, was a Croat from Bosnia-Herzegovina who pursued a policy of genocide and ethnic cleansing. "This is now the Ustashe Independent State of Croatia," Pavelic declared on August 14, 1941. "It must be cleansed of Serbs and Jews. There is no room for any of them here. Not a stone upon a stone will remain of what once belonged to them."

In contrast to the ethnic fanaticism of the Ustashe and of the Serb royalists known as the Chetniks, Tito remained committed to the Yugoslav idea. He organized and led an uncompromising wartime struggle against the Germans and Italians, and he won recognition from the United States and Britain in 1943. In 1944, Tito seized power in Belgrade and established a Communist-style dictatorship. But his foreign policy was too independent for Stalin's taste and the Russians began quietly infiltrating Yugoslav institutions, planning to replace Tito and his colleagues with more pliable men.

Tito's defining moment in foreign affairs came in 1948, when by refusing to take orders from Moscow, he became a modern-day David fighting a Soviet Goliath. He survived. He then proceeded to build relations with all countries, promoting trade and various other forms of cooperation and trying to construct a network of links that could serve to ward off possible blows by the world's mighty nations. He set into motion the so-called Third World Movement of non-aligned nations.

It was the United States that provided this David with his slingshot. The colorful heretic was quickly embraced by Washington as an ideological threat directed at the heart of Stalinism. Over time, driven by strategic considerations, the American role deepened steadily and Tito became one of the main recipients of U.S. military and economic aid. From the early 1950s until the end of the 1980s, the United States was publicly committed to supporting the "independence, territorial integrity and nonalignment" of Yugoslavia. In so doing, the United States effectively checked the thrust of an aggressively confident Soviet military toward the Mediterranean.

After Stalin's death in 1953, Tito began a long process of reconciliation with his successors that started when Nikita Khrushchev flew to Belgrade in 1955 to publicly apologize and formally acknowledge Tito's right to his own brand of socialism. In the memorable image of former U.S. Ambassador Laurence Silberman, Tito became Europe's Fiddler on the Roof, treading a conceptually narrow path: on one side was a slide toward Bolshevism, on the other toward pluralism. Since he could not go either way and retain power, he became a balancing artist. All his instincts favored courses offering the least possible disturbance to the East-West status quo. When Henry Kissinger called on him in 1974 to complain that Yugoslavia seemed to be tilting too far toward the Russians, Tito reassured him that was not the case. "You see, they are so close, and you are so far, far away."

Throughout his life Tito was bored by abstractions, and he never took ideology very seriously, at least not as a means of interpreting the actions of others or his own reactions to problems. He was passionate about music (he learned to play the piano late in life), young women (each of his three wives was more than twenty years younger than he), and the good life. He was a true Yugoslav: he abhorred tribalism. His new Yugoslavia was to be based on his concept of "Brotherhood and Unity" for all its peoples. Before and during World War II, he was the only political leader in Yugoslavia whose party appealed to all the ethnic groups. He insisted throughout his life that any form of national chauvinism was a poison that must be eradicated.

Tito's Yugoslavia was by any measure unique: an independent Communist country within Moscow's reach but beyond its grasp. He made real strides toward democratization, at least when measured by Soviet bloc standards; gave people a long-coveted freedom of movement; opened the country's borders and invited Western investors. In reaching out to his people, he came closer—at the expense of Marxist doctrine—to the point of view of the South Slavs. The doctrine had to be adjusted; he realized he could reach them not through appeals to their class consciousness—they had none—but through a sympathy to all ethnic groups, the idea of equality and respect, and physical courage, which they respected and to which they responded. And even though Tito insisted all along that he was an orthodox Marxist, the benign Western view was summed up by the late *New York Times* foreign affairs columnist C. L.

Sulzberger: "Sure Tito is a Marxist, but his dogma was written by Groucho, not Karl."

Most Western observers feared that Yugoslavia might not survive Tito's death and that his successors—lacking his authority, his native wit and diplomatic skills—would soon stumble. But most wanted Yugoslavia to succeed. Such poignant wishful thinking was reflected in the 1974 edition of the *Encyclopaedia Britannica,* which maintained that "The Yugoslav system is so deeply rooted, and the survival of a strong, independent, nonaligned Yugoslavia is so vital to the maintenance of European stability, that the country will undoubtedly survive the shock of Tito's departure."

At least initially, after Tito's death in 1980, Yugoslavia absorbed the shock. Its foreign and domestic policies proceeded along the established groove and were managed by well-trained technocrats and experienced diplomats. But the nation was on automatic pilot. Tito's successors all clung to a Titoist rhetoric, and ambitious politicians like Milosevic more so than others. It is worth noting that Milosevic's rallying cry in the 1987 power struggle was his condemnation of Ivan Stambolic's "anti-Titoist policies."

By temperament and experience, Milosevic was not the man to assume Tito's burden; it was too heavy for him. He was a tactical genius, but without a strategic sense. He was too secretive; diplomats who negotiated with him said there were never more than two or three other persons inside the cavernous, gloomy presidential building. He lacked Tito's broad concept of Yugoslavia and its place in the world. He was not a natural diplomat: he seemed incapable of entering into the minds of his neighbors or understanding their fears. Rather, his arrogance inspired fears in others. On a different level, the man was a perfect expression of communism's failure to nurture new generations of competent and imaginative officials. He was far more ambitious and ruthless than Communists from Tito's generation. His was a new type of dictatorship: a television dictatorship, backed up by police. He turned television and radio into a narcotic—the words, the sound chosen to numb your brain—

the chauvinistic message permeating everything like a poisonous miasma.

In contrast to Tito, who was comfortable with delegating authority and at ease with people who exercised their own judgment (provided they did not challenge his personal authority), Milosevic was a man who wanted to be in total control of every detail. He was exceedingly vindictive, destroying all whom he perceived as a challenge. And by all accounts he took great pleasure in the misery he brought to others and in the sense of power and control this afforded him.

Milosevic's lack of foreign experience led him to ignore the changes around him. The information age had dawned; the slow disintegration of the Soviet Empire was evident; the old certainties were disappearing. And yet he dismissed his own advisers who counseled a careful subordination of Serb ambitions to the maintenance of good relations with neighboring states. These were people who did not oppose his goal, but merely urged patience and careful calculations before action was taken.

Above all, Milosevic misjudged the United States; why, he wondered, should Serbia defer to an unwieldy democracy whose establishment he could always distract by tactical concessions? He did not understand—as Tito had understood intuitively—that no reconfiguration of Balkan borders could be achieved in the face of opposition from Washington. Still, he was proud of what he considered his familiarity with America and his personal relationship with many important Americans, including Lawrence Eagleburger, now deputy secretary of state in the Bush administration.

Milosevic flaunted his friendship with Eagleburger, who was a greatly admired figure in Yugoslavia. Eagleburger's local fame dated from 1963, when an earthquake ravaged the Macedonian capital, Skopje. Though he was just a junior officer in the U.S. Embassy in Belgrade, Eagleburger helped orchestrate the Western aid program to the city. He was thereafter known as "Lawrence of Macedonia."

When Eagleburger returned to Belgrade as the U.S. ambassador from 1977 to 1981, Milosevic was a young bank president who talked liberal economics. He was a frequent guest at Eagleburger's dinner table and the two men established a rapport that continued after Eagleburger left Belgrade. In 1988, while Eagleburger was in the private consulting business, he visited Belgrade and called on Milosevic. "They talked about old times," recalled John Scanlan, Eagleburger's former deputy.

But by 1989, Eagleburger's view of Milosevic had changed. The man he had known in the late 1970s was different from the man he read about in diplomatic dispatches and press accounts. Eagleburger found Milosevic's new rhetoric abhorrent. As deputy secretary of state, he was deeply concerned by Milosevic's policies, which could lead Yugoslavia into catastrophe. He expressed his annoyance with Milosevic to Scanlan, who called on him in May 1989 upon the end of his tour in Belgrade.

"Your friend Milosevic is beginning to cause a lot of trouble over there," Eagleburger growled.

"But Larry," Scanlan replied, "I met Milosevic at your dinner table."

Scanlan's replacement, Warren Zimmermann, was sent to Belgrade with new instructions. President George Bush's view was that Yugoslavia no longer enjoyed its former geopolitical importance and therefore should not expect special consideration from Washington. But for more than a year Zimmermann was not able to deliver this message to the most powerful man in Belgrade; Milosevic simply would not see him. If there was a major change in American policy, he confidently told intimates, his "friend Larry" would forewarn him.

In the back of Milosevic's mind there was always another superpower card to play—the Soviet Union—even though Mikhail Gorbachev's policies had unnerved him. He took it as an article of faith that he could always count on Moscow's backing; "Nas i Rusa dvjesta miliona" ("We and the Russians together are 200 million strong") was an old Montenegrin saying that was always revived in times of crisis.

His diagnosis was not quite correct. Certainly, Moscow's links to the Serbs were strong, but Milosevic failed to detect the changes underway in Russia. He would make an astonishing miscalculation on

August 19, 1991: hours after hard-line plotters staged a coup against Gorbachev, Milosevic's chief ideologue, Mihajlo Markovic, announced Yugoslavia's support for the hard-liners. Only Iraq's Saddam Hussein and Libya's Moammar Qaddafi followed suit. Within a few days, when it became clear that the attempted coup had turned into a disaster for the plotters, the scope of Milosevic's misjudgment became abundantly clear to the Belgrade establishment, indeed to Milosevic himself. Having alienated the progressives around Boris Yeltsin, Milosevic would spend an enormous amount of effort and money to repair the breach over the next few years. He would never quite succeed until the NATO bombardments of Serbia in 1999 galvanized Russian public opinion against the United States.

But it was in the domestic political arena that Milosevic departed most drastically from Tito's principles.

The stability in Tito's Yugoslavia was based on a delicate ethnic equilibrium, buttressed by his personal authority. But his authority may not have been sufficient had he not been a master at balancing ethnic interests. He advanced the cultural and political rights of non-Slav minorities more than anyone else in Eastern Europe—especially with regard to the Bosnian Muslims and the Kosovo Albanians.

In Tito's view, the Yugoslav kingdom between the two world wars was a "prison of nations" because it was dominated by the Serbs and their king. But even before he wrested power, Tito had to confront the ethnic issue at a constitutional assembly held in the Bosnian town of Jajce in the middle of World War II.

At issue was Bosnia, a triangle-shaped territory which was literally and metaphorically the heart of Yugoslavia. Apart from an Eastern Orthodox Serb majority and a Roman Catholic Croat minority, Bosnia contained a large Muslim community (at that point amounting to one-third of the total population). All three were ethnic Slavs speaking the same language, Serbo-Croatian.

Although they professed to be internationalists, the Communists could not agree on what to do about this state of affairs. Serb representatives insisted that Bosnia belonged to Serbia; their Croat colleagues argued that it was rightfully Croatia's. The Muslims were poorly represented in the assembly, and they were apprehensive about their future status.

Tito's Solomon-like solution—indeed, the only rational solution for a Yugoslav leader—was spelled out in a single sentence that shaped the constitutional future of the Bosnia republic: "Bosnia does not belong to either Serbs *or* Croats *or* Muslims; it belongs to Serbs *and* Croats *and* Muslims."

It was not the solution Milosevic would have proposed.

The first three years of Milosevic's rule suffused Serbia with a dizzy optimism. Just as Mira had predicted in 1968, his photograph or portrait hung in every store window, in offices and government buildings, in trucks; it was impossible to walk through Belgrade without constantly meeting his confident gaze. Tito's image began to disappear—except in Kosovo and Bosnia. At the end of 1988, Milosevic began a sustained attack on Marshal Tito when he told a huge rally in Belgrade that "even before his death the [Yugoslav] system didn't function—Tito functioned."

The tabloid press selected Milosevic as "The Man of the Year" in 1988. A popular song of the period hailed him as a saviour, with a refrain that rhymes in Serbian:

*We now know who is the second Tito*
*His proud name is Slobodan.*

In the course of 1988, mass rallies—known as "truth rallies"—were held in many towns and cities. They took on the aspect of national festivals. Patriotism was reflected in the number of assembled citizens. Government institutions no longer functioned. This was, Milosevic said, a new form of freedom—a "democratic, honest and expected reaction" of citizens who "feel threatened." They served his political purpose: the masses were prepared to mow down any political opponents of Milosevic; and there was no small element of Nazi-style pressure tactics in all of this.

In the aftermath of the fall of the Berlin Wall in November 1989, Yugoslavia embarked on a series of reforms to adjust to the new situation. But the Yugoslav Communist Party was disintegrating. Party bosses from the six republics were constantly quarreling; most of them were afraid of the powerful Serb strongman.

Milosevic's actions accelerated the process of disintegration. When the Communist leaders of the northernmost republic of Slovenia sided with the striking Albanian miners in Kosovo, Milosevic imposed an economic embargo on Slovene goods. *Politika* and other newspapers led the assault on Belgrade stores that featured Slovene-made goods in their shop windows, thereby "insulting the patriotic feelings of customers."

Having tamed Kosovo, Vojvodina, Montenegro, and Serbia itself, Milosevic had not expected much resistance from Slovenia (population 2 million). A proclamation of the boycott of Slovene goods included an arrogant assertion that foreshadowed the frightful collapse of Yugoslavia in the years to come:

> We want you to know that not a single citizen of Serbia will plead with the Slovenes to remain in Yugoslavia.

The proclamation was issued on December 1, 1989—exactly seventy-one years to the day after the Kingdom of the Serbs, Croats, and Slovenes was created. According to Borisav Jovic, Milosevic's senior deputy at the time, Milosevic was planning to punish the other Western republic—Croatia—by imposing an embargo on deliveries of electrical energy from Serb power plants.

The Slovene Communists, who had led the drive to adopt the constitutional amendment which laid the ground for elections and Slovenia's sovereignty, changed their party's name in December—becoming the Party of Democratic Reforms. The republic was in a secessionist mood. At sports meetings in Slovenia, the crowds were shouting "Srbe na vrbe" ("Hang Serbs from willow trees"). The party's message was "Europe Now"—Slovenia wanted to quit Yugoslavia and join Europe. Milosevic's boycott merely reinforced the secessionist sentiments. It was also a prelude to the formal collapse of the Yugoslav Communist Party, which took place at an extraordinary party congress in late January 1990.

While he had blamed Stambolic for "anti-Titoist" policies three years earlier, Milosevic by 1990 no longer had any use for Tito. The Serbian media now cast the famous marshal as a former intelligence agent with links to Hitler; the weekly magazine *On* topped a list of outrageous crimes by asserting that Tito had been involved in "repeatedly raping young Serb girls."

The Slovene Communists, for their part, came to the congress with a firm mission to demolish the old Communist Party, and to use Milosevic to do it. They correctly counted on his inflexibility. After two chaotic days of a Serb-Slovene rhetorical war, they walked out. "Have a good journey," Serb delegates cheered. It was later discovered that the Slovenes had already checked out of their hotels in order to avoid paying for an extra day.

"What are we going to do?" asked the presiding officer. "This is a new situation."

"I propose we continue with our work," an unperturbed Milosevic replied.

Suddenly, an unexpected blow was delivered by the Croatian Communists. They called for an indefinite postponement and announced they would not take part in any decisions. The congress was indefinitely adjourned. It was the final debacle of Tito's "brotherhood and unity" dream and the beginning of the end of Yugoslavia. Milosevic's ploy to gain control of the Communist Party through a majority of votes at the congress had failed. From this point on, he knew that his hope to replace Tito as the undisputed master of Yugoslavia was a mirage. And so he began to think in terms of a Greater Serbia, which he articulated in a meeting with Serbian regional officials a few months later: "We have to do everything to have a united Serbia if we want to have the republic, which is the largest and most populous, dictate the future course of events."

After the congress ended abruptly on January 22, 1990, only

one man seemed unconcerned. The federal prime minister, Ante Markovic, noted that the Yugoslav Communist Party had died, but "Yugoslavia is going to continue to exist."

Markovic, a Croat technocrat, had been appointed prime minister the previous year. His job was to administer the country's economy, finances, and foreign relations; but his political backing was the Yugoslav Communist Party, which was now dead. His optimism was quickly to prove unfounded and naive.

After January 1990, Yugoslavia entered a chaotic period of slow disintegration as the first free elections in the republics brought nationalist leaders to the fore.

"There will be war, by God," Milosevic told his aide Borisav Jovic on February 13. The third man present, Yugoslav defense minister General Veljko Kadijevic, added his own view: "There won't be the kind of war they want, but it will be the kind of war which it must be, and that is that we shall not allow them to beat us." Four days later, Milosevic's agents helped organize a Serb political party in the Krajina section of Croatia.

By June, Milosevic's strategy was taking practical shape. Jovic recorded in his diary that on June 28—St. Vitus Day—Milosevic had outlined his plan to him: Slovenia and Croatia would be "ejected" from Yugoslavia, but the Serb-populated areas of Croatia would remain in the federation. The defense minister had already accepted the idea that the army must "defend the right of the people who want to remain" in Yugoslavia. Milosevic had become the de facto commander of the Yugoslav federal army, which in the preceding months had turned into a Serbian army. Even General Kadijevic did not realize when the transformation took place. "There were no precise dates," he said, "because decisions were ripening with events."

Milosevic assigned the practical work to his most trusted aides in the police and security services: Radmilo Bogdanovic, Jovica Stanisic, Mihaly Kertes, and Radovan Stojicic-Badza. But while preparing for war, he talked of peace. His Socialist (formerly Communist) Party emerged victorious from the 1990 elections, with

Milosevic engineering a nearly total fragmentation of the body politic—fifty-three parties fielded candidates for parliament, more than half of them so-called mosquito parties run by his agents to divide and weaken any opposition. Milosevic was easily elected president—there were thirty-one other presidential candidates in the running—and that was the only election he truly won, even though his party machinery engaged in electoral fraud and vote stealing.

A Radio Belgrade journalist, Dusan Radulovic, ambushed Milosevic as he was leaving a rally, surrounded by bodyguards, demanding a statement about the election. Milosevic halted for a moment as if something totally extraordinary was happening—didn't the journalist know that he never talked to the press or responded to their questions?—then walked away without saying a word.

The persistent journalist phoned Milosevic's home that evening, asking whether he wanted to say something to the Serb people.

"I don't want to!" came the reply.

"Thank you," said the journalist.

"You are welcome," said Milosevic.

He was still, though, a popular figure in Serbia.

The adulation of his people had been intoxicating for Milosevic. It had fueled his transformation from lifelong gray Communist Party apparatchik into a fervent nationalist, obsessed with his need, his duty, to preside over the disintegration of Yugoslavia and to secure most of its territory for Serbia—his interests and Serbia's interests becoming identified in his mind.

Thus was the Yugoslav crisis carried to a higher level. The smaller Yugoslav republics rejected the "Greater Serbia" idea and announced intentions to seek independence to protect themselves from Milosevic's predations. In December 1990, the new government of Slovenia held a referendum on independence. An overwhelming majority endorsed the proposal that the tiny republic should formally declare independence six months later. The leaders of the republic of Croatia obliquely hinted they would follow suit, but lacked the confidence to hold a referendum on the issue. The leaders of two other republics—Macedonia and Bosnia—became alarmed.

Milosevic had become resigned to letting Slovenia go, for it had no Serb minority of any significance to provide a plausible pretext. The conflicts of the preceding year had also taken their toll. When Italian foreign minister Gianni de Michelis in early 1991 questioned him about the prospect of Slovenia's secession, Milosevic told him, "They can go. If they want, they are free to go."

The other Yugoslav republics, however, had significant Serb minorities, and Milosevic could not release them so easily. His idea that the new Yugoslavia—which he would rule—would be the old Yugoslavia minus Slovenia was soon stated in an unequivocal way in banner headlines across the country. When Vasil Tupurkovski, the Communist leader of Macedonia, warned that "if a single republic leaves the federation then Yugoslavia will cease to exist," Milosevic replied in the slang of the underworld: "Malo morgen." ("Just forget about it.") The reply suggested a man deeply confident that the fate of the country was in his hands.

The optimism was short-lived. Milosevic's critics in Serbia began issuing warnings that he was leading the nation into a disaster. They were promptly silenced. In March 1991, Belgrade University students mounted massive anti-war demonstrations, singing "Give Peace a Chance." The most wonderful thing about these thousands of young men and women was a fresh bright interest in human rights, faith in themselves, and a sense of humor which they brought to expose the nasty reality and disperse the lies and illusions the media had fed them. They were joined by tens of thousands of ordinary citizens, teachers and scientists, artists and clerks, and democratic opposition leaders. The situation called for a new political figure to channel the whole thing in a fruitful direction.

Up to this point, there had been no serious fights between Milosevic and the opposition, because the opposition was not organized and the democratic leaders had allowed themselves to be picked off one by one—either arrested, or intimidated, or corrupted.

This time, on March 9, 1991, the capital city was buzzing with rebellious energy. The writer Vuk Draskovic and other opposition leaders, standing on the balcony of the National Theater, demanded press freedom and an independent judiciary. The police unexpectedly turned water cannons on the crowd and lobbed tear gas canisters into the central square. The protesters were enraged. Draskovic, a striking figure with an unkempt mane of black hair and flowing beard, urged the protesters to resist. "Charge! Charge!" he shouted when the riot police surged forward.

The demonstrators found iron bars, sticks, and bricks; the police beat a retreat. For several hours, the protesters were in control of the city and the regime appeared to be faltering. Rumors that a coup d'état was underway circulated throughout the city. But the opposition leaders suddenly appeared paralyzed by their very success: they gathered in the Serbian parliament trying to get in touch with Milosevic and his aides.

Milosevic replied by calling tanks to the streets of Belgrade, arresting and torturing opposition leaders, and closing down a local independent television station and the student radio station B92.

The brutality shocked Belgrade. Angry students the next day left their dormitories at midnight and began round-the-clock demonstrations in the heart of the city. Thousands of residents supplied food, blankets, and other necessities. Leading nationalist intellectuals including the poet Matija Beckovic, president of the Serbian Writers Union, joined the students.

Milosevic phoned the seventy-seven-year-old Orthodox Patriarch Pavle and successfully persuaded him to plead with the students to abandon the protest. But the protesters jeered when the frail old man made his appeal.

Clearly shaken by the scope and intensity of the new protest, Milosevic agreed on March 11 to meet with student representatives in an effort to defuse the crisis that threatened to inflame the country.

The meeting took place in a vast government hall. The students demanded the immediate release of Draskovic, one of the March 9 protest organizers, and the firing of propaganda chief Dusan Mitevic and of security czar Radmilo Bogdanovic.

Milosevic tried to appear reasonable and accommodating. "People should not destabilize things," he said, "at a time when we are trying to stop the resurgent Ustashe Fascists, Albanian secessionists, as well as other forces of the anti-Serb coalition who are endangering people's freedom and rights."

He had, Milosevic said several times, no authority to do anything about their demands.

"Are you currently responsible for anything in this country?" a tall, gangly psychology student named Zarko Jokanovic asked him bitterly. "You are behaving like the queen of England when you have the power of a Russian tsar!"

The atmosphere remained tense. Another student asked permission to open the window for some fresh air. Chants of "Slobo You Are Saddam" suddenly filled the room.

Jokanovic then produced a photograph of a young man who had been killed by police two days earlier. "Is there anything human left in you?" he asked Milosevic, who turned red but did not reply.

On March 13, Draskovic was released from jail. Mitevic and Bogdanovic, Milosevic's two closest aides, agreed to step down and were quietly assigned different duties (while remaining Milosevic's top aides). The students believed that they had won. "Freedom for Serbia!" bellowed Draskovic, looking out at the huge crowds in central Belgrade celebrating his release.

It was particularly painful for Milosevic to sacrifice his friend Dusan Mitevic, the man who had been a mainstay of his struggle for power. They met alone at Milosevic's Tolstoy Street private residence, reminiscing about the old days. Milosevic was apologetic. The students had to be pacified; but nothing, he said, was going to change between the two friends.

Milosevic had a gift for Mitevic, he said, handing him a Colt pistol of white steel with a chamber holding six bullets. Mitevic later recalled his own quip at that point: "It holds too few bullets for the number of enemies I have." They both broke into laughter.

Three days later, Milosevic invoked emergency measures. He addressed the country by television, declaring that he was taking Serbia out of the Yugoslav federation and ordering "the mobilization of special reservists and the urgent formation of additional Serbian militia units." He said: "Yugoslavia has entered into its final phase of agony. The Republic of Serbia will no longer recognize a single decision reached by the Presidency under existing circumstances because it would be illegal."

Milosevic's meaning could not be clearer. "Yugoslavia," he stated, "is finished." Serbia, in effect, had seceded.

The country was thrown into disarray. That same day, the Serb rebels in Croatia proclaimed the independence of Krajina, the banana-shaped agricultural region of Croatia in which the Serbs were a majority.

The goal of these maneuvers by Milosevic was to impose his will on the Serb-dominated Yugoslav Army. Up to that point, at least in theory, the military chiefs led by Defense Minister Kadijevic had been under the control of the collective eight-man presidency. Since Milosevic controlled four of the eight votes (those of Serbia, Montenegro, Kosovo, and Vojvodina), the presidency was frequently paralyzed. Now, by proclaiming that "Yugoslavia is finished," and announcing that he was planning to create his own military, Milosevic forced the Serbs who dominated the Yugoslav officers corps to come to his side, giving him control of the military.

The fires of protests died down in Belgrade, but only after Milosevic consented to another meeting with two hundred students and professors from Belgrade University who demanded to know his plans for Yugoslavia. A clearly uncomfortable Milosevic faced the young people, his staunchest opponents, who boldly asked him to resign.

In turn, he talked about "all Serbs living in one country" as his goal.

"You have to understand," one student, Nebojsa Milikic, replied, "that there is only one national interest—that Serbia and Yugoslavia become democratic states."

But nothing happened. Tens of thousands of Serb professionals began moving abroad. The novelist Vidoslav Stefanovic was the harbinger of the mass exodus: he moved to Greece and vowed not to return before democracy was established. Speaking of Milosevic, the novelist said: "I believe he'll destroy everything!"

A course had been set. Milosevic's 1989 prophecy in Kosovo that war would come had a self-fulfilling quality. He made sure it would happen: he would incite the Serb minority in Croatia to provide the spark, then use the remnants of the Yugoslav Army against Croatia.

Milosevic had come to realize that in a land of such deep differences, no single leader could take Tito's place without resorting to brute force. He would not flinch from such a requirement.

He made his new intentions clear at a closed meeting of regional Serb leaders on March 16, 1991. "Borders are always dictated by the strong, never by the weak," he said. "We simply consider it as a legitimate right and interest of the Serb nation to live in one state. This is the beginning and the end." Milosevic proceeded to list the areas in other parts of Yugoslavia where Serbs lived. "And if we have to fight, by God we are going to fight. I hope that they will not be so crazy as to fight against us. If we do not know how to work properly and run an economy, at least we will know how to fight properly."

One of those attending the meeting, Slobodan Djukic, the mayor of Valjevo, said later that Milosevic made clear that he was preparing to drive out the Croats and the Slovenes, the two Roman Catholic republics. "I understood after the meeting that he was ready to form a Yugoslavia without the Catholics," Djukic said.

The Croats, however, would not submit to Milosevic's will. And they had a leader who could counter him point for point, Franjo Tudjman.

Tudjman was in a sense a perfect match for Milosevic. A former general in the Yugoslav Army, Tudjman had come to power in the first free elections in 1990, riding a wave of Croatian nationalism that arose in response to Milosevic's fierce Serb nationalism across the border.

Tudjman had channeled the emotions of Croat nationalism onto himself and used them without scruples to establish his power. Like Milosevic, he was a consummate cynic, a politician of authoritarian mien whose natural expression was a scowl, only rarely replaced by an awkward chuckle or a nervous smile. Neither man showed much understanding of, or interest in, democratic values. But whereas Milosevic was driven solely by power, Tudjman was also obsessed by nationalism of the most narrow-minded kind.

The key to Tudjman's success was an alliance with the militant nationalist émigrés who had been associated with the Ustashe, who fled to North and South America and Australia after World War II. In Croatia, the Ustashe spirit had been driven underground by Tito, but not destroyed.

Tudjman openly courted the Ustashe exile organizations. He invited Ustashe émigrés to Croatia and issued visas upon their arrival at the airport in Zagreb. This was, he said later, his most crucial political decision. It was so risky, he said, that he and his associates "waited till the last minute to see whether we would be arrested or not."

It was, he added, "a turning point in my life. . . . Great deeds, both in individual and creative terms, and especially in social innovation and even militarily, are created on the razor's edge between the possible and the impossible. It is in such moments that judgment is important to achieve something that seems impossible for most people."

His rhetoric echoed the Ustashe commitment to the "Aryan blood and honor" of the Croatian nation, which alarmed the Serbs in Croatia, who accounted for 13 percent of its 4.5 million population. "Thank God my wife is not a Jew or a Serb," Tudjman baldly declared during his 1990 election campaign.

The new Croatian political platform was the destruction of Yugoslavia and hatred of the Serbs. It was reflected in such slogans as "Mi Hrvati ne pijemo vina/nego krv Srba iz Knina" ("We Croats don't drink wine, rather we drink the blood of Serbs from Knin") or "Srbe na vrbe" ("Hang Serbs from willow trees"), which appeared all over Croatia.

Milosevic was no longer devoted to maintaining the unity of Yugoslavia, but he knew it could be a bargaining chip in his power game. He kept his options open. A note from the diary of one of his aides, Borisav Jovic, makes that clear:

> We thought, Milosevic and I, that there was no reason to keep Croatia by force in Yugoslavia and we thought the Army should have withdrawn to the Serb territories. But the Army could not understand this because they still believed they should defend Yugoslavia.

Within a few short months, however, there would no longer be a Yugoslavia to defend.

# 4
# Croatian Intrigues

The land known as Bosnia and Herzegovina is one of those unresolved custody cases left by history and compounded by all the shifting powers that have bid for this strategic piece of real estate.

Prior to 1878, Bosnia was a geographic entity in the Ottoman Empire, a regime that classified its subjects by religious affiliation, not nationality. The Sultan's army occupied the region in 1463 and imposed a harsh and brutal rule on its Christian population. Muslims alone enjoyed the rights of citizenship, and so a substantial number of the local Slavs accepted Islam. The fact that their descendants are still called "converts" reflects the self-serving political arguments of Croatia and Serbia, both of whom have insisted that Bosnian Muslims are erring Slavic brethren who have strayed from Christ. Nobody refers to, say, the Lithuanians as "converts" because they accepted Christianity in 1368. Nor do we question the authenticity of Islam in, say, Indonesia, where it arrived even later than it did in Bosnia. Although not a model of religious freedom, the Ottoman Empire did allow non-Muslims to maintain their churches and synagogues and in fact showed more religious tolerance than the Muslims would be accorded later by Bosnia's Christian rulers.

By the mid-nineteenth century, the Ottoman Empire had grown steadily weaker, and the Balkan Slavs became pawns in an international power game. The ardent pan-Slavists in Russia encouraged Serbia and Montenegro to go to war against Turkey and to help their brethren in Bosnia. But if Russia were to advance into the Balkans, it would have to do so by closing all avenues to the expansion of the Austro-Hungarian Empire. Great Britain believed further that it had an interest in preventing Russia's breaking through to the Mediterranean, which might threaten British commercial interests.

To forestall wider conflicts and reach a satisfactory accommodation, the great powers convened at Berlin in 1878 to redraw borders and manage the decline of the Ottoman Empire, which the newspapers had taken to calling "the Sick Man of Europe." Bosnia was placed under the administrative control of Austria-Hungary, a fortunate development for its mixed population. The first Austrian census, in 1879, showed the Muslims with 38 percent, Orthodox Serbs with 42 percent, and Roman Catholic Croats with 18 percent. Vienna introduced the idea of the acceptability of diverse forms of social behavior, and promulgated new forms of human rights, including freedom of worship and civic equality. The Habsburg rulers also introduced the idea of parliamentarianism. These were major steps forward for a province oblivious to the values of the European Enlightenment.

The Bosnian Croats welcomed the new colonial masters; being Roman Catholic meant a higher social status for them. But the two largest groups—the Serbs and the Muslims accounted for 80 percent of the total population—were wary, for Austrian administrators had no experience in dealing with these groups. The confusion in Vienna over how to integrate the new province was reflected in the fact that Bosnia was placed under the authority of the Imperial Ministry of Finance, which some saw as reflecting its colonial status but others regarded as a pragmatic decision to avoid conflicts between the foreign policy and military elites.

The abrupt end of Turkey's rule left the Muslims in a state of shock. They were facing an uncertain future, demoted, and for the first time under Christian rule. Under the Ottomans' tradition, the fusion of political sultanate and religious caliphate had given the Turkish polity a sacred character. Politics was a means to create a just social order as defined by the Koran. The only legitimate political processes were those sanctioned by the shari'a, the Islamic law.

The Muslims assumed the superiority of their faith and were resolutely hostile to Christian ideas and practices. The secular social rules were at odds with Islamic teachings on dietary habits, alcohol consumption, the role of women, and other things. Shari'a was no longer the source of law. Tens of thousands—mostly families of men employed by the Ottoman administration—gradually migrated to Turkey. Feeling threatened, those who remained quickly coalesced into a coherent unit.

The Muslim community circled the wagons and firmly insisted on maintaining a way of life based on the Islamic religious law. Religion—rather than ethnicity—defined them and shaped their collective memory; they had no other national image nor did they have a historical state to look back on. (Medieval Bosnia had been Christian.)

Faced with such opposition, the Habsburgs changed tactics. The first move was to detach their new Muslim subjects from the religious authorities in Istanbul; to this effect Vienna created the position of a reis-ul-ulema, the local supreme religious authority, backed up by a four-member religious council, the mejlis-al-ulema, appointed by the Austrians and not the Ottomans.

This was a fateful decision. Initially, many Muslims did not regard the council members as authentic religious leaders. More fundamentally, they were divided on the question whether the Koran allowed them to live under, and cooperate with, the new Christian rulers. But over the next two decades, the office of the Muslim spiritual leader in Sarajevo became accepted by the Muslim community. Eventually this became the basis for the creation of the Slav Muslims of Bosnia as the only nation nominally identified by their religion, and not their language or ethnicity.

The Muslims also learned to play parliamentary games. The Bosnian assembly showed itself not so much a vehicle for expressing the province's popular will as a means for mobilizing it behind the imperial administration. The three religious communities—Catholics, Muslims, and Orthodox—formed three ethnic parties and were initiated into the art of political dealmaking.

The substitution of religion for national identity had a lasting influence on Bosnia's political and social development. The religious political orientation not only set out divinely ordained obligations of individuals but also emphasized the rights of the community rather than the rights of individuals. The Muslims quickly learned the practical value of their swing votes on a variety of divisive issues; the Austrians, on the other hand, were all too eager to extend to the Muslim elite their previous privileged status, provided they collaborated with the Austrian authorities. In practice this meant that the Muslim-Croat coalition had a thin majority over the Serbs.

By the time Austria annexed Bosnia in 1908, in a direct violation of the Treaty of Berlin, the Muslims fully supported the Austrian move; in 1910, they formally swore allegiance to the Habsburg emperor.

But this sequence of events aroused the profoundest misgivings among the Serbs, both in Bosnia and in neighboring Serbia. Once again the Bosnian Serbs were buzzing with rebellious energy. Their talk grew wilder, with demands for liberation of the parts of the Serb nation in Austria-Hungary and Turkey.

The Serbian government in Belgrade was deeply involved in fomenting Bosnian unrest. There has been speculation that Serbian and Russian agents were involved in the conspiracy that ended with the June 28, 1914, assassination of Archduke Franz Ferdinand and his wife, Sophie, but that was never fully documented. What is documented is that a Russian military attaché in Belgrade, Colonel V. Artamanov, had given money and encouragement to a secret Serb nationalist society known as the Black Hand, which in turn supplied weapons to a conspiratorial Bosnian Christian organization known as Mlada Bosna ("Young Bosnia"). On Serbia's most sacred day—St. Vitus Day—an eighteen-year-old conspirator named

Gavrilo Princip fired the shot that killed the heir to the Habsburg throne as he visited Sarajevo. When Austria subsequently rejected as insufficient Serbia's all but complete submission to the terms of its ultimatum, war became inevitable. Russia was too deeply committed to allow the Serbs to be wiped off the map. Germany backed Austria, France sided with Russia. Within six weeks the continent was at war.

In 1918, Bosnia became a part of the new Yugoslav kingdom; this time, however, the Serbs were in charge. The Muslims, like other minorities, had to subordinate their sense of community to the dominance of the three main tribes: the Serbs, the Croats, and the Slovenes.

During World War II, the Bosnian Muslims sided with the Croatian Fascists and fought alongside the Ustashe and the Germans in the genocidal struggle against the Serbs and Serb-dominated Tito Partisans. The Serbs were decimated. After the war, however, the Muslims were first given the status of a minority before Tito elevated them, in 1971, to the status of a nation.

The meeting at Tito's splendid hunting lodge at Karadjordjevo on March 25, 1991, was so secret that Milosevic never admitted it took place, much less the diabolical plan that was hatched there.

His guest was Franjo Tudjman. The topic was Bosnia. In a strange way, the two men were bound together; they were like Siamese twins who had one heart. And that heart was Bosnia.

Both Tudjman and Milosevic had decided that the old Yugoslavia was dead and that three or perhaps four successor states would emerge. Where they differed was on the matter of territory. Both wanted the whole of Bosnia. Since any scramble for Bosnia meant war, they decided to reach an agreement at the expense of the Bosnian Muslims. The two men shared the view that the Muslims were not a distinct nation, although Tudjman contended they were actually Croats, whereas Milosevic insisted that they were Serbs.

Tudjman had staked his claim the previous year, first by asserting that Bosnia was "a national state of the Croatian nation," but then modifying his position slightly by insisting that Bosnia and Croatia formed one natural economic and geographic entity. He had been afraid to push the matter further, torn between greed for more territory in Bosnia and anxiety that a militarily stronger Serbia might upset his plans for Croatia's independence.

He was prepared to accept Milosevic's new plan for a Greater Serbia as amounting to Belgrade's control over Yugoslavia minus the two Catholic republics (Croatia and Slovenia), provided that Croatia was accorded a share of Bosnia.

The understanding they reached at Karadjordjevo was that the Bosnian republic should disappear from the map. Details were to be worked out later. Indeed, the two men soon held another secret meeting on the Serb-Croatian border, and then had their personal envoys (Croatian prime minister Hrvoje Sarinic and Milosevic's counselor Smilja Avramov) discuss details of the Bosnia division. According to Stipe Mesic, Tudjman's top deputy at the time, the envoys met secretly more than thirty times to discuss maps and population movements (a euphemism for what later became known as ethnic cleansing).

At the same time, Milosevic told Tudjman to come to terms with the Serbs of Krajina, the Serb enclave inside Croatia, hinting that he would not go to war to defend their interests.

Following the Karadjordjevo meeting, U.S. Ambassador Warren Zimmermann met with Tudjman for what he later described as the "most astonishing single discussion" of his three years as ambassador. It was in fact a monologue, Zimmermann recalled. Tudjman asserted—with echoes of Milosevic's paranoia—that the Bosnian Muslims were planning a Greater Bosnia which would spread to Turkey and Libya; that their leader, Alija Izetbegovic, was a fundamentalist front man for Turkey; that Catholics and Orthodox alike would be eradicated; and that Tudjman himself had planned with Milosevic to divide Bosnia between them. "Let Milosevic take the larger part, he controls it anyway," Tudjman told Zimmermann. "We can do with less than fifty percent."

Publicly, Milosevic never acknowledged the existence of any understanding with Tudjman. But after Karadjordjevo, he claimed he never had any intentions "to dispute the right of the Croatian nation to secede from Yugoslavia. But I want to make it absolutely clear that it should not occur to anyone that a part of the Serbian nation will be allowed to go with them."

What he told his top advisers may only be surmised from the published diary of his aide Borisav Jovic, who noted, after a meeting with Milosevic: "The only problem I see is what to do with the Serbs in Croatia."

But Milosevic intended to grab as much territory as possible around Croatia's edges. Jovic reports:

> Milosevic and I decided we would limit our military activities to those territories in Croatia where the Serbs wanted to remain with us. We would protect them from the Croatian authorities and the Croatian paramilitary units. We knew we would have to withdraw the army from those parts which evidently could not remain in Yugoslavia, and to close our eyes as far as the arming of the Serbs [in Croatia] was concerned.

It was difficult for Muslim politicians to imagine a Muslim future in a purely Serb or Croat state. In the immediate aftermath of Karadjordjevo, they were immobilized: like the heroes of the old Greek tragedies, they seemed condemned to an ineluctable fate from which there was no escape. There was no one on the scene strong enough to put the brakes on; the old Yugoslav military, which was stationed in Bosnia, was on Milosevic's side.

The Muslims' sense of survival was extraordinarily powerful. They rightly regarded any division of Bosnia as an intolerable threat to their security and interests. By 1991, they comprised the largest ethnic group in the republic, 44 percent to the Serbs' 31 percent and the Croats' 17 percent. The rest identified themselves as Yugoslavs. Assailed from both sides, their room for diplomatic maneuvering was almost nonexistent.

The choice between Milosevic and Tudjman was hardly a choice;

as Alija Izetbegovic put it, it amounted to "choosing between leukemia and a brain tumor."

Izetbegovic was a unique person on the Yugoslav political scene, the only leader who had been an active anti-Communist throughout his life. He was drawn by his religious beliefs into politics and went to work to create an underground Muslim organization almost immediately after the end of World War II. He was jailed eight years for this.

He was an unassuming and likable man, but his mild manners, vacillations, and fumblings belied a far tougher and shrewder politician. As the leader of a Muslim minority in a sea of Christians, he was prepared for a compromise. But he also understood that compromise was not possible with such men as Milosevic, whom he viewed as the "Serbian Stalin," and Tudjman, whom he described as the "Croatian Hitler." In a speech to the Bosnian parliament on February 27, 1991, Izetbegovic declared: "I would sacrifice peace for a sovereign Bosnia-Herzegovina, but for that peace in Bosnia-Herzegovina I would not sacrifice sovereignty."

He was determined to resist. He understood that nations are made by the force of arms and ideas, that there are winners and losers, and that the Muslims were outgunned and outnumbered. Having grasped the meaning of Milosevic's deadly game, he also discovered the Serbs' Achilles' heel: Milosevic's propaganda revealed him as a narrow-minded apostle of intolerant nationalism.

Izetbegovic pursued political preparations with skill and imagination. Part of it was to get the Muslims to understand the threat; of no less importance was the pursuit of alliances among concerned nations. But the crucial element in his strategy was to make the idea of "multiculturalism" his rallying cry.

The "multicultural" platform was a brilliant tactical move that endowed the Muslims with a higher claim to public virtue. It also set Izetbegovic apart, in Western eyes, from his Serb and Croat opponents, the two predatory neighbors who wanted to destroy the republic and divide it between them.

While preaching multiculturalism, Izetbegovic embraced Islamism as his ideology. His Party of Democratic Action was to be an exclusively Muslim party. "For now, unfortunately, our Party must be sectional [that is, sectarian]," he said. "The parties that try to represent everyone are small and weak. Until now, Muslims have had no political leaders. We need a big party, then we need political power."

Early on, some Bosnian Muslim intellectuals issued public warnings: Izetbegovic, they said, was against a modern, multicultural Bosnian state; he was exploiting religion for political purposes; and his "hidden agenda" included the partition of Bosnia and the creation of a purely Muslim state in Europe.

"Izetbegovic is not interested in becoming part of Bosnia's history, but a part of the history of Islam—the man who established the Muslim state on European soil in the style of one-man-against-the-world," maintained a 1993 White Paper on Alija Izetbegovic written by two critics, Musadik Borogovac and Sven Rustempasic.

This argument was given additional force by Mustafa Sehovic, a prominent Muslim figure who was a physician, writer, university professor, politician, and member of the Bosnian parliament. Close to eighty, he had a noble bearing and a brisk, lively sense of humor, the prototype of a European intellectual with a magnanimous soul and a far-reaching and acute mind.

Sehovic had been a part of the Muslim leadership all along, but he openly favored younger Muslim politicians, especially Haris Silajdzic, Bosnia's first foreign minister, who was Western-educated and who saw Bosnia's future in Europe. Sehovic too wanted to see the Bosnian Muslims integrated into a cosmopolitan Europe rather than a rump ecclesiastical state beholden to Iran and Saudi Arabia.

Izetbegovic, he said, "wants the whole of Bosnia. And don't pay much attention to his multiculturalism."

But Milosevic never even attempted to form an alliance with the pro-European Muslim intellectuals in Bosnia. By the late spring of 1991, all political maneuverings—feverish, complex, muddled—were in the last resort irrelevant. A course had been set.

Milosevic's propaganda machinery made war seem inevitable. "Freedom is acquired only by blood," shrilled the broadcasts of nationalist agitators trying to create the sense of immediate threat from Croat and Muslim duplicity. Whose blood? Nobody asked the question, for there was nothing to counter the hectoring and denunciatory messages laden with rapturous references to Serb mythology and poetry.

It is hard from present perspectives to understand how anyone could succumb to such messages. The only explanation is that Milosevic controlled the masses by controlling the flow of information, and that the skills he acquired during his years as an information officer and propagandist were now being applied to advance his agenda.

Milosevic kept himself in the background, as was his style, allowing his minions in the media and parliament to do the work.

Serbia's parliamentary sessions, carried live on radio and television, turned into jingoistic harangues. "The Croats hate us, and so do the Shiptars and the Macedonians," cried socialist deputy Batric Jovanovic. "But thank God, we Serbs are strong enough and nobody can do anything to us."

To which the deputy Zivorag Grkovic added: "Now when we've got the right man in whom we all believe, we are ready to die" for the cause.

War had become a necessary preliminary to paradise. At its root was an induced masochism, identification with the redeeming blood, the unconscious belief that the "national cause" demands immersion in pain.

When war finally came on June 25, 1991, less than a year after the first free elections, it was fought first in Slovenia. The Slovenes had followed through on their decision to declare independence on that date. They also provoked war by forcibly seizing control of the border posts; they opted for war as a way to get what they wanted. But the Slovene leader Milan Kucan had a personal assurance from Milosevic—the two men had discussed the matter on January 24 and reached agreement—that Serbia would not oppose Slovenia's right to secede.

The Yugoslav government ordered two thousand troops to secure control of the border posts.

The "ten-day war" was probably unique in the history of warfare: about fifty people—mostly Yugoslav Army soldiers—lost their lives in what was an almost theatrical but skillfully staged propaganda war for Slovenian independence. The propaganda effort was boosted by German foreign minister Hans-Dietrich Genscher, who arrived in the Slovene capital of Ljubljana at the start of the war and accused the Yugoslav Army of "running amok" in Slovenia. In Washington, Republican Senate leader Bob Dole called on the Bush administration to "compel" the Milosevic regime to "halt its violent crackdown on democracy and human rights."

This, indeed, was Milosevic's war, but only in a perverse sense. He had honored his pledge to Kucan. "I am going to repeat a hundred times that I am for peace," Milosevic kept saying. But Milosevic did not even try to block the army's halfhearted move. The Slovenian "war" was useful to Milosevic for other reasons: it discredited the last two figures committed to the preservation of Tito's Yugoslavia. One was the prime minister, Ante Markovic, who had ordered the army into action but then categorically denied ever having done so; the other was the defense minister, General Veljko Kadijevic, the last Titoist general, whose incompetence had degraded what was once a formidable military force. A discredited Kadijevic and the other generals now had to shift their allegiance to Milosevic.

Later in the summer, however, the real conflict erupted between the Serbs and the Croats, the two largest tribes, again under the pretext of the Yugoslav Army's efforts to keep Tito's union from falling apart but in effect to solidify and expand the position of the Serb rebels in Krajina, who had earlier declared their independence from Croatia.

The war with Croatia was brief, brutal, and mostly confined to border areas with mixed Serb-Croat populations. It started several weeks after Croatia declared its own independence on June 25. According to Tudjman's propaganda, the Roman Catholic Croats were fighting against "hegemonism" by the Eastern Orthodox Serbs, who were not only Communists but also an inferior, Oriental culture.

Milosevic's propaganda asserted that his heavily armed proxies in the Krajina and the Serb-dominated Yugoslav Army were defending a "defenseless Serb people" from a reemerging Croatian fascism. Both sides expressed a strain of fanatic idealism; nationalists fought side by side with Communists.

Lord Peter Carrington, the former British foreign secretary, was called by the European Union to help Cyrus Vance, the former secretary of state who was now UN Special Envoy to Yugoslavia, to negotiate an end to the Serb-Croat hostilities. Carrington was struck by the cynicism of both Milosevic and Tudjman. When he first met them, he recalled, "it was clear to me that both of them had a solution which was mutually satisfactory—which was that they were going to carve it [Yugoslavia] up between them. They were going to carve Bosnia up. The Serb areas would go to Serbia, the Croat to Croatia. And they weren't worried too much, either of them, about what was going to happen to the Muslims. And they didn't really mind about Slovenia."

Milosevic publicly insisted that Serbia was not involved in the war in Croatia. But, in reality, he micromanaged events from behind the scenes, personally directing strikes by the Yugoslav Air Force in support of the Serb rebels in Croatia and using the Yugoslav Army to prepare the ground for the coming Bosnian war.

An extraordinary record of a telephone conversation may be perhaps the only documentary evidence of Milosevic's operational style during these wars. It is unclear who taped the August 1991 exchange between him and Radovan Karadzic, the Bosnian Serb leader who was preparing for war in Bosnia. Its transcript was presented at one of the last sessions of the Markovic federal government, on September 19, 1991, by critics of Milosevic's war policy:

> MILOSEVIC: . . . You just talk to General Uzelac [Nikola Uzelac, the commander of the Banja Luka Corps in western Bosnia] and he will tell you everything. If there are places where you experience problems, you should contact me personally.

KARADZIC: I have a problem with Kupres [a western area of Bosnia]. One part of the Serbs there are pretty disobedient.

MILOSEVIC: Don't worry. That's easy, just tell Uzelac.

KARADZIC: Hm.

MILOSEVIC: You'll get everything, don't worry. We are the strongest.

KARADZIC: Yes, Yes.

MILOSEVIC: Don't worry. As long as we have the army, nobody can do anything to us.

KARADZIC: Hm.

MILOSEVIC: And don't worry about Herzegovina. Momir [Bulatovic] has sent the message to the people that those not prepared to die for Bosnia should take five steps forward. Nobody did.

KARADZIC: That's fine. But what about that bombing near . . .

MILOSEVIC *(jokingly):* Today is not a convenient day to use the air force, the European Community is meeting.

The Yugoslav Air Force carried out air strikes against Croatian forces that summer and fall, and the world watched Milosevic's forces pulverize the Croatian town of Vukovar. Only an attack on Dubrovnik, the jewel of the Adriatic, provoked an international outcry. With the rebel Serbs aided by the remnants of the Yugoslav Army in control over large disputed parts of Croatia, Milosevic calculated that the time was ripe to agree to a UN peacekeeping presence to protect his gains. Meanwhile, the preparations for war in Bosnia intensified and a Sarajevo newspaper, *Slobodan Bosna,* reported on November 21, 1991, that Karadzic's party was readying its paramilitary forces to surround the Bosnian capital and that they were getting guns and other equipment from the Yugoslav Army.

Milosevic's position in Serbia was deteriorating, however. The economy had come to a standstill. More than 500,000 refugees from the war were living in miserable conditions in camps around Belgrade. Angry parents' complaints could no longer be drowned in a televised torrent of patriotic euphoria. The conscripts from Serbia proper did not want to fight.

The very fact that the vastly stronger and better armed Yugoslav Army could not defeat poorly armed Croatian troops demonstrated Milosevic's failure to inspire the Serbs to a national crusade. Instead, paramilitary troops—the Tigers, the White Eagles, the Chetniks—spearheaded the Serb campaign in Croatia, motivated by the prospect of plundering. "They were types who would kill a man of ninety for a lamb," General Slavko Lisica, the commander of Yugoslav Army forces on the Dalmatian front, recalled later. "My men in the front lines would come to me and say, 'The paramilitaries rob, they rape, they steal. Why are we fighting and what are we fighting for?' "

The army's performance was disappointing. Inevitable delays became longer. Nothing could be properly synchronized. Commanders frequently resorted to a peculiarly vicious method of "motivating" their troops: they would fire on their own positions to make the men fight for "self-preservation." General Lisica conceded that he had ordered his artillery chief to open fire on his own men to "motivate" them. "If somebody gets killed, so be it."

In one such incident, after one of his units had seized the strategic Maslenica Bridge north of Zadar, the general quickly summoned them for a pep talk. He wanted to shame the conscripts into fighting. All those who are not prepared to "defend the glory of the Serbian nation" had better lay down their arms and take off their uniforms, the general told them.

"And, incredibly, they all did, including their commanding officer," Lisica recalled. "They were standing there and I got furious and shouted at them to remove everything including their underpants, and with the exception of one man they all removed their military issue underpants and marched off completely naked. I was still hoping that they would change their mind, but they didn't."

The next day, the men must have found clothes in neighboring villages and commandeered a cannon somewhere, which they used to shell Lisica's headquarters.

In a similar incident on the Vukovar front, the commander of a unit of raw recruits demanded to know who wanted to fight and who wanted to return home. The company promptly split into two. But one soldier, Miroslav Milenkovic, from the town of Gornji Milanovac, could not make up his mind and instead blew out his brains in front of his comrades.

A strong and sullen resistance was particularly strong in the heartland of Serbia—a region known as Sumadija—whose people are less inclined to extremism. Only one out of every four young men responded to a call-up—26 percent, according to published figures. A majority refused to "volunteer" for the front. Desertions were rampant. Reservists refused to fight; some staged dramatic anti-war incidents. About seven hundred reservists from the town of Velika Plana returned their weapons and uniforms to the military. Others went into hiding or fled abroad. Milosevic sent police through the streets of towns and cities to haul in men for "voluntary" military service; late one night, the American journalist Jonathan Landay was hauled out of his car and taken before a recruiting officer. Menfolk were also systematically snatched from their workplaces and homes and pressed into the army; in the provinces, paramilitaries arrived with trucks at factory gates for the end of work shifts and simply loaded men in, without giving them the opportunity to go home and tell their families.

Some dramatic protests were staged in major urban areas. When Air Force Captain Zdravko Vidakovic saw one of Milosevic's key political allies, Montenegrin leader Momir Bulatovic, in a street in Podgorica, he pulled a revolver and committed suicide in front of Bulatovic without uttering a word.

More typical was the protest of Vladimir Zivkovic, a student from Valjevo who was sent to the front against his will. Announcing, "I've had enough," he climbed into an army armored personnel carrier and roared out of the Vukovar front along fifty miles of country roads to Belgrade, where his vehicle briefly careened out of control and smashed two sedans before Zivkovic parked it in front of the federal parliament building. The military police quickly hustled him away and an official statement declared him in a state of temporary insanity. When they heard the statement read over the radio, Zivkovic's comrades-in-arms were enraged. Brandishing weapons, nine of them stormed into the local radio station and demanded airtime to denounce Ministry of Defense claims. They said Zivkovic was sane, demanded his release, and served a litany of complaints against the regime. "We are not traitors," one of them declared on the air. "But we do not want to be aggressors."

The regime vigorously suppressed all news about malcontents and desertions. The media's patriotic euphoria offered the spectacle of a united people embarked on a holy crusade. At the same time, Milosevic unleashed paramilitary gangs, which he had thus far used only outside Serbia proper, on his own population. All dissenting voices were to be silenced. In one instance, six men wearing black ski masks over their heads stormed into the dingy offices of the Center for Anti-War Action in the heart of the city and wrecked everything they could find. Those who ignored such intimidation faced beatings or even assassination, usually by men with black stockings over their heads. In Belgrade, the most notorious of the paramilitary forces were the Tigers, led by Zeljko Raznjatovic, known as Arkan, and the Chetniks, led by Vojislav Seselj. Two other notorious warlords—Dragoslav Bokan and Mirko Jovic—operated mainly outside Belgrade.

Press accounts quoted Arkan as warning "Serb traitors" that his Tigers would deal with them once "we are done with the outside enemies." Jovic's message to the population was that his dog could "smell Serbian traitors in Belgrade." In this climate of Fascist-style intimidation it was never certain who the real killers were—whether the police itself or the notorious paramilitary formations.

An example was the gangland slaying of a wealthy businessman, Branislav Matic, who had initially supported Milosevic but switched his financial backing to Vuk Draskovic's Serbian Renewal Movement. In August 1991, Matic, George Bozovic, and several other critics of the regime were fingered in the parliament by Milosevic's ally, Vojislav Seselj, who warned that "something should be done about" them. Three days later, Matic was gunned down in front of his wife and their two young children; his assassins left the scene in a white Mercedes.

The same day, about twenty paramilitaries marched into the Slavija Hotel restaurant in the heart of Belgrade where Bozovic was having dinner. Bozovic saw them coming, fled through the service entrance to the second floor, and hid in an unlocked room. When his would-be assassins began searching the area by shooting off the locks, Bozovic leaped out of a second-floor window onto a moving truck. He hurt his leg but saved his life.

Funeral services for Matic were attended by some ten thousand people, who heard orators lay the blame at the feet of Milosevic. His regime, Draskovic said in his eulogy, "feeds and thrives on blood and can only through blood keep itself in power." Bozovic, who also spoke at the funeral, was more threatening. "Once the war in Croatia ends, vengeance will come," he said.

But nobody except those attending the funeral heard these words.

Milosevic, however, insisted that the paramilitary formations did not exist. "As is well known, they are banned here," he repeatedly said, even though Arkan's Tigers were using the stadium of Red Star Belgrade, the European soccer champions, for their military exercises. When Ambassador Zimmermann noted that Arkan's trail of pillage and murder in Croatia had been shown on Belgrade Television, Milosevic replied that "our television is free to broadcast what it wants." He added, "As I understand it, he [Arkan] is no more than a simple sweetshop owner."

Shortly afterward, when Thailand closed down its embassy in Belgrade, Arkan and his family moved into the elegant former residence of the Thai ambassador, the building owned by the Foreign Ministry's Diplomatic Housing Office.

Arkan was an extreme example of the unsavory characters Milosevic used for his purposes. Nicknamed the "baby-faced killer," he kept his men well trained, well armed—and well rewarded. They sent home plunder from their victims, from refrigerators to foreign currency. Milosevic granted Arkan an oil concession in the easternmost part of Croatia which the Serbs seized in 1991; Arkan also took over a winery.

Under Tito, Arkan had been a hit man for the Yugoslav secret police, the UDBA, charged with eliminating anti-Communist exiles in Western Europe. Interpol has outstanding arrest warrants for him on charges including robbery, extortion, drug smuggling, and murder. He was convicted of armed robbery in Belgium, Holland, and Germany, but always managed to escape from prison. This was never mentioned by the Serb media, which lionized him. Magazine photographs from 1991 show him posing with dozens of his Tigers—all except Arkan are wearing black ski masks, clutching AK-47s, and raising their hands in the three-fingered Serb salute.

To intimidate the Kosovo Albanians, Arkan was made a parliamentary deputy for Kosovo, where he would swagger around town and broadcast TV messages to the Albanians to leave. In Belgrade, his presence could not be missed: he maintained his headquarters at an ice cream parlor near Milosevic's home which he had restructured into a five-story pink marble folly with glass elevators on the outside and a balcony overlooking the Red Star stadium.

Since the paramilitaries belonged to no formal military structure, Milosevic was able to claim that he had nothing to do with them. Arkan, when asked by journalists who he was reporting to, replied: "My commander-in-chief is Patriarch Pavle." For Milosevic, the man who liked to leave no traces, the paramilitary groups were the perfect hired accomplices. Even Richard Holbrooke seemed to have accepted his argument that he had nothing to do with them, describing Arkan as a "freelance murderer" and a "racist fanatic run amok."

The reality was far different. Arkan and other paramilitary leaders were in the Yugoslav chain of command. Seselj told journalists assembled at the Writers Club Restaurant that, "Milosevic organized everything. We gathered the volunteers and he gave us special barracks at Bubanj Potok, all our uniforms, arms, military technology and buses. All our units were always under the command of . . . the Yugoslav army. Of course, I don't believe he signed anything, these were verbal orders. None of our talks were taped and I never took a pencil and paper when I talked to him. His key people were the commanders. Nothing could happen on the Serbian side without Milosevic's order or his knowledge."

This view of Milosevic's relationship with the paramilitary "volunteers" is confirmed by Dobrila Gajic-Glisic, the executive secretary of Serbia's defense minister, General Tomislav Simovic. In her autobiographical book, *Serbian Military,* she recounts the minister's daily conversations "via a special telephone" with Milosevic, who micromanaged many aspects of the paramilitary activities in Croatia. Arkan, she said, was occasionally provided with helicopters during certain operations.

"Arkan operated within the Territorial Defense system," she wrote. "He had his own group which acted under his command, but all actions were cleared and coordinated with the Yugoslav army [high command]." The ministry also provided "clothes, weapons and basic equipment" for other paramilitary groups; they all received military training at the Bubanj Potok military camp outside Belgrade. When professional officers returning from the front warned the minister that Arkan and his men were committing atrocities against civilians, she quoted Simovic as replying, "I support anyone who is actively fighting. I'm not in a position to control who does what on the ground. I leave that to each man's conscience."

What did infuriate the minister was his discovery that some paramilitaries were under the direct control of the Yugoslav security services and that they worked together with special commando units of the Serbian police controlled by the deputy interior minister, Radovan Stojicic-Badza, and security czar Radmilo Bogdanovic, both close associates of Milosevic.

General Simovic insisted he should have been warned about this command structure. But Milosevic liked to compartmentalize his activities, never giving any one subordinate too much control or understanding of the bigger picture. He took extra care to keep a formal distance, to make it seem as if others, outside his control, were responsible. He was the type of politician who leaves no traces. He never wrote an article under his name; his short speeches contained no plans; his interviews were slogans designed for the primitive nationalist ear. His style was conspiratorial. Everything was moved by word of mouth—without a paper trail. He never delegated to those around him defined areas of responsibility that could be regulated by a clear-cut statutory code.

Simovic's outburst proved the end of him. It was provoked by an incident involving a Belgrade-born Australian mercenary known as Captain Dragan (his real name was Dragan Vasiljevic). The Serb media had turned Captain Dragan into a folk hero in the fight for a Greater Serbia. It described him as a mercenary who carried a swagger stick, kept a young leopard as a mascot, and insisted on the strictest discipline. Though born a Serb, he had emigrated with his family to Australia and joined Australian forces fighting in Vietnam before training armies in Africa as a soldier of fortune.

General Simovic had selected Captain Dragan to train his own paramilitaries in Belgrade. He ordered his reassignment at the end of December 1991. But Captain Dragan refused, citing "obligations toward the State Security Services of the Republic of Serbia" and said that "my engagement must have complete approval of the service mentioned."

General Simovic was furious. "For me, the role of the interior ministry is an enigmatic one," he complained as he appealed for an urgent meeting with Milosevic. "They are becoming more and more secretive. The most enigmatic is Radmilo Bogdanovic."

Milosevic declined to meet him. Instead, the general was promoted—he received his third star—and then sent into retirement.

# 5
# The Abdication of the West

One can only marvel as to how a rational and responsible administration such as that of President George Bush could ever become entangled in a sequence of missteps that led the United States first to an open-ended military commitment and then to a war in the Balkans. Whatever the reasons, they did not include lack of information.

It is certain that the last thing Bush wanted was a war in Europe. It is also certain that in 1989–91 his mind was focused on the gradual collapse of the Soviet Empire and on the Persian Gulf War. But the level of inattention to the burgeoning crisis in the Balkans was quite remarkable. And even after the hostilities in the former Yugoslavia began in the summer of 1991, the president and his secretary of state, James Baker III, simply ignored them.

Any account of Yugoslavia's collapse that is based on a record of the diplomatic exchanges and news dispatches is incomplete, perhaps even meaningless, because it leaves out the mood and attitudes of Bush and Baker. They made all decisions. They had the best advisers money could buy. Their key associates had been steeped in Yugoslav affairs, had served in Belgrade, and were expert's experts on the Balkans. Deputy Secretary of State Lawrence Eagleburger had served twice in Yugoslavia; he was seen by all as "Mr. Yugoslavia," and everybody kept coming to him for advice. National security adviser Brent Scowcroft, who had once served as a U.S. military attaché in Belgrade, managed to keep himself out of the limelight even though his credentials matched Eagleburger's. Indeed, Scowcroft had written his doctoral dissertation on Yugoslavia.

Despite such wealth of knowledge and experience, Bush and Baker decided to do nothing.

"Eagleburger and I were most concerned about Yugoslavia," Scowcroft said later, revealing much more than his loyalty to Bush would normally permit. "The President and Baker were furthest on the other side. Baker would say, 'We don't have a dog in this fight.' The President would say to me once a week, 'Tell me again what this is all about.' "

Warnings also came from prominent figures outside the administration. The éminence grise of American diplomacy, George F. Kennan, who had served as ambassador to Yugoslavia from 1961 to 1963, spoke already in 1989 with the prescience that he had shown so often in his long career. With the cold war over, he told Ambassador Zimmermann, people in Washington thought that Yugoslavia was no longer in a position to destabilize the international order. "They are wrong," Kennan said. "I think events in Yugoslavia are going to turn violent and to confront Western countries, especially the United States, with one of their biggest foreign policy problems in the next few years."

The problem was that Bush saw Yugoslavia as a local problem rather than a European problem. A country once of great importance to the United States had become—owing to the collapse of the Soviet Empire—a country of relative unimportance to America. The message to Milosevic was that the world had changed, old relationships had outlived their time, and that Belgrade could no longer expect special treatment. Beyond that, nobody had a clear vision as to what the new U.S. policy toward this "relatively unimportant" country should be, which meant that Zimmermann had to improvise. Put bluntly, the United States had no policy at all.

Zimmermann arrived in Belgrade in the spring of 1989 in the midst of frantic preparations for festivities commemorating the six hundredth anniversary of the battle of Kosovo. Milosevic oversaw in detail the planning of the extravaganza. It was highly important to him as a demonstration of his undisputed mastery over Yugoslavia following his reconquest of Kosovo, Montenegro, and Vojvodina. Yugoslav dignitaries as well as members of the diplomatic corps were invited.

Zimmermann declined the invitation. An erudite and highly moral diplomat, he was put off by the inflammatory rhetoric and chauvinistic crudities that dominated public discourse; he found Belgrade a wholly different city from the one he had known in the 1960s when he served as a junior officer in the embassy. But the real reason for his action was based on his belief that his presence at Milosevic's mass celebration in an area predominantly populated by ethnic Albanians would violate the spirit of his instructions.

While he had been given no specific guidelines as to his overall approach to Yugoslavia, the instructions with respect to Kosovo were very specific. Both Eagleburger and Scowcroft had been alarmed by Milosevic's repressive policies and the possibility of an armed Albanian rebellion. They had calculated the likely destabilizing effect an inflamed Kosovo could pose to U.S. interests, in particular the likelihood of a major regional war involving, among others, the NATO countries of Greece and Turkey on opposite sides. "This was one real U.S. national interest with respect to Yugoslavia," Scowcroft said later. This was also something the president understood and was determined to prevent at all costs. Zimmermann was instructed to convey that to Milosevic and to press him to seek accommodation with the Albanians.

Zimmermann had to wait for more than a year to see Milosevic.

The ambassador's refusal to attend the Kosovo festivities infuriated Milosevic. To rub salt in the wound, several other Western ambassadors also decided to stay away when they learned that Zimmermann would not attend.

A petulant Milosevic immediately decided that this was a calculated snub. He retaliated by freezing out the ambassador and blaming him for organizing a "boycott." For the rest of his term, Zimmermann was subjected to incessant barrages of insults in the press and in parliament. Comedians and talk show hosts—on state media controlled by Milosevic—ridiculed him for his concern over the violation of human rights of Kosovo's Albanians. (A joke on Radio Belgrade: "The housing shortage in Kosovo can be solved easily," the disc jockey said. "The Albanians can all find a place in Zimmermann's heart.") Zimmermann handled it all with amazing grace and dignity.

Milosevic's behavior was an example of the way he treated anyone who crossed him or stood up to him, anyone who showed him he may not be the chess master in ultimate control of the pawns and pieces on the board he was playing.

Years later, Milosevic would describe his "feud" with Zimmermann as "one of his greatest personal mistakes" that cost him dearly. "I acted as a stupid, stubborn fool," he said on two separate occasions. This private admission was offered as his explanation for the subsequent American hostility toward him and his policies. Zimmermann had, he decided, poisoned the minds of American policy makers and thereby helped in the destruction of Yugoslavia.

In fact, Zimmermann fought vigorously to keep Yugoslavia together even after his superiors had given up. He strongly supported the last Yugoslav prime minister, Ante Markovic, whom he saw as offering an avenue to block Milosevic and other ethnic warriors. A silver-haired man who radiated optimism and good humor, Markovic was voted into office in March 1989 with a mandate to curb runaway inflation and introduce radical reforms. His rather spectacular economic performance over the next two years gave him a fighting chance to deal with the ethnic crisis. He consulted various American economists—among them Jeffrey Sachs of Harvard, famous for helping other former Communist countries make the transition to capitalism—as he sought to turn Yugoslavia into "a Western democratic country with a capitalist system." By early 1990, the Yugoslav dinar was fully convertible; trade was liberalized allowing free imports; and Markovic was pressing to remove the limits on private ownership. What he needed desperately, he told Zimmermann, was support from the West and particularly from the United States.

Zimmermann fought hard to focus Washington's attention on the problem; but his views were ignored. He flew to Washington in hopes of conveying to Baker personally his assessment that the collapse of Yugoslavia would lead to extreme violence and would eventually involve the United States one way or another. But Baker had no time for Zimmermann; the administration was fully preoccupied with Operation Desert Storm. Zimmermann then engineered an official visit to Washington by Markovic, but nobody had time for the Yugoslav prime minister. Markovic was probably the only head of government who had to pay for all his meals in Washington; nobody was willing to offer a dinner or lunch in his honor.

In May 1991, the so-called Nickles Amendment, sponsored by Senator Don Nickles (R-Okla.) and Senate Republican leader Bob Dole, became law. It prohibited all economic assistance to Yugoslavia unless it ceased its human rights violations in Kosovo. The legislation affected only $5 million of assistance, but it had a devastating impact on the Markovic government, which was automatically denied access to loans from the World Bank and International Monetary Fund and other credit markets.

Zimmermann felt defeated. Moreover, his State Department colleagues sought to blame him for the ultimate failure of American policy. "He was in the lead among those fighting to keep Yugoslavia together, even after the CIA prediction that the country was about to collapse," one official said of Zimmermann. "He kept supporting Ante Markovic. He changed his views reluctantly and late."

Once the Croatian war started, Markovic was finished and his government existed only on paper. He formally resigned on December 20, 1991. The collective Yugoslav presidency also collapsed as the representatives of four republics—Croatia, Slovenia, Bosnia, and Macedonia—no longer took part in its work. The rump presidency, with the representatives of Serbia, Kosovo, Vojvodina, and

Montenegro, was now a wholly owned subsidiary of the Milosevic regime.

Washington's indifference removed whatever restraints existed and encouraged Milosevic to press forward with his plan for a Greater Serbia.

His generals and intelligence agents operated behind the scenes to provoke conflicts. They consciously permitted secret shipments of weapons from Austria and Hungary to reach Croatian secessionists. We can only speculate about Milosevic's motives. One particular transfer of forty thousand Kalashnikov assault rifles and other weaponry—clandestinely arranged by the Hungarian government—was filmed by Yugoslav Army intelligence operatives and shown with great fanfare three months later on Belgrade Television. Instead of seizing the illegal shipments, the generals were providing Milosevic with the evidence he needed to convince the Serb nation that the whole world was conspiring against them and that for the Serbs to accomplish anything meant that they had to do it by themselves and through the use of their military force.

The mass influx of weapons turned the country into a vast armed camp. Zimmermann urged forceful action; since the country was doomed, the United States and the Europeans should help arrange for a peaceful change. He also raised a troublesome question with regard to the ethnic warriors' claims to the right of self-determination: should the United States encourage the breakup of states or seek to prevent them? But nobody paid attention, since an active U.S. role also meant the possible use of force. The problem was, as Zimmermann put it later, that "the Bush administration was really dug in against the threat of force, for Vietnam reasons, for Persian Gulf reasons. Nobody wanted to do anything, even on a contingency basis. It was a very strong principled position."

Scowcroft admitted later that the tragedy might have been prevented or at least sharply reduced by the weapons of diplomatic and economic blandishments that lay so easily at hand. "At one point we could have made a difference, before the fighting had started," he said, "if we had sat down with the Europeans and said, okay, if this country is going to break up, this is how it should be done, and then forcefully present these ground rules to the Yugoslavs. This was the last chance."

But Bush's head-in-the-sand response, as far as Milosevic was concerned, amounted to a tacit approval for him to use force. By doing nothing, the United States effectively acquiesced to the carnage in Croatia and in Bosnia, even when it degenerated into mass murder.

The burgeoning problem was left, be default, to the Europeans, who were buoyed by the wave of euphoria that had followed the collapse of communism and the preparations for the European Union (EU). They believed that they could settle the Balkan problem. "The age of Europe has dawned," declared the EU chairman, Jacques Poos of Luxembourg.

A plan developed by EU negotiator Lord Carrington recognized the six republics as the constituent units of the former federal state, and proposed that each unit be accorded as much sovereignty as it wanted. This opened the possibilities of a common currency, economic ties, defense, foreign affairs, and other links. Carrington's plan guaranteed a wide gamut of cultural and political rights to the Serbs outside Serbia; in areas of Bosnia and Croatia where the Serbs were in the majority, they were to be granted the rights of their own parliament, and their own administration, including local police and judiciary. Carrington said later: "It seemed to me that the right way to do it was to allow those who wanted to be independent to be independent, and to associate themselves with a central organization as far as they wanted to. Those who didn't want to be independent, well, they could stay within what had been Yugoslavia. You could do it, so to speak, à la carte."

Milosevic accepted the plan "in principle" on October 4, 1991, but when he arrived in the Hague on October 18, he was firmly against it. All other Yugoslav chieftains were for it, including Milosevic's protégé in Montenegro, Momir Bulatovic.

Milosevic was stunned. Dutch diplomat Henri Wejnaendts later said he talked to Milosevic in the men's room about Bulatovic's position. "Bulatovic will not stay president of Montenegro for long," Milosevic remarked.

Bulatovic immediately came under attack at home. "There was a series of unpleasant meetings in Belgrade," he recalled. "The press labelled me a traitor. I was asked whether I was a spy, had I received money from a foreign country." A browbeaten Bulatovic was forced to change his position to keep his job.

The Carrington plan failed. Milosevic insisted that the nationalities—and not the republics—were the legitimate constituent units of the Yugoslav federation.

"Here was a massive weakness," said Lord Owen, the former British foreign secretary. "We never owned up to that reality. Any military action that was substantive had to involve the United States. The Europeans weren't sufficiently strong, they weren't committed." Moreover, they had no common approach. Only the Germans from the very beginning had insisted that the European Union should promptly extend diplomatic recognition to Croatia and Slovenia. The British and the French held that recognition was the most potent weapon in the hands of peace negotiators. Hans van den Broek of the Netherlands, who was intimately acquainted with the complexities of the Yugoslav problems, warned that premature recognition would be disastrous.

At the December 15–16 meeting of European foreign ministers in Brussels, Genscher announced that Germany had decided to break ranks with the rest of its European partners on the issue of diplomatic recognition of Croatia. This meant ignoring the recommendations of a European Union panel under the chairmanship of the French jurist Robert Badinter. Under the Badinter criteria, republics seeking recognition would have to have adequate protection for national minorities and demonstrate control of their own borders; Croatia did not meet either one. (The commission recommended that only Slovenia and Macedonia be granted recognition.)

Carrington, who also attended the meeting, was furious. John Major's Conservative government did not even send Foreign Secretary Dougles Hurd to the meeting; his deputy Douglas Hogg went in his place. It was a signal that Britain had decided to go along with Germany. It was a quid pro quo matter: only a few weeks earlier the Germans had helped Britain secure favorable terms in the Maastricht Treaty. Carrington felt that his entire mission was being destroyed. "The only incentive we had to get anybody to agree to anything was the ultimate recognition of their independence; otherwise there was no carrot," he said. "You just threw it away, like that."

The Americans were equally surprised when German chancellor Helmut Kohl, on a visit to Washington shortly before Christmas 1991, relayed the German decision to President Bush. The president asked Eagleburger to make the American counterargument.

A participant in the Cabinet Room meeting recalled Eagleburger being "very tough on premature recognition" for the reasons stated by Carrington. Moreover, Eagleburger forecast an escalation of conflict.

"Then Kohl said in effect, I've heard you but it won't be very long before we recognize Croatia," the participant in the meeting said. "And the president said nothing."

Scowcroft, who was also present, failed to grasp the chancellor's position and felt it probably had to do with the past German-Croat relationship; but this was hardly a complete explanation since the only close ties between the two nations had been those during World War II, though Croatia had been part of the Roman Catholic Austro-Hungarian Empire. A strong factor may have been the influence of a large Croatian guest worker community and a strong Croatian lobby within Germany itself. Moreover, public opinion in Germany is traditionally anti-Serbian. Scowcroft realized just how much importance Kohl assigned to Croatia when he asserted "something to the effect that Germany was prepared to risk the breakup of the European Union if necessary."

Once Germany acted, the United States sought to make the best of a bad job for the sake of Western unity. It followed the Germans and other Europeans in recognizing the independence of Croatia and Slovenia without securing human, civil, and political rights for minorities. Carrington complained loudly and publicly. "This was our greatest failure," he said. A few months later, he quietly resigned as the European Union peace envoy.

By the end of 1991, it had become clear that European diplomacy would only go so far, and that there was little political will for a military intervention. Instead, the deteriorating crisis was deposited into the even more ineffectual hands of the United Nations. Milosevic and Tudjman at that point accepted Cyrus Vance's plan for a cease-fire (that would freeze the existing front lines) and UN troop deployments in several disputed territories. Milosevic agreed to order the Yugoslav Army out of Croatia—which also meant out of Krajina.

The leader of the Krajina Serbs, a dentist called Milan Babic, rejected the Vance plan. His action was a thoroughly unexpected obstacle from a leadership Milosevic had nurtured and sustained for several years and which now refused to do his bidding.

The army, Babic argued, was the single guarantor of Krajina's security. He said the Vance plan would isolate Krajina.

Babic was summoned to Belgrade. The meeting dragged on for seventy-two hours. The Bosnian Serb leaders, Radovan Karadzic and Biljana Plavsic, were also called in to reassure Babic that Bosnia would remain in Yugoslavia and that he should not fear isolation. Borisav Jovic gave Babic guarantees that in case of an attack on Krajina, the army would be sent to defend it.

But Babic would not budge.

Jovic then tried intimidation. "If you don't accept this," he told Babic, "we'll be forced to get rid of you."

Babic, who knew that Milosevic's secret police occasionally resorted to assassinations and feared that his defiance might cost him his life, went pale. "What do you mean?" he blurted out.

Jovic, instantly grasping Babic's fears, said: "Oh, don't worry. We'll do it legally, through the parliament."

Within weeks, Milosevic did just that. The media denounced Babic in the strongest terms. The Krajina leadership was ordered to call the Krajina assembly into session; the assembly endorsed the Vance plan and voted Babic out of office. He was replaced by a more pliable storeroom clerk named Goran Hadzic. In January 1992, the United Nations arranged a cease-fire and placed fourteen thousand peacekeeping troops between the Serb rebels and the Croatian government forces.

Serbia's nationalist dreamers saw Germany's recognition of Croatia as a watershed. The dream of a Greater Serbia had suddenly shrunk. The international recognition of Croatia's borders meant that the 350,000 Krajina Serbs were now subjects of a hostile government, unreachable except through continued war.

For several months the flames of war stopped at Bosnia's borders. All sides knew that Bosnia was a powder keg, but everybody—especially the Bosnian Muslims themselves—hoped that Bosnia's harmony could be preserved. But if the multinational federation was doomed and Serbs and Croats were shooting at one another, what future could Bosnia have, being, as it was, the microcosm of the failed state of Yugoslavia?

In November 1991, prompted by Milosevic, Bosnian Serb leader Radovan Karadzic and his supporters organized a Bosnian Serb plebiscite on independence and won an overwhelming approval. On January 9, 1992, the Bosnian Serbs proclaimed their own republic, separating themselves from the rest of Bosnia.

Like Milosevic, the wild-haired Karadzic came from a Montenegrin family, the son of a farmer-soldier steeped in the epics that still have a grip on the people from his native Mount Durmitor. He was over six feet tall, with a broad, sad face and a weak chin. During World War II, his father first fought on the side of the royalist Chetniks—who started the Serb uprising against the Nazis—but later switched to Tito's Partisans. After the war, though, he was imprisoned and jailed for several years on unclear charges. That coincided with the early years of Karadzic's life—he was born in 1944. A family friend recalls the Karadzic family as "poor, primitive people, with a village mentality." But Radovan was smart and was sent to Sarajevo, at age fifteen, to finish his schooling. He received a university degree in medicine, married a classmate, studied psychiatry in New York, and become a psychiatrist in Sarajevo.

He was also a poet of some renown, with four published volumes of gloomy verses. In retrospect, one of his poems (published in 1970) appears to forecast the deadly events in which he himself would be a key actor:

> *I hear misfortune walking*
> *Vacant entourages passing through the city*
> *Units of armed white poplars*
> *Marching through the skies.*

In 1987, he went to jail, charged with writing fake medical certificates for state construction employees and getting free materials for a weekend home he was building. He served eleven months, but was acquitted and would later claim that he was framed because of his political views. With the emergence of Milosevic, Karadzic became a faithful acolyte and helped organize the 1989 Kosovo celebrations. Now wholly convinced that the salvation of the Serb nation lay in Milosevic's hands, he embarked on a course charted by Milosevic as Bosnia's champion of the Serb national cause. Before the first free elections in 1990, he was one of the founders of the Serb Democratic Party (SDS). Exuberant and bold—some would see a wild streak in his personality—Karadzic loved the limelight and was given to exaggerations and blood-curdling rhetoric. Milosevic viewed him as a talented and loyal young politician; they spent long hours together scheming and plotting the division of Bosnia.

By early 1992, the Yugoslav Army had withdrawn from Slovenia and Croatia mostly to Bosnia. Milosevic at that point issued a secret directive ordering the creation of a new Bosnian Serb army; all Serb Army officers born in Bosnia were transferred to the new army. Although this clashed with the Yugoslav Army's tradition and regulation as a non-ethnic force, the order was carried out "quickly and efficiently," according to Borisav Jovic. By March, Karadzic had at his disposal a force of ninety thousand well-equipped troops supported by modern firepower.

The slide to war now gained momentum.

Once again the Serb people were gradually being prodded into a single mind by a determined minority of radical fanatics who controlled the media. Once again Milosevic's spin doctors whipped up the crudest national feelings—how glorious it was to die for Serbia—while suppressing any debate about the possibility of peaceful accommodation.

In the initial stage of the Yugoslav disintegration, even as Milosevic and Karadzic were making their plans, the other leaders of Bosnia refused to heed the siren songs of nationalism. Indeed, a Bosnian Serb, Bogic Bogicevic, representing Bosnia in the federal Yugoslav presidency, prevented Milosevic's plans of staging a coup d'état against the federal government. In January 1991, Milosevic and the Military High Command had prepared detailed plans for a military takeover of the entire country. On March 12, the army was placed on full alert. Defense Minister Veljko Kadijevic was ready to move, but the generals, many of them non-Serbs and still loyal to Tito's legacy, demanded approval by the collective presidency. Milosevic could count on four "yes" votes (Serbia, Montenegro, Vojvodina, and Kosovo); Croatia, Slovenia, and Macedonia were automatic "no's."

Everything depended on Bogicevic, who represented Bosnia. As a Serb, he was counted upon to cast the decisive vote in favor. But Bogicevic voted no, and held firm despite the fury of the plotters who came up short of a majority for the military intervention. Bogicevic, moreover, was not an isolated figure; a majority of urban Serbs were unswayed by Milosevic's propaganda. There was a certain pride in the uniqueness and diversity of Bosnia, reflected in a crude saying, "Jebes zemlju koja Bosnu nema" ("Screw the country that hasn't got a Bosnia"). The three communities had more than an emotional stake in the place. Some 27 percent of all marriages in the republic were mixed. The question remained whether the nationalist manias could have spread like a cancer into Bosnia without direct acts of subversion and terrorism from the outside, from Belgrade and Zagreb, which created a climate in which there seemed to be no retreat possible from the extreme positions that had been taken by everyone.

Milosevic sensed that the West was preparing to extend diplomatic recognition to the Muslim government in Sarajevo, but he regarded it as an empty gesture. He reassured a nervous Karadzic over the prospective recognition by likening it to the Roman emperor Caligula's appointment of his horse to the Senate; the horse never became a senator. The Bosnian Muslims may have their diplomatic recognition, Milosevic said, but they would have no country.

This time, the Americans took the lead, recognizing Bosnia on April 6, 1992. The Muslim nations, and Saudi Arabia in particular, had been instrumental in nudging President Bush to throw America's support behind the Bosnian Muslims. The Saudis had been crucial to Bush's great foreign policy triumph by providing the essential ground base (as well as money) for the Gulf War against Iraq. Other Muslim nations such as Egypt and Syria had also played important roles in preparing Desert Storm, and they too were fully behind the Bosnian Muslims.

The recognition was grounded in a misreading of Milosevic and his intentions. "Mistakenly we thought Milosevic would not cross the [Bosnian] border," Scowcroft said later. It amounted to the sanctioning of a divorce without an agreed property settlement, a prescription for violence. In the end, nothing could stop the Serbs and Croats from starting another war.

As in Croatia the previous year, Milosevic gradually prepared the conflict, using his Bosnian Serb proxies with a sinister calculation. He authorized the arming of Serb paramilitary gangs who initiated conflicts. "We had specific agreements with Milosevic," said Vojislav Seselj, whose paramilitary Chetniks—along with other paramilitary outfits such as the White Eagles and Arkan's Tigers—were the first to start fighting in Bosnia and were responsible for some of the worst atrocities of the wars. A 1994 UN report identified eighty-three different paramilitary organizations operating in

Bosnia. Some were criminals from Serbia's jails who were equipped with sheepskin hats and Kalashnikovs and bundled off to Bosnia to kill the infidels and redeem themselves as true Christian soldiers.

The pattern was always the same: a group of flag-waving, bearded brigands, frequently inebriated, would come into a village to help local Serbs organize their "defense" and distribute arms. Nobody quite knew who these people were, but they dispensed "patriotic" exhortations. Agents of Milosevic's secret police, always under assumed names, were usually in charge. At night, Muslim neighbors would get anonymous phone calls threatening their children and women and ordering them to abandon their homes and relocate. One or more murders in cold blood—usually of prominent Muslims—were sufficient to send the Muslims fleeing.

The ethnic cleansing of larger towns and cities began after April 5, when the Croatian Army moved into Bosnia and seized the town of Bosanski Brod, on the Sava River. The general conflagration began the following day. The Serb paramilitary gangs, spearheaded by Arkan's Tigers, drove Muslims from a swathe of territory in eastern Bosnia, ransacking the towns of Visegrad, Zvornik, and Bijeljina along the Drina River and razing mosques (in Zvornik, all eight mosques were demolished).

Karadzic's army quickly seized almost 70 percent of Bosnia's territory and surrounded Sarajevo, the capital, which it pounded with heavy artillery from the hills. The Croatian nationalists, sporting Ustashe symbols and supported by Tudjman, seized more than 20 percent of the territory, mainly in western Herzegovina, which they cleansed of its Serb and Muslim population. The Muslims held Sarajevo, Tuzla, and a few other towns.

But after those first triumphant advances, things started going wrong for the Bosnian Serbs. The steady bombardment of a city that was the home of the 1984 Winter Olympics was a stroke of astounding criminality and stupidity; there were immediate protests about this barbarity from everywhere. A turning point was the May 27 "bread-line massacre" in Sarajevo, in which people standing in a line for bread were killed by the Bosnian Serb gunners; after that date, Western public opinion swung firmly behind the Muslims. The United Nations dispatched twenty-seven thousand peacekeepers into Bosnia to secure humanitarian aid; but the force lacked the authority and strength to impose order and their efforts to arrange cease-fires were flagrantly violated.

By the summer of 1992, most of Bosnia was aflame, with people taking up arms, setting whole villages alight. Hate and fear were the principal forces at work. Bosnian Serb intellectuals in particular were in the grip of a hypernationalist rapture. Biljana Plavsic, the university professor who later would replace Radovan Karadzic and be viewed as a "moderate" in the West, argued on television—"speaking as the biologist that I am"—that Serbs were genetically superior to Muslims. And Karadzic, the poet-psychiatrist turned politician, frequently recited blood-curdling passages from old epics to the troops at the front—accompanying himself on the single-string gusle—to evoke past heroism. He would quote the Montenegrin poet Njegos's absolute certitude that the ancient internecine strife would lead to redemption:

*Let come these things men thought could never be;*
*Let Hell devour; let Satan swing his scythe;*
*Still graveyard turf shall bring forth many a flower,*
*For coming kindreds in Time's later Hour!*

This encouraged Serb fighters who, complete with medieval symbols and Old Testament beards, began demolishing mosques in Bosnia and seeing themselves as descendants of the ancient heroes. Hundreds of thousands of Muslims were forced from their homes, tens of thousands were killed or injured. It was the worst humanitarian catastrophe in Europe in half a century.

Detention camps appeared that summer. The notorious Serb-run camps—Omarska, Keraterm, Manjaca—soon became known throughout the world, but there were many more camps that remained anonymous. In the eyes of the rest of the world, the Serbs stood accused not only of mass detention but of organized extermination.

But the Serbs seemed oblivious to it all. Indeed, a popular song that year glorified the exploits of the worst of the paramilitary ethnic cleansers, and its refrain daily jammed the airwaves:

*They protect Serb glory,*
*They guard Serb lands,*
*Arkan's Tigers,*
*Brave warriors without a flaw.*

Apart from anecdotal press accounts and testimony of Muslim refugees, clear evidence linking the Milosevic regime to Bosnian atrocities emerged during the only war crimes trial ever held before a Serbian court. Milosevic had organized the trial in the town of Sabac, near the Bosnian border, in November 1994, presumably to deflect Western demands to deliver potential war criminals to the international tribunal that had been convened in the Hague.

Seeking to demonstrate that Serbia was prepared to punish war criminals, the authorities brought war crimes charges against Dusan Vuckovic, a thirty-one-year-old mechanic from the village of Umke, near Belgrade, who went as a "volunteer" to Bosnia one day after the outbreak of the war "to help the Serb people there."

Prosecutors charged that Vuckovic crossed into Bosnia on April 7, 1992, and was assigned to a Territorial Defense unit which was engaged in disarming the Muslim population in order to "prevent" ethnic conflicts. They described Vuckovic, who had been discharged from the Yugoslav Army for mental instability, as an alcoholic who was very angry because of mistreatment he had suffered at the hands of the Muslims. On June 27, 1992, Vuckovic was said to have "showed intolerance toward the Muslim civilians" by torturing, killing, and maiming them. The incident took place at the Hall of Culture in the village of Celopek, outside Zvornik, where some two hundred Muslims were housed and guarded by the police. The indictment charged that, while interrogating the Muslims, he had cut off a man's ear, then turned his automatic rifle on the prisoners, killing sixteen and wounding twenty others. Vuckovic was also accused of raping and robbing a Muslim woman.

The indictment was carefully worded to exclude any possible implication of Serbia in the Bosnian war. The brutal murders were cast as actions of an angry and deranged man. A psychiatrist, Dr. Svetislav Jekic, testified that Vuckovic was a "psychopathic personality who suffered from chronic alcoholism," and that "his capacity to control his actions was sharply reduced as was his ability to understand the meaning of his actions." The prosecution did not present a single witness to the killings.

A vastly different picture emerged during the trial, although none of the defense arguments were published in the government-controlled media. Before the judges, Vuckovic argued that he was being "set up" by the Serbian secret service and that he had been forced to sign his confession. He had entered Bosnia as a member of the paramilitary group called the Yellow Wasps, he said; the group was "closely linked" to high Serbian Interior Ministry officials and was armed before entering Bosnia. The Yellow Wasps were provided housing by the commander of the Zvornik Territorial Defense, Marko Pavlovic.

Perhaps the most interesting aspect of the trial was revealed by Vuckovic's defense attorney, who was unable to establish the identity of Marko Pavlovic or to discover who had appointed him the military commander of Zvornik. The defense quoted witnesses as saying that "Marko Pavlovic" was the alias for an agent of Milosevic's secret police named Branko Popovic. A journalist for the small independent weekly *Vreme* said the mysterious commander had told him that he was reporting directly to Radmilo Bogdanovic, Milosevic's confidant and security czar.

A policeman who was on duty in the Hall of Culture at the time of the incident could not recall whether Vuckovic had actually killed any Muslims. He told journalists that "various Serb fighters have been coming in and out of the Hall of Culture, armed and many of them drunk, and they would take groups of Muslims out and kill them to avenge their murdered relatives. Perhaps Vuckovic killed them too." Vuckovic's older brother, Vojin, who was also with the Yellow Wasps, said that Arkan's Tigers had executed about seventy Muslim civilians a day after the incident involving his brother; he said he was told by the Territorial Defense commander that Arkan's people had killed fifteen and wounded seventeen others a few days later.

A Muslim prisoner, Hama Tahic, who was wounded by Vuckovic and later managed to escape to Austria, recalled sustained torture and executions carried out by Vuckovic over a period of several months. "He would place the victims on the stage and force them to sing Chetnik songs. Dusan passionately enjoyed the mixture of music and the cries of victims—they would be finished off with the plunge of the knife into their mouths."

The trial was adjourned indefinitely after the prosecutors suggested new psychiatric tests for Vuckovic. Milosevic's clumsy public relations ploy had failed.

# 6

# The Summer of Discontent

For Milosevic, the year 1992 was a critical one. It had become apparent to the nationalists as well as to the bureaucratic establishment that Serbia was in complete diplomatic isolation. Moreover, the consequences of his contempt for world public opinion were beginning to have a disastrous impact on the country in general and its economy in particular.

With the economy in shambles, a wave of protests swept through what remained of Yugoslavia at the end of the Croatian war in early 1992. It became apparent that the government was broke. For weeks, millions of state employees had not been paid but continued to go to work day after day. The population suffered a major blow when it became known that the regime had spent foreign currency deposits from private savings bank accounts to finance the Croatian war. The printing presses at the Yugoslav mint went into extra overtime; day by day the dinar was becoming more worthless. Columns of marchers, singing hymns and unarmed, had converged for months on the great square in front of Belgrade's National Theater where they shouted the usual anti-Milosevic slogans:

"Slobo You Are Saddam" and "Out with the Red Bandits." A morbid joke making the rounds in Belgrade—referring to the family history of suicides—held that Milosevic would do the greatest service to his country by following his family's tradition.

There was a widespread realization that the ruling elite was compromised and that the impetus for change had to come from outside the former Communist bureaucracy. This sentiment touched off, of all things, a monarchist revival. Various politicians had put out clandestine feelers to Crown Prince Alexander, son of Peter II, the last Karadjordjevic king, who had been overthrown by the Communists in 1945. Alexander had been born in London, where his family had escaped in 1941, had never lived in Yugoslavia, and spoke only broken Serbo-Croatian. His ancestor and founder of the dynasty, George Petrovic, known as Karadjordje, was a cherished national icon.

Alexander had made a brief visit to Belgrade—his first—in the fall of 1991 and left a good impression: he was charming, intelligent, and somewhat courtly. Occasionally he displayed a shade of Serb arrogance: when asked if he was related to the Windsors, he replied: "It's the other way around, the Windsors are related to us!"

The dynasty had always had a strong following among the rural population, but this time the restoration was favored by the educated classes as well. The hope was that someone untainted by the Communist past could help Serbia free itself from a ruling oligarchy of former Communists and repair its appalling image abroad. For his part, the prince was eager to regain his royal patrimony, taking as his model the constitutional monarchy of Juan Carlos of Spain, who had succeeded the dictatorship of Francisco Franco in 1975.

Milosevic became genuinely alarmed by the prince's challenge. When the nationalists began to tilt toward Alexander, Milosevic set out to disrupt and split the monarchist movement, his acolytes spreading rumors that the prince was a simpleminded British soldier. To further derail Alexander, Milosevic orchestrated a division within the royal family, encouraging Alexander's uncle, Prince Tomislav, to advance his own claim to the throne.

Tomislav, in his seventies, also living in England, was accommodating. He enjoyed the attention. "Tomislav is coming today," a military intelligence colonel reported to the Serbian defense minister. "We will keep him longer in the country and give him great publicity, then let the Karadjordjevics slaughter each other."

The publicity, indeed, was great as Tomislav was featured on television, on the radio, and in the newspapers. There were speculations in the media about Tomislav becoming the ruler of the Bosnian Serb state as a preliminary to reclaiming a role in Serbia proper. Alexander's supporters became confused and disheartened.

The opposition parties invited Prince Alexander to return to Belgrade in March 1992 for a mass rally to commemorate the victims of Milosevic's brutal suppression of the mass protest on March 9, 1991, in which army tanks were called to help riot police. The prince agreed.

Milosevic sensed a threat from this strange and formidable confluence of forces. He was so worried about the patriarch joining the rally that he asked Dobrica Cosic for help. Milosevic suggested that the novelist, who was respected by the church, should urge the old cleric to stay away from the protest outside St. Sava Cathedral. Even without Milosevic's prompting, Cosic had contacted a senior bishop to question the wisdom of the patriarch's participation.

But the patriarch decided to ignore warnings and appeared at St. Sava to officiate at the services for the victims of the 1991 demonstration.

Radio Television Belgrade had begun live coverage of the proceedings when its acting director, Dobroslav Bjeletic, received a call from Milosevic ordering the broadcast pulled from the air. Bjeletic, a former provincial Marxist lecturer, ran breathlessly along the long corridors of the television headquarters yelling at the top of his voice, "Break off the program! Cut it off!"

Bjeletic himself was new in the job and had no idea where to go. He ended up in a room where machinery and circuit breakers were located, still yelling, "Cut it off, cut it off!"

"A written order is required for that," a technician replied.

"I'm giving the order and you are fired," Bjeletic shouted.

"I'm sorry, but I have to follow the instructions."

"How do you turn it off?" Bjeletic demanded from another technician.

"You can press that button," the technician replied.

The interruption of the program angered the city. It only produced more mass protests.

More worrisome to Milosevic was the growing discontent within the ranks of the nationalist intellectuals who had been his earliest supporters.

By early 1992, Dobrica Cosic and other nationalist intellectuals understood that the idea of a Greater Serbia was dead in the face of the diplomatic recognition of Croatia and Bosnia by the United States, as well as by Germany and other European countries. They became genuinely alarmed that Milosevic was leading Serbia toward catastrophe and self-destruction, and so they distanced themselves from the Serb leader.

After the debacle at St. Sava Cathedral, Cosic reached the decision that Milosevic had to go. Silence was his way of registering opposition, and so he withdrew from public life. Cosic's political allies, while ostensibly still in Milosevic's corner, were secretly plotting against the dictator. In an atmosphere of murmuring intrigue and Fascist-style public pronouncements, Cosic's villa became the conspiratorial meeting place for all types of disaffected nationalists.

The conspirators had cast a wide net throughout the political, military, and security establishment, including Milosevic's proxies in Bosnia and Krajina. The consensus among the conspirators was that Cosic should replace Milosevic. Just how this scheme was to be realized was kept secret. Cosic's allies and co-conspirators in the military commanded sufficient firepower to stage a coup, but needed a clear signal from him to move into action. The writer, however, was temperamentally inclined toward procrastination and analysis. For all his failings, he was a decent man and he shrank from power, probably in genuine anguish. He seems to have been possessed by two ideas, mutually exclusive: he longed to bring peace and prosperity to the Serb nation and he lacked the political single-mindedness to assume responsibility for the use of force.

Even though the times were nervous and disturbed, and senior military officers counseled a conciliatory policy, Milosevic and his accomplices in Bosnia headed into another war in April 1992. The new Serbian defense minister, General Marko Njegovanovic, was one of the military's smartest officers; until 1991, he had served as head of military intelligence. Shortly after replacing General Simovic, the new minister addressed his top aides with the following assessment: "Serbia's economy has collapsed. Serbia is alone. We have had only bad results; that is because we embarked on the path of using force. The basic objectives have not been achieved. We should now be using peaceful means to resolve the existing problems."

But Cosic was unable to act. Instead, he decided to warn Milosevic personally that his despotic leadership had reached a dead end and to urge him to share power through a government of national concord. His complaint was directed not against Milosevic's ultimate objectives but against his failure to achieve them.

His letter to Milosevic, dated April 8 (shortly after the outbreak of the Bosnian war), was on the whole a litany of scathing criticisms. Serbia was heading into a catastrophe—the country was completely isolated and fighting enemies who were supported by the United States and Europe. He said that only an all-party government of national unity could mobilize the nation: Milosevic "alone can no longer lead" Serbia. He demanded new elections and a role for the opposition in shaping Serbia's policy. Despite his undisputed political skills, Milosevic was burdened "with heavy and unfortunate flaws." Cosic criticized Milosevic's Kosovo policy, asserting that the fate of Kosovo could not be decided by the Serbian president and the Kosovo Serb nationalists but by the "most responsible people of the Serb nation."

Immediately upon receiving the letter, Milosevic summoned Cosic for a talk. The meeting was attended by Kosta Mihajlovic, one of the authors of the 1986 Memorandum, who was close to both men.

Milosevic accepted Cosic's stinging criticism with calm good humor and discussed "lateral" issues the novelist had raised without tipping his hand.

Dissatisfied with the result of Cosic's direct approach, the conspirators decided to proceed with soliciting the support of the great powers. They first contacted senior nationalist politicians in Moscow. Key Western capitals and intelligence services were approached, including the CIA, with inquiries about their attitude toward a planned coup against Milosevic.

Warren Zimmermann recounted in his memoirs how Cosic's political ally, Shakespearean scholar Nikola Koljevic, made the approach. Koljevic appeared at the front gate of the U.S. residence one Saturday morning in May 1992 and demanded to speak with the ambassador urgently. Koljevic refused to identify himself but insisted that embassy guards summon Zimmermann over the intercom:

> I went out to see. It was Nikola Koljevic, the number two Bosnian Serb. I invited Koljevic in and gave him a glass of wine. After some aimless conversation, he came to the point. He had been talking to Dobrica Cosic . . . and the two of them agreed that Milosevic had become a liability for Serbia. It was time to replace him. Koljevic told me that Cosic would be a much better president of Serbia. He said that such a change would eliminate a major problem for the United States and the West.

The ambassador feared some kind of provocation, since Koljevic had been Milosevic's creature and wholly identified with his policies. "I gave him no encouragement," the ambassador continued, but instead made it clear that the United States regarded Koljevic himself, along with the other leaders, "as major problems."

The whole episode quickly became irrelevant when Zimmermann was recalled two weeks later in protest over Milosevic's Bosnia policy. At the end of May, the United Nations imposed a total economic embargo against Yugoslavia.

The sanctions, Milosevic instructed his propaganda chiefs,

should be presented to the Serbs as a proof of "a worldwide conspiracy" against them. The press and television promptly launched a campaign aimed at strengthening the pride and endurance of the Serb nation and their belief in the ultimate victory—"The more they hate us, the stronger we get!"

His propagandists quickly produced a popular ditty in the style of Serb epics:

*Oh, Slobodan, you of Serb faith*
*You penetrate foreign designs*
*Lightning is flashing from your eyes.*
*Dear brothers, we are in a new age*
*Slobodan Milosevic is born.*

But this did not work. The impact of sanctions was immediate. Serbia was completely cut off from the rest of the world. Long lines at gas stations testified that people had started hoarding gasoline; canisters were kept in basements and halls. Nationalist euphoria had given way to discontent, despair, and bristling bad temper. The opposition once again was galvanized into action.

Throughout May and June, students led mass protests against Milosevic's war policy. On one occasion they wrapped a black ribbon of mourning, more than a mile long, around the parliament building to protest the siege of Sarajevo. One of the main targets of the demonstrators was the headquarters of Radio Television Belgrade, where they set up a statue of a man staring at a television set; the inscription read: "Murderer by remote control." On another occasion a line of young men, many of them wearing death masks and black gym clothes emblazoned with skeletons, converged on Milosevic's home on Tolstoy Street. Thousands of riot police prevented the protesters, who were stretched over several miles, from approaching the house, but this only touched off new student sit-ins modeled on the Tiananmen Square pattern. They were joined by angry parents demanding the return of their sons from the Bosnian front; there were rumors of significant casualties in Bosnia.

Alarmed by the possible spread of unrest, Milosevic himself

made a rare appearance on television in late May 1992, insisting that "Serbia is not at war" and that "not a single soldier who is a citizen of the Republic of Serbia is outside Serbia's borders."

But death notices nailed on neighborhood trees told a different story: "Died in Travnik, as soldier in a tank unit, from the Ustashe hand, helped by politicians and their followers." Notices mentioned various Bosnian locations—Mostar, Bratunac, Kakanj, and others—where Serb soldiers had died fighting alongside the Bosnian Serb military.

Even *Politika,* which was under Milosevic's complete control, occasionally failed to censor material on its obituary pages.

One such notice, on November 20, 1992, read:

> Six months have passed since the death of our cheerful and beloved brother and son
>
> MARKO HRNJAK
>
> born July 5, 1972, freshman class, Engineering Faculty of Belgrade University, soldier-paratrooper on active service.
>
> He died on May 23, 1992, in the suburbs of Mostar, at a time when "Serbia was not at war," at a time when "not a single soldier who is a citizen of the Republic of Serbia was outside Serbia's borders," and at a time when many residents of Mostar, including those of the same age, were becoming citizens of Marko's native Belgrade. So we ask: who killed Marko? His unfortunate young adversary, the Muslim sniper, or his own general?

Faced with adversity, Milosevic became cunning and inventive, like a cornered animal looking for ways to save himself. As he had in the past, he proceeded to throw his opponents off guard with a series of dramatic and totally unexpected decisions.

He first had his aides float rumors that Cosic would be elected president of Yugoslavia to replace the remnant of the old collective presidency.

Then, in the first week of June, Milosevic offered Cosic the position of president. He appealed to Cosic's patriotism and vanity; he was a master at stirring such passions in others like a calculating grand master moving them across a chessboard.

Cosic raised several conditions: he wanted new elections, a government of experts, constitutional changes, and a more flexible foreign policy. Cosic said Milosevic agreed to everything. "We talked for a long time," Cosic confided to the journalist Slava Djukic, "and I told him that I wanted to see real changes. I had the impression that we were in full agreement." Cosic realized, when it was too late, that this was all an act, that Milosevic was "a type of man who made all decisions alone, or in secret consultations with a few people close to him." The overriding impression, in retrospect at least, was of calculated deceit and duplicity in which Milosevic proposed to share power with a politically inexperienced seventy-two-year-old writer, but that he did so in order not to lose power completely.

On June 15, Cosic was elected president of Yugoslavia. He watched the televised parliamentary proceedings at his home, then ordered a cab to take him to the parliament building. He received a standing ovation upon entering the chamber. Among those standing was Milosevic, who seemed exceedingly uncomfortable in this new role. Since becoming Serbia's unchallenged master, he was accustomed to entering the chamber last and leaving it first.

Under the constitution of Milosevic's Yugoslavia, the federal presidency was a largely ceremonial job, but with important residual powers: the president was commander in chief of the armed forces. The office of prime minister was given greater responsibility for the conduct of foreign, fiscal, and economic policy. Milosevic's built-in insurance policy was the provision that both the president and the prime minister were elected by the parliament, which was dominated by men who served Milosevic. He held all the threads of power in his hands, even though, as president of Serbia, he was supposedly outranked by the top federal officials.

Outsiders frequently found this confusing. But Milosevic was not interested in titles or pomp: his only interest was the real thing—power. And he wielded power by virtue of his control of the old Communist Party machinery, police, and the media. His preeminence was best summarized by a later Yugoslav prime minister, Radoje Kontic, the man constitutionally responsible for the conduct of foreign affairs, when he was asked by journalists to explain why his government was not involved in the negotiations leading up to the Dayton accords.

"Negotiations with foreign countries are conducted by the person who is the wisest, and that is Slobodan Milosevic," Kontic replied.

Cosic, with a novelist's eye, recalled details of his first day as president; he had not quite understood before then to what extent the rump collective presidency was a sham, a rubber stamp serving Milosevic. He did not quite know what to expect when he entered what was to be his new office where the transfer of power was to take place. The office was slightly larger than a basketball court—it was Tito's former office.

What was to be transferred? he asked. What unfinished business was left for him to deal with?

"We have nothing to submit and nothing to leave," replied Sejdo Bajramovic, the token ethnic Albanian who represented Kosovo on the rump presidency. Bajramovic was a former non-commissioned officer in the Yugoslav Army who had no political standing among the Kosovo population.

"The secretary Nada knows everything," said Branko Kostic, the Montenegrin representative on the rump presidency, who was rushing to catch a plane back home to Montenegro.

Cosic was left alone in the vast room behind a huge desk with a battery of telephones. The secretary, Nada, explained their use.

Cosic began his presidential activity that day by phoning and summoning to his office the chief of military intelligence, the chief of general staff, and the chief of the federal police—in that order. He said he could not explain to himself why he began with the chief of military intelligence.

Even as he was turning Cosic's nationalist rebellion to his own purposes, Milosevic was engaged in another high-level political maneuver to provide cover for his warmongering in Croatia and Bosnia. In March 1992, he turned his attention to Milan Panic, a wealthy Serb-American businessman from California who had invested in a pharmaceutical company in Serbia.

The idea, both bizarre and brilliant, had come from Milosevic's propaganda czar, Dusan Mitevic. It gives an insight into how Milosevic keenly understands the vanities and weaknesses of others and how he uses these for his own purposes. Eventually, however, he always discards such people (the way he abandoned Stambolic) when he no longer needs them—or when they become a threat to him, or too close to him.

Panic was a proven economic manager with a colorful biography widely known in Serbia. A refugee from Tito's Yugoslavia, he had enjoyed a meteoric business success in California as the founder, chairman, and CEO of ICN Pharmaceuticals. His rags-to-riches story appealed to the Serb imagination. A native of Belgrade, Panic was only fourteen when he joined Tito's Partisans to fight against the Germans; after the war he became a prominent sportsman and a member of the Yugoslav Olympic cycling team. In 1955 he defected and two years later arrived in America as a penniless refugee. Now he was an American, a fabulously rich one who hobnobbed with the mighty and the famous.

Panic, who was visiting his new factory in Belgrade, was invited to a private dinner with Milosevic. They ate alone in the dictator's office and in short order both men were inebriated.

As the wine flowed and the conversation grew more intimate, Panic realized that he enjoyed Milosevic's company. They clicked, perhaps because they misunderstood each other's interests. Milosevic saw Panic as a wealthy American businessman with access to powerful figures in Washington and thus someone who could be valuable to him. Milosevic's own experience was that access equals influence. Panic, on the other hand, played up his access to Washington's mighty and powerful because he saw Milosevic as a means for him to short-circuit horrendous Balkan bureaucratic procedures involved in the purchase of a pharmaceutical company.

"Why don't you come over and run our economy?" Milosevic

said in a remarkably breezy fashion. "You'll be prime minister! Why not?"

Panic dismissed the offer, but only after discussing the matter at some length and making the point that he felt he indeed could do something to help Serbia's economy.

"No, no, no, I'm not kidding," Milosevic said. "You run the economy and I'll do the rest. Think about it."

Panic went to bed having decided against it and woke up the next morning having decided to go for it. He confided in Jack Scanlan, the former American ambassador who was now a vice president in his firm. Scanlan viewed the drunken episode as Balkan hot air. Yet he felt it necessary to warn Panic: "I don't think you want to get involved in the politics of this country. It's a mess and it's getting worse. Civil war is already underway."

A few days later, back in California, Panic contacted Warren Zimmermann, who was visiting Los Angeles to address the World Affairs Council. "He told me about Milosevic's offer," recalled Zimmermann. "Obviously I could not give him any advice but I could tell him one thing; Milosevic is not somebody who was going to share power with anybody. That's just the way the man is."

"He doesn't know Milan Panic," Panic replied.

He had already decided to accept Milosevic's offer, but when it was formally announced in Belgrade on June 14, 1992, one day before Cosic was elected president, Panic unexpectedly set his own two conditions. He would take the offer provided that he could keep his U.S. citizenship, and he wanted the offer publicly endorsed by all political parties in Yugoslavia.

Milosevic quickly agreed. So did all the political leaders. But Panic needed Washington's approval for his plan, and could not accept the offer until he was assured that his U.S. citizenship was not endangered. The country held its breath, not knowing whether a Panic premiership would become a reality.

Meanwhile, the unrest continued. The nationalists may have been mollified by Dobrica Cosic's elevation to the Yugoslav presidency, but the students, liberals, and opponents of the Bosnian war were unwilling to pin their hopes on Milan Panic, who might never make it to Belgrade. Thousands of protesters set up tents in a park outside Milosevic's office for a long vigil and also to accommodate their supporters from the provinces who kept pouring into Belgrade for a St. Vitus Day protest that was scheduled to last for eight days.

Trying to stem the tide, Milosevic held an unprecedented face-to-face meeting on that day, June 28, with the opposition leaders. Among them was his old boss in the university party organization, Nebojsa Popov, now a leading liberal opposition figure.

Milosevic at this meeting was a different man, the very picture of calm and tolerance, and eager to make concessions. Opposition politicians felt somewhat uncomfortable—disarmed is the right word—because their complaints were met with short affirmative exclamations—"But of course"; "I don't see any problems"; "Correct." They sensed that he was in full retreat. Only at one point did Milosevic lose his cool. That was in an exchange with Popov, who addressed Milosevic with the familiar *ti* rather than the formal *vi*, and demanded his resignation.

A rattled Milosevic countered by saying, "And why didn't you go to the front?"

Popov replied sarcastically: "Let's go together, if you want, with you leading the way!"

Their exchange continued.

"There are lots of people, groups and parties who are dissatisfied," Popov said. "We should talk about it."

"Of course."

"So we propose a round table discussion between the opposition and the regime."

"Aren't we talking now?"

"Well, yes, but we want to hear your views."

"Can you first give me an idea of what you are going to say?"

"We propose that you submit your resignation. This is one of the preconditions for a change in the situation."

"But you know that is decided by those who elected me [as president of Serbia in 1990]," Milosevic asserted, as if shocked. "I should hope you are not counting yourself among them. The authorities in Serbia, I think, should be chosen by elections and their removal from a position of authority should be the same way, by the will of the electorate."

"We want elections," Popov went on.

"Of course, why not."

"We have in mind new presidential elections."

"Of course, why not."

"Well, let's talk about that," Popov persisted.

"This possibility is always there," Milosevic said.

"You have to state it."

"Well, I'm stating it."

"You are stating it!"

"Any time. The constitution provides for this possibility—to test the confidence in the president."

"Including provisions for his resignation," Popov continued.

"Including that request," Milosevic replied. "Don't you worry about it. What is important for me is the view of the citizens, and not conjectures by a small group of people about what they [the citizenry] think."

Popov told the gathering that the president of Serbia had agreed to new elections.

"Dear gentlemen," Milosevic said with a note of incredulity in his voice, "but this is not the first time I have stated this."

After the session, the opposition was jubilant. Popov and other opposition leaders were convinced that Milosevic had just signed his own political death warrant by agreeing to a new election.

A few days later, at a midnight rally with protesters carrying burning candles, the crowd chanted a ditty threatening Milosevic with the fate of the late Romanian Communist dictator Nicolae Ceausescu, who had been summarily executed together with his wife during the 1989 revolution in Bucharest:

*Just you wait, Slobodan.*
*Ceausescu awaits you!*

A week later—fittingly on the Fourth of July—Milan Panic arrived from America to assume the post of prime minister of Yugoslavia. Milosevic now truly appeared to be tamed, boxed in on the left and on the right. With the installation of Panic and Cosic in the two top jobs of the Yugoslav state, the pressures eased and the protests subsided.

Milosevic had reached a turning point in his dominion of Serbia. It was the worst summer of his life. He understood that power was flowing away from him. By the end of the year he himself was publicly branded a potential war criminal by Secretary of State Lawrence Eagleburger. Not only his legacy but his own personal survival was at stake.

He had seriously misjudged the West. He was totally convinced until the last minute that the Americans and the Europeans were bluffing by threatening to impose economic sanctions against Serbia in May of 1992. When the sanctions were imposed, he promptly dismissed them, saying, "The economic blockade will only accelerate the restructuring of our economy."

He was also stunned by the scope of domestic opposition. When the people turned against him in May and June, he watched huge crowds of protesters on television and asked Dusan Mitevic, his friend and propaganda chief, with genuine incredulity, "Who are those people?" No longer sustained by the emotionalism of popular acclaim and with many black marks against him, Milosevic appeared to his friend a lost and broken man who had no sense of what was going on.

He succumbed to depression and practically disappeared from public life. For the first time he seriously considered leaving politics and going into exile.

Rumors began to circulate about his state of mind. Some attributed his mood swings to diabetes, type II, from which he had suffered since the early 1980s, but in reality few people saw him in his black moods, when he would hurl streams of profanities at those around him. He was given to seizures of apoplectic fury when crossed or when confronted by the brutal stupidity of his proxies which he thought gave him a bad name. He was exceedingly vindictive, his soul full of one black passion—to get even, to avenge.

"I think he is a lonely man," said Slava Djukic, the veteran journalist who had written a political biography of Milosevic. "He never opens his soul to anyone, he does not know real sadness."

Several of his former friends and classmates also spoke of pathology. The man, they said, was subject to serious depressions, sometimes staying at home for a couple of days to hide the condition. He was incapable of remorse, they said. He had not shed a single tear over the atrocities his paramilitary had committed. Serb psychologist Zarko Trebjesanin described him as the "cold narcissus," whose burning power-lust had obliterated not only the memory of his family's self-destruction but also his capacity to empathize; over the years he had dissociated himself from all violence to keep his ego intact, so much so that he had become oblivious to his own use of violent means.

He was also possessed by the sense of his lonely destiny, a modern-day messiah who wanted to restore the fourteenth-century Serbian state of Tsar Dusan. "What does it matter if 200,000 or 300,000 people die if we can restore Dusan's empire," he had told a company of inebriated intimates, according to Ted Olic, a former Yugoslav news executive, but quickly corrected himself, saying, "I was only joking."

The most striking thing about Milosevic was the absence of any ideological motivation at all. He was a chameleon: he inspired public support for his nationalist policies while the old Communist establishment viewed him as never having left their ideological ramparts; both failed to grasp that behind a bleakly rigid exterior was a man in love with himself and completely consumed with the pursuit of unchallenged personal power. "Ideology has never meant as much to my husband as it does to me," Mira once wrote. "He would never say, 'I'll die for socialism, I'll die for internationalism,' like I would."

He was a superb tactician, someone capable of reacting rapidly to events, and thoroughly unscrupulous. But he operated by flashes of insight based on his experience, always seeking to ground them in the Serb mythology which resonated in the villages and small towns. He intuitively knew the secrets of demagoguery. He expanded his power as much by the fear he incited as by the nationalist fervor he inspired. Not content with surrounding himself with sycophants, Milosevic went one step further in his restless determination to subordinate the entire population of Serbia to his stern discipline: he dealt with any matter that caught his attention by cutting clear across the usual ministerial channels.

He used his personal aides in much the same way—suddenly, without warning, moving one young man or another to top jobs. In this way he elevated his office into the sole center of power: it initiated all actions. In late 1991, younger officials in his entourage began talking about the need to hire a Western public relations firm; the Serb propaganda machine was so mired in lies that it was completely discredited. A deputy prime minister, Darko Prohaska, the bright former manager of a major export-import firm, opened talks with Saatchi & Saatchi. But once Milosevic heard about it, Prohaska was fired and the negotiations terminated.

He alone conducted negotiations with foreigners, sometimes having only his confidential secretary in attendance. U.S. diplomat Rudolph Perina confessed that he could not understand how Milosevic was running the country: "There are no staff around him, no hangers on. Only [executive secretary Goran] Milinovic and a secretary. In his office there was only one large photograph, that of his wife, Mira. We spent a lot of time in his dacha. He had no office equipment there, nothing. Once, after we concluded an important agreement, we had to send a driver to Belgrade to get a typewriter to get it down on paper."

Nobody who dealt regularly with Milosevic ever doubted that he was saved that summer by his wife. She stiffened his spine; she could not imagine herself living in exile. She has always been his main adviser, but during his ascendancy she had remained out of view, insisting that she was merely a college professor of sociology and a housewife. But in 1991, when Milosevic's troubles deepened and he appeared to be losing his grip, Mira emerged into the limelight. In December 1990, she had founded a new Communist party under the name of the League of Communists-Movement for Yugoslavia, which she later renamed the Yugoslav United Left (YUL). She also began writing a column in the biweekly magazine *Duga*. People in Belgrade soon learned that the most effective way to reach Milosevic or get anything done was through Mira.

In the summer of 1992, Mira Markovic came out fighting. She assailed nationalists and their leaders, declaring that her husband had never been a nationalist. She rejected public complaints about the forced mobilization, saying it did not exist. The Yugoslav wars were "unclear, unnecessary and immoral," she said.

The writer Radivoje Lola Djukic agreed with her, but then publicly asked: "Well, who came to power and began to lead us down that path? Where have you been, Madame and Comrade Markovic? Why are you addressing world public opinion instead of asking your husband, during a dinner, why he permits the children of Serbia to be sent to die in such a war?"

Mira had no answer, and deflected the question by saying, "How does Radivoje Lola Djukic know what I ask my husband at dinnertime?"

By the end of the summer, Milosevic had regained his bearings. To save himself, he decided his course should indeed be reversed. It was to become a learning experience that made him change the way he dealt with foreigners; there was to be no fundamental shift, but rather a change of tactics, a sharpening of his wiles that took into account the mortal danger foreigners now posed not merely to his grip on power but also to his own future.

Western nations, he realized, were not pawns. He had to treat them as far more dangerous queens, rooks, or knights on the chessboard of which he fancied himself the ultimate master. First and foremost, he understood that he had to repair his relations with the United States.

He had been so arrogant, so intoxicated with his own power, that he had gone out of his way to be rude to the Americans. His wounds, he saw, were self-inflicted. He had gleefully humiliated the Senate Republican leader, Bob Dole, and a group of eight U.S. senators in the fall of 1990; Milosevic had refused even to receive them. From now on, he would treat foreigners with conspicuous courtesy.

Americans who met with him after 1992—among them Richard Holbrooke and the two men who were in charge of the U.S. Embassy in Belgrade, Rudolph Perina and Larry Butler—found him charming. A tough, often petulant negotiator, yes, but charming. Senior British Foreign Office official Douglas Hogg was also taken in by the charm. "I had to keep reminding myself of all the terrible things he has done," Hogg said.

This approach—the charming face and the conciliatory tone that made him appear as a shining light of sweet reason—was designed to disarm. Instead of refusing to meet with foreign critics, Milosevic would now greet them with lavish hospitality and respond to their concerns with exclamations of "Of course, of course" or "I'll have my people look into it." When confronted with unpleasant facts, he insisted that his interlocutors had been "misinformed."

International negotiators David Owen and former Norwegian foreign minister Thorvald Stoltenberg, who both met with him frequently, described him as a considerate host. "He always appeared to have plenty of time," Owen said later. "Meetings were long and were usually accompanied at his insistence by lunch or dinner." Milosevic took to remembering small things: what his visitors drank; the name of a diplomatic note taker's new baby. He presented himself as knowledgeable about the rest of the world, discussing the changing importance of the New Hampshire primary with American visitors. At times he would earnestly talk about the need for elections and for the validation of any politician at the ballot box. Holbrooke, in his memoir *To End a War,* notes with approval a colleague's belief that Milosevic would have made a good Western politician if he had grown up in different circumstances.

Only Zimmermann has been consistent in his assessment of Milosevic as a con man, an arch dissembler. "As with all natural actors," he later recalled, "it was impossible to tell how much consciously he deceived others and how much he deceived himself." That may have been the reason why Milosevic had found it easy to con others.

Indeed, the more one contemplates his advisers and allies, the more one is struck by their narrow-minded nationalism or sheer brutishness. Milosevic knew how to control and use such men, and did so. Always aloof from his subordinates, he carefully staged his rare appearances. He enjoyed the power game in the raw, the drama of it, the unexpected moves; he rarely disclosed his intentions. "Milosevic knows only servants and enemies," his former information minister Aleksander Tijanic said. "Partners and allies do not exist for him."

Vojislav Seselj, leader of the ultra-nationalist Radical Party—who urged his followers at the outbreak of the Yugoslav wars to use "rusty spoons" to gouge out their enemies' eyes—provided him with a safe parliamentary majority and paramilitary Chetnik forces. Milosevic had once described this fanatical hawk as the politician he "admired most." That bit of flattery, a rare public comment about another politician, was likely calculated at the time to give tacit approval to Seselj's brand of extreme nationalism. Another ally was the paramilitary leader Arkan.

His trusted aides were few. Milosevic demanded mindless loyalty. His approach was businesslike: he discarded those who worked for him when the job was done. Only a handful of men stayed on for a long time. One was Dusan Mitevic, the propaganda chief, who performed many delicate tasks for Milosevic. Others included his security chief Radmilo Bogdanovic; his two assistants, Mihaly Kertes and Radovan Stojicic-Badza; and Jovica Stanisic, the secret police chief.

Below them was a very important layer of courtiers, including about one hundred economic managers who lived well and enjoyed unusual freedom and privileges in return for undivided loyalty. But none of these was a close friend. They helped Milosevic swindle the entire country by spending people's savings from their hard currency accounts in Yugoslav banks. After that they soaked up what remained in private hands through a scam involving a series of "private" banks, all linked to Milosevic. Dobrila Gajic-Glisic, the executive secretary of the Serb Defense Ministry, has detailed the activities of one private banker, known as "The Boss" Jezda (real name Jezdimir Vasiljevic), who won government concessions in exchange for obtaining military equipment from Israel despite the UN sanctions. (Among other items the Boss brought in were special infrared mine-clearing equipment, the most modern equipment for monitoring telephone and telefax communications, and various types of ultra-modern miniaturized bugging devices.)

The Boss struck a blow against Yugoslavia's isolation by sponsoring a Bobby Fischer–Boris Spassky chess world championship rematch on the Montenegrin coast in the fall of 1992. The inevitable crash would come in April 1993. The Boss announced from Budapest that anyone with claims to money in his Jugoskandik Bank should deal with the government of Serbia. Rumors circulated that, in the middle of the night, government agents had removed strongboxes with hard currency from all banks. The next morning, long lines formed in front of private banks, which immediately shut their doors for "temporary restructuring."

These banks were in essence pyramid schemes that functioned for more than a year before crashing, but not before Milosevic cronies, tipped off in advance, withdrew their funds.

Milosevic then got the Central Bank to print money until the dinar became utterly worthless. It is not hard to imagine what destruction these economic steps wrought on the fabric of the society. The relentless pauperization would soon sap the capacity for defiance among the public. The decline in living standards since 1991, when an average monthly salary was about $845, was staggering. The average monthly salary in October 1992 was $85; in December, it was $50, and in January 1993, it stood at $22.

The only established fact about Milosevic's personal profiteering involves his purchase of an elegant villa in Belgrade. His mortgage application, dated July 26, 1991, was approved the same day, and by the next day Milosevic was the proud owner of the villa on Tolstoy Street. The building was subsequently renovated and equipped with government money. The timing and speed involved in the transaction—the purchase was made just as the Croatian war was beginning to escalate—suggest that Milosevic knew about the coming Weimar-type inflation. Two years later, his entire mortgage amounted to less than his monthly salary.

But neither financial gain nor the pomp and trappings of power were of interest to him; he was motivated by power itself.

# 7

# The Unquiet American

Milosevic's odd choice of Milan Panic as prime minister was part of his effort to curry favor with the West, even as he tossed a bone to the nationalists by elevating Cosic to the Yugoslav presidency. Panic was a major contributor to U.S. political campaigns, and he cherished the symbols of this status: White House dinner invitations, photographs with presidents and presidential aspirants, senators, cabinet members, and other dignitaries. Milosevic seems to have thought that Panic's word carried great weight in Washington. Or perhaps he was blinded by Panic's wealth and the Communist notion that moneymen were the real rulers of America. Like most Serbs, he may not have understood that a self-made immigrant millionaire stood several orbits outside America's power elite.

More likely, Milosevic had to work with what was available to him.

Whatever the motives, the day Panic arrived in Belgrade, Milosevic knew that he had made a serious mistake.

Milosevic had dispatched his confidant Dusan Mitevic aboard a

Soviet-made Yak-40 trijet to Budapest to meet the new prime minister on July 3, 1992, and accompany him back to Belgrade. But Panic and his entourage refused to be seen together with this completely discredited spin doctor, for fear of sending a wrong signal to the Serb nation.

Mitevic, left alone at Budapest airport, had to rent a car and drive himself back home. After crossing the frontier into Yugoslavia late that evening, he rushed into the border police office to phone Milosevic at home and report the incident. "I thought I was looking at a conspiratorial group," he said, describing Panic and his associates.

Milosevic was stung, Mitevic later recalled. He kept silent for a while, then groaned: "Holy shit, what are we going to do now?"

Milosevic fancied himself a shrewd judge of character. Before offering Panic the prime ministership, Milosevic had noted Panic's ostentation, his appreciation of press attention and flattery, and his restlessness. He expected Panic to become Belgrade's public relations general—a happy second banana with a very important title—who would deflect international criticism and present a smiling, reasonable face to the world.

Panic, however, had different ideas.

Although not a politician, he had keenly followed developments in Eastern Europe and Russia after the collapse of the Berlin Wall: he saw a vast new market opening up. In 1990, he bought Serbia's largest pharmaceutical factory and rapidly proceeded to acquire more than a dozen similar facilities (six of them in Russia) over the next few years. The purchase of the Belgrade plant brought him into direct contact with Milosevic.

Having gained business success and wealth, Panic viewed his new job as an opportunity for higher destiny. He wanted to leave a mark of another kind: stop the Bosnian war, recognize the independence of all the former Yugoslav republics, and turn his energy to economic reconstruction of his native country. Once the fighting was over, he reasoned, he could create an environment conducive to economic growth—low inflation, stable rules of the game for business, and a climate friendly to foreign investors. He would entice multinational corporations with their crucial dowry of technology, skills, and access to markets. A number of his business friends had already committed themselves.

All that was needed was common sense: rationality, intelligence, hard work, and persistence could solve any problem. He imagined himself turning Serbia into the California of Europe, overhauling its internal arrangements and introducing the American system. He believed with a kind of holy passion that the American political system was the only rational one. But before he left the United States, he had reached the conclusion that the removal of Milosevic was mandatory if anything like this could be accomplished.

What lent Panic additional credibility was the presence in his entourage of John Scanlan, who had been American ambassador to Yugoslavia from 1985 to 1989; it reinforced the image among Serbs of a native son who had vaulted himself into the magical circle of the American establishment.

Scanlan was a quintessential State Department man: self-effacing, distinguished-looking, someone with a practical sense as well as a capacity quickly to define the root of the problem. He spoke fluent Serbo-Croatian and was familiar with the country and all its leaders, including Milosevic. After retiring from the Foreign Service in 1991, Scanlan was hired by Panic as a vice president of ICN Pharmaceuticals to supervise the firm's rapid expansion into the former Communist world.

Immediately upon arrival, before he was sworn in, Panic confronted Milosevic, telling him that he must resign in order to clear the way for the lifting of UN economic sanctions. To make this palatable, he offered Milosevic the job of director of a new American-Yugoslav bank he was in the process of putting together. Milosevic would move to California, where, in addition to a $150,000 annual salary, he would be given a mansion, a yacht, and a variety of other perks.

Dusan Mitevic attended one of the crucial conversations and

tried to sway his friend to take the deal. "You are going to become a new hero in the people's eyes, because you are resigning so that the sanctions can be lifted," Mitevic told Milosevic.

"It's fantastic," Milosevic replied, noncommittally.

"I felt like I was playing Russian roulette," Mitevic later recalled, describing a meeting at which Milosevic's peaceful departure was discussed and agreed upon. "I think Milosevic felt cornered. Before the UN sanctions were imposed we did not quite grasp what that meant. Some people even said they would be good for Yugoslavia. But a month later we were suffocating, there was no oxygen. Milosevic looked at Panic's proposal as a way out."

Panic insisted that a formal agreement be drafted, and Mitevic and Scanlan were assigned the job. After two long meetings at the Belgrade Hyatt Regency Hotel and arguments over each phrase, the document was presented to the principals.

Milosevic, whom Mitevic described as looking ashen and abandoned, pronounced it okay, and expressed readiness to put his signature on it, but even so he did not sign. Milosevic's emotional distress was so convincing, Panic said later, that he felt sorry for the Serbian leader. Panic consoled him, telling Milosevic that he would be remembered for making "a personal sacrifice for the Serbian people."

There are those who insist that Milosevic never intended to give up power in this fashion—testimony of the only three people directly present on this occasion notwithstanding—but there is no doubt that he must have been fully aware of his vulnerability. It is also likely that his wife, Mira, could not envisage life in American exile and that she believed he was still stronger than his adversaries.

For his part, Panic promptly contacted the Bush administration with a request for a visa for the Milosevic family. Full of optimism, he rushed to Helsinki on July 10 to meet with Secretary of State Baker, who was attending a ministerial conference of the Conference on Security and Cooperation in Europe (CSCE). The day before, CSCE nations had agreed to suspend Yugoslavia's membership in the organization.

The meeting with Baker went badly. Panic informed Baker that Milosevic had agreed to resign and asked for Baker's help in the removal of UN sanctions, at least the crippling oil embargo against Yugoslavia. "We have to give something to the Serbian people," he said.

Baker would not consider the request, saying, "That is a question for the United Nations."

Here's what we expect you to do, Baker continued, and started reading from a single sheet of paper. Panic interrupted him, saying, "Why don't you just give me your paper and we talk."

Baker, accustomed to greater deference, bristled: "Mr. Panic, you've got to stop interrupting me, I've got to get through these ten points."

Almost immediately after the meeting, Baker aides leaked a story to the press that Panic was Milosevic's Trojan horse and a Serb apologist who had "crashed the party" in Helsinki. The truth was that Panic had indeed been formally invited by Baker, with the invitation relayed through the U.S. Embassy in Belgrade, but Panic could not produce a copy of Baker's invitation without undermining his standing in Serbia.

Before departing Helsinki, Panic was mobbed by journalists who questioned his subservience to Milosevic. Panic responded by declaring his intention to carry out his policies, which encompassed the recognition of all former Yugoslav republics including Bosnia. He was prepared to recognize Bosnia as an independent and sovereign state provided it guaranteed equal political, civic, and human rights to all of its people. Under the constitution, he insisted, the prime minister was in charge of foreign affairs.

But what if Milosevic decides differently? the questioners persisted.

"I am like the president of the United States and Milosevic is like governor of California," Panic repeated several times. "If he gets in my way, God help him."

"Why did you have to say such a thing about me?" Milosevic demanded over the phone when Panic returned to Belgrade. "Why did you have to say it over and over again, that 'If he gets in my way, God help him'? You know, Milan, that is not the way to talk about me."

Milosevic as yet had no inkling that Panic was acting without political support from Washington and that, in fact, the Bush administration had come to view him as an unexpected impediment to its policy (or lack of policy) toward the Balkans. But he could not have failed to register that Panic had returned empty-handed from Helsinki. For someone with so developed a sense for self-preservation as Milosevic, this was a significant signal.

The problem was that the Serb public had welcomed Panic with enthusiasm. People in the street yelled, "Save us, Milan!" and "You are our hope!" He was an exotic visitor in a monogrammed white shirt and freshly pressed blue suit, looking very healthy, face sun-burnished, his hair carefully groomed, not a strand out of place. But he was also *nash*—one of ours—and therefore good. He may have spoken Serbo-Croatian with a heavy accent, but that did not matter.

Throughout these tiring summer months Milosevic was drifting along on the political waters, taking cover behind silence and petulance, and dodging the agreement on his voluntary departure. He no longer had any intention of abdicating; yet he had to bide his time. But in the meetings of top leadership Milosevic oscillated between "angry elation and manic depression," according to Sveta Stojanovic, who was Cosic's top adviser.

The swollen tide of public opinion was pressing against Milosevic: Panic's ratings in public opinion polls were soaring, while his were plummeting. Except for Radio Television Belgrade, Milosevic's grip on the media was weakening. The cover of the weekly *NIN*, once firmly in his corner, was emblazoned with the headline:

MILOSEVIC = FEAR
PANIC = HOPE

Even inside the entrenched Communist bureaucracy, where Milosevic had residual support, the mood toward him was changing: Balkan bureaucrats tend to go with the winner, and Panic looked like a winner. Power gravitated toward him. Sveta Babic, who ran the Diplomatic Housing Authority, perhaps the government's major hard currency source, and one of Milosevic's coterie of company directors and party hacks, was coming around. Initially he had dismissed Panic as an inconsequential figure, a "confidence man," but gradually this changed, and by August he was trying to arrange a meeting with Scanlan to offer his services. "Milosevic has got to go," he said. Someone as worldly-wise, as cynical and sardonic as Babic used to talk about Milosevic only in superlatives, or not at all. If he could be swayed, anyone could.

But without American support, Panic was doomed, and Milosevic knew it. Scanlan urged contacts with as many Western leaders as possible to offset Baker's hostility, and this produced frenetic diplomatic activity but few tangible results. Panic's activism—he met with the leaders of dozens of countries to plead his case—generated a gush of optimism from his supporters that he would succeed and that the West was behind him.

Even so, the Bush administration remained unyielding. Panic flew to New York and tried to arrange a meeting in Washington with Eagleburger, who was now the acting secretary of state; but Eagleburger relayed an acid message through Scanlan: "Jack, I want to make sure you get this message clear to Panic. I don't want him to come to Washington tomorrow so that there would be no impression that we back the deal of swapping Milosevic's removal for the lifting of sanctions. Baker is not going to negotiate this. He cannot. This is a matter for the United Nations. Tell him please not to question my friendship. This is not a matter of friendship. I feel I am his friend, but he is in the big leagues now. That's the way it is."

Apart from Scanlan and Dr. Ljubisa Rakic, a well-known physician who was a member of the Panic cabinet, nobody else knew about this demoralizing setback. Given the proclivity of Balkan minds to search for hidden meanings, the Serb public was not distressed, for they considered that Panic's American trip must have had a hidden significance that would be revealed later.

Next, Panic dispatched Rakic to see Eagleburger. They had been old friends, ever since the 1963 Macedonian earthquake relief. Eagleburger warmly embraced the doctor, greeting him as "old friend," but was blunt in his refusal. Rakic had argued that he wanted to rid his country of Milosevic and the Communists, and the Americans were hampering this by undermining Panic and thus bolstering Milosevic's position. "Larry, you've got to help us," he pleaded. "We are the first non-Communist government in Yugoslavia since 1945."

"You are only a decoration, you are a smokescreen," Eagleburger replied. "You prevented us from bringing Milosevic down. We would have brought him down. This way it's going to take a bit longer. He deceived us; we had a great confidence in him before. Don't worry, we are going to do our own thing. He is neither a Communist nor a nationalist. He likes power and he lies."

But the last thing that President Bush wanted was any involvement in the Balkan mess. The war in Bosnia was no longer a foreign policy problem but a political problem: it had become an issue in the 1992 presidential campaign, offering the Democrats an opportunity to criticize Bush in the field he was strongest—foreign policy. Governor Bill Clinton, Bush's Democratic opponent, attacked the Bush administration for "turning its back on violations of basic human rights" and urged air strikes against the Serbs; his aides argued that Belgrade and other places in Serbia proper should be targeted. If elected president, Clinton insisted, he would make the United States "the catalyst" for a collective stand against aggression. "In a world of change, security flows from initiative, not from inertia," he added.

Bush responded by accusing Clinton of "recklessness," but the administration adjusted its rhetoric, calling on the United Nations to use force, if necessary, to secure deliveries of food and medicine to Sarajevo, the besieged Bosnian capital.

Eagleburger, who had daily access to intelligence reports, knew that Milosevic was the main force behind the Bosnian war. He never doubted the sincerity of Panic's intentions, but he was convinced that Panic was no match for Milosevic. Given the president's firm view that America not get involved in Bosnia, Eagleburger had no specific policy course to recommend. "If we had known what we wanted to do we could have gone to the allies and strong-armed them," one of Eagleburger's top aides said later. "But we didn't."

Panic enlisted the help of President Dobrica Cosic, and the two debated ways of removing Milosevic from power without outside help, but could not reach a decision. Cosic was not averse to the use of force. "He was prepared to have Milosevic arrested," Panic said later. "That was one possibility; the other was to defeat him in the elections," which Milosevic had agreed to hold for the Serbian presidency in December 1992, in fulfillment of his promise to Nebojsa Popov on June 28.

Panic secretly raised the issue with his tennis partner, the chief of general staff General Zivota Panic (who was no relation). The two men drove to Karadjordjevo, Tito's old hunting lodge, and went for a walk in the woods. The general listened intently as the prime minister outlined his argument for the removal of Milosevic, whom he described as a millstone around Serbia's neck. His policies would destroy the nation. He must be removed, Panic said, "but I don't want any bloodshed."

"That can be done," the general said after a long pause.

"You could arrange to have him picked up while he is having a late-night drink at my house," Panic said.

"Yes," the general said. "We have no choice." But then the general made a remark that provides a glimpse into the thinking of a man whom Milosevic had handpicked for the most sensitive job in the Yugoslav military. "It can be done," the general added, "but you go to Washington and get support for us. If you tell me everything is okay, I'll do it."

Panic was in no position to do that.

Milosevic must have been warned by his allies that something was afoot, and he fell into a deep depression.

One evening, he arrived unannounced at Panic's residence,

where they sat on the veranda overlooking Belgrade and drank wine. By now Panic had become convinced that Milosevic was the kind of man who respects and fears only those who are not afraid of him.

Serbia needed a dramatic change, Panic began to argue. He himself was not interested in power: all he hoped to do was to achieve peace and then return to his waterfront house in Newport Beach. Milosevic had to resign—for the sake of Serbia.

Panic kept laying into him: "The people who are guiding you into this mess are not your friends. You are responsible for what is happening in Bosnia. You are responsible for the catastrophic economic conditions in Serbia. Resign. You have to resign!"

"When I get going like this," Panic later recalled, "I can't stop, you know. When you believe something emotionally, intellectually—when you believe it—you become a powerhouse even if you are not."

Milosevic listened for a long time. He seemed shocked by such bluntness. "Why are you going after me like this?" he finally said.

"Because you lied to me! You agreed you'd resign."

"I don't do to you what you are doing to me," Milosevic said, almost bitterly. Then, Panic continued, "suddenly he looks at me and says, 'Enough.' I have never seen him so despondent. So he takes a revolver—he always carries a revolver—and hands it to me. 'Shoot me,' he says. 'Get it over with.' And I am stunned, of course. I can't believe my ears."

"'Are you crazy?'" Panic cried. "'You've got to be sick! You have children, you have family. You want me to shoot you? You are sick. Resign! That's what I want you to do. Stop doing this wrong thing.' And I thought I was dealing with a madman. So we had more to drink. . . ."

A few days later, Milosevic returned to Panic's residence, this time pleasant but aggressive. He began intimidating Panic by hinting that Panic was under constant surveillance. (Milosevic would tell the ranking American and British envoys details about their clandestine conversations or moves to put them on the defensive.) "The first thing in the morning I get a report about what is happening in your life," Milosevic kept telling Panic. "I know everything, everything!"

In their last private meeting, which lasted nearly seven hours, Milosevic provided what, by all appearances, was a rare insight into his soul. Panic was disturbed by reports from Bosnia of babies butchered and mothers and daughters raped in a hideous cycle of Bosnian revenge, by casual brutality of former neighbors that was spreading to Serbia itself. "What you are doing in Bosnia is wrong," Panic said. "We must end it immediately." He repeated his offer to arrange for a graceful way out for Milosevic. "You must step down for the sake of Serbia."

"You don't understand what I mean to Serbia," Milosevic replied. "I'm the Ayatollah Khomeini of Serbia. The Serbs will follow me no matter what!"

"How can you say something so stupid?" Panic replied angrily.

"Milan, you don't understand. You work for me! Don't you realize it?"

"That's even more stupid than you being Ayatollah Khomeini. You are crazy! We are adversaries!"

Until that day, the ostensibly cordial relationship between Milosevic and Panic had remained undisturbed, at least on the surface. A covert struggle had been waged from the very beginning. Panic was in charge of the federal police and secret service, but Milosevic controlled the Serb police. Early on, Panic's own security people discovered that his phone lines were bugged. They assumed that some bureaucrats were reporting about the goings-on inside his office and residence: how else would Milosevic know of cabinet decisions even before they were taken? Panic had all of his American staff (except John Scanlan) move in with him to the prime minister's villa, which put an additional burden on everybody. Their workload doubled. The daily government business transactions—cabinet sessions, meetings with individual ministers, planners, delegations—ended at six or seven in the evening. Then, after dinner at the residence, their real working day began.

But Panic's lack of success in producing any dramatic changes helped Milosevic recover his narcissism and his sense of invincibility. In his own mind, Milosevic had assigned himself a lordly entitlement and moral free passage which was reflected in startling levels of arrogance and complete arbitrariness. When Panic again pressed him to resign, Milosevic bluntly informed the prime minister that he had no intention of doing so.

"But we have an agreement," Panic shouted.

"No such agreement exists," Milosevic shot back.

"Let's call in Mitevic. He is your friend. He is a witness," Panic said.

Mitevic was sitting down to his dinner when a phone call summoned him urgently to Milosevic's office. A limousine already was on its way to pick him up. "I immediately saw that the president and the prime minister had argued, and I thought they were both drunk," he recalled later. He noted the empty bottles of whiskey and wine.

He was instantly accosted by Panic. "Now, Dusan, tell him about the agreement"—stressing the word "agreement" to indicate he was talking about the document that Mitevic and Scanlan had drafted and Milosevic and Panic had verbally approved.

"Is there any such agreement?" Milosevic asked acidly.

"Yes," Mitevic replied. His stomach clenching, Mitevic found himself wishing to disappear into thin air. He knew full well the vengeful streak in his friend.

"You see," Panic turned triumphantly to Milosevic. "There's your witness!"

"Did I sign it?" Milosevic asked.

"No," Mitevic replied.

"Did you sign it?" Milosevic asked.

"No."

"So you see," he looked at Panic with a flash of sardonic humor, "that's a worthless piece of paper!"

Mitevic was promptly dismissed. As he was leaving, he could hear the two men hurling ugly epithets at each other. They were at drawn swords, Mitevic concluded.

A few weeks after that conversation, Mitevic, the former director of Radio Television Belgrade who was now a member of the Serbian government in charge of resources, was relieved of his duties.

The conflict between Milosevic and Panic would burst into the open a week later at the International Conference on the Former Yugoslavia.

The conference, which was held in London on August 26 and 27, 1992, assembled the leaders of more than thirty nations. Panic intended to use it as a forum to press his political program, as well as to impress upon a skeptical Western community that he was not a puppet of Slobodan Milosevic.

In the weeks preceding the conference, the British organizers had insisted that the Yugoslav delegation include Milosevic. Panic, who did not want to have Milosevic in his delegation, insisted that as prime minister he was solely responsible for the conduct of foreign affairs. By dealing with Milosevic, he argued, the West kept him as a player on the world stage as well as strengthening his position in Serbia. But the British were insistent: the Western officials wanted to talk to Milosevic.

Panic, who was fighting to head off a move to expel Yugoslavia from the United Nations, ultimately agreed. He was keenly conscious that a failure to retain the UN seat would have unhappy consequences for his political future.

But when the conference chairman, British prime minister John Major, called on Milosevic to address the plenary session, Panic vigorously intervened.

"You speak when I tell you to speak," he told Milosevic. Then, turning to Major, Panic added: "This is my delegation and I will speak for my delegation. If I think Mr. Milosevic should speak I'll tell him to speak."

Milosevic looked on uncomprehendingly. Nobody had ever said such words to him in the presence of other people, let alone at a gathering of world figures. Self-effacement in such situations was for him the most unnatural of roles, yet he remained mum. His pride wounded, he was further humiliated by other speakers, and the London conference remained in his memory as the two most miserable days of his life. "He was like a beaten dog," one of the participants recalled later.

In his speech, Panic said: "Some participants at this conference still have agendas that bear the potential for fueling the flames of a broader conflict rather than furthering the quest for peace. I am not one of them. I do not speak for Greater Serbia. I speak for greater peace." Panic also met with Ibrahim Rugova, the leader of the Kosovo Albanians, and openly condemned Serbia's repressions in Kosovo.

After the plenary session, Panic, Cosic, and other members of the Yugoslav delegation, meeting in a hotel room, insisted on Milosevic's resignation. Cosic said that the announcement should be made in Belgrade, not London. A humiliated Milosevic left the conference early, in a huff and without informing anyone that he was taking one of the Yugoslav government's two aircraft.

Immediately upon his return to Belgrade, Milosevic convened his closest allies, led by Radmilo Bogdanovic, to a meeting at his weekend home in Pozarevac. They agreed that Panic should be ousted immediately. The main role in this effort was assigned to Vojislav Seselj, whom Milosevic used as a cudgel against his domestic critics and whose paramilitary Chetniks spearheaded Serbia's aggression in Croatia and Bosnia.

The London conference, like so many international meetings on the former Yugoslavia over the years, seemed to have accomplished a great deal, but in actuality amounted to nothing. A triumphant Panic felt vindicated by the fact that its final document in effect had endorsed his political program. Indeed, Milosevic himself had agreed to the twelve-point document, expressing "reservations" only on one point dealing with the acceptance of the administrative borders of Tito's Yugoslavia as the new international frontiers. In Belgrade, however, when questioned about the conference, Milosevic declared: "I didn't agree to anything! What are you talking about!"

On August 31, Seselj and a group of Milosevic allies tabled a no-confidence vote in parliament and unleashed a campaign of vitriol against Panic. They accused the prime minister of "sellout," and in particular objected to the provisions on Kosovo and the acceptance of Tito's borders, which left sizable Serb minorities in Bosnia and Croatia. Panic, they said, was an "adventurer" who "knows more about California than about Kosovo." The rhetoric quickly assumed an anti-American tone and focused on former U.S. Ambassador John Scanlan, Panic's foreign affairs adviser. Scanlan was attacked as a "dark figure" and part of an American plan to destroy Yugoslavia. He was linked to another former ambassador, Lawrence Eagleburger, who had led the U.S. delegation at the London conference. "One former American ambassador was orchestrating things on one side of the table while the other former American ambassador was doing the same on the other side of the table," Seselj said.

As was his habit in emergencies, Milosevic summoned a group of Kosovo Serbs to Belgrade to stage anti-Panic demonstrations. But this time Milosevic miscalculated and made a tactical error.

Public opinion polls conducted in Belgrade showed Panic's approval rating at 82 percent. More ominous, from Milosevic's point of view, were threats of mass demonstrations by Belgrade University students. In addition, he simply lacked the votes in one of the two chambers of parliament where the Montenegrins had the power to block the move to oust Panic. The Montenegrins, in fact, announced their support for Panic. "All these parliamentary maneuvers call to mind the atmosphere of a lynching," said Montenegrin parliamentary leader Svetozar Marovic. Cosic also issued a forceful statement asserting that the motion was "ill considered and damaging" to Serbia.

Milosevic quickly reversed himself. On September 2, his spokesman announced that the ruling party would not support the motion. An embarrassed parliament, after three days of sharp denunciation of the London conference, had to endorse its results with an overwhelming majority.

As a result of Milosevic's error, Panic seized the initiative and fired Foreign Minister Vladislav Jovanovic, a Milosevic creature, after removing an even more important henchman, Mihaly Kertes, whose title was deputy federal interior minister. A malevolent ethnic Hungarian, Kertes was one of the handful of people who had direct access to Milosevic's home and was trusted by his wife. Through Kertes, Milosevic controlled special secret police units that were engaged in ethnic cleansing and other covert operations in Bosnia.

For a few weeks, Panic saw his authority rise among high officials who were testing the prevailing winds. He would see it falter rapidly when he failed to prevent Yugoslavia's expulsion from the United Nations. The UN seat represented the continuity of Yugoslavia and as such was Milosevic's obsession. "It was an enormously important matter for him," Panic's new foreign minister, the veteran diplomat Ilija Djukic, recalled. "To Milosevic it meant that he salvaged what could be salvaged from Yugoslavia; the others destroyed it, not he. He saved Yugoslavia."

Other former Yugoslav republics were duly admitted to the world body and UN Secretary General Boutros Boutros-Ghali urged Panic that his government also apply for membership. Panic, a pragmatic businessman, was prepared to do so, but given Milosevic's absolute intransigence on the issue, tried to postpone and deflect a confrontation. On September 21, in a letter to all UN members, Panic urged that the General Assembly postpone the decision; but the matter had already been decided upon in the Security Council. The next day, Panic met with the foreign ministers of the five permanent members of the council—the United States, Britain, France, China, and Russia—at the Russian mission in New York.

"Panic was brilliant," Scanlan recalled. "He was convincing and I thought he was at the edge of turning things around. All except Eagleburger were beginning to be swayed by him." But the U.S. secretary of state would not have it. "If we deviate from what we have agreed to, we are going to have a problem and the outcome would be worse," Eagleburger said. "We don't want to reopen that."

For Eagleburger and Scanlan, once close friends and now sitting on opposite sides of the table, the meeting in the Russian mission was personally painful. At one point, Eagleburger turned to Scanlan and said in a low voice: "Jack, five years ago would you have thought that you and I would be sitting here in these respective positions?"

"No," replied Scanlan.

On September 23, in an atmosphere of Serbophobia and tension, the assembly turned down Panic's last-minute appeal. The vote was 127 to 6.

Milosevic had come to a conclusion after Panic had failed to derail the UN move against Yugoslavia or to obtain any visible backing from Washington: Panic, he now knew, was not the exponent of some secret American design.

His method of reasserting himself was predictable and familiar. Milosevic's tools, as always, were television and the police. His tactic was surprising and totally unexpected.

On October 9, he arranged an interview on Belgrade Television to publicize his conflict with Panic and Cosic, but made it sound like a legitimate part of the political process leading up to the December presidential elections in Serbia. The interviewer was the new director general of Radio Television Belgrade, Milorad Vucelic, an intelligent and thoroughly cynical sycophant who elevated organized lying beyond the wildest imagination of his predecessor, Dusan Mitevic. Under his leadership, according to Belgrade intellectuals, "television became worse than the lie itself." Belgrade TV journalists themselves were making the point by saying privately, "Give us back Dusan Mitevic!"

One of the first exchanges provides the flavor of the "interview":

> VUCELIC: I think neither Serbia nor you and the leadership has ever advocated the war option.
>
> MILOSEVIC: I'm glad that you are reminding the citizens of that fact.
>
> VUCELIC: One gets the impression that President Cosic is getting much better at diplomacy, that he is having spectac-

ular successes, that everything is developing in a more attractive fashion, with congratulations and applause, but that the results are getting worse and worse. Do you share this impression?

MILOSEVIC: Well, in short, yes.

In the course of this bizarre interview, Milosevic suggested that Panic was controlled from Washington, while "it remains to be seen" who controlled Cosic. The interviewer then turned to Kosovo and Cosic's idea that the territory should be divided by peaceful negotiations between Serbs and Albanians.

"What division are you talking about?" Milosevic replied, ostensibly incredulous but in reality to give the interviewer the opportunity to repeat and elaborate on the proposal that Kosovo be divided between the Serbs and the Albanians.

"This is out of the question," Milosevic finally replied. "Absolutely out of the question. I could never support such a thing."

The capital was now openly split into two camps.

Cosic responded to this attack a few days later, in an interview with *Politika* on October 15 in which he called for Milosevic's resignation. "If my resignation were discussed as much at home and abroad as Milosevic's, I would step down," he said. "Milosevic and I differ essentially in the understanding of democracy and ways of pulling the country from the abyss in which we find ourselves." Cosic had already agreed to run against Milosevic for the post of president of Serbia.

Meanwhile, Panic on that same day flew to Kosovo to meet with the ethnic Albanian leaders whom he was determined to win over. In an extraordinary scene, he embraced Ibrahim Rugova on the steps of the Pristina Town Hall and endorsed all Albanian demands except secession. "Dr. Rugova and I are going to democratize the Yugoslav system," he declared. He also publicly berated the Serb nationalist zealots who had wielded power in the province since 1989.

In private talks, Panic urged the Albanian majority to take part in the forthcoming election in order to defeat Milosevic. The solid

Albanian bloc of nearly 900,000 votes, he said, would prove decisive. He vowed to give Kosovo's Albanians full autonomy on the pattern of Tito's "limited sovereignty"; there was no issue on which a compromise could not be found, he insisted, provided each side respected the other's interests. Rugova and his colleagues, however, were in a secessionist mood and eventually turned him down. If they were to reenter Serbia's political process, they would effectively be abandoning their quest for independence—something they were not prepared to do.

Late Saturday night, October 19, the duty officer in the headquarters of the federal secret police received a phone call from a good friend, an agent of the Serbian police whose offices were located across the street. The caller wanted to return to the federal police a special camera capable of taking photographs at night from a great distance. The federal police were equipped with the latest technology; local police frequently borrowed equipment for special use.

"There's no need to rush," the federal policeman said. "We won't need it over the weekend."

"I'd just like to get it done. It takes five minutes."

"Fine," replied the duty officer.

"One more thing. Please phone your guys and tell them to let me in." The federal police headquarters, built of solid granite, was virtually impenetrable, with steel doors and the latest coding devices.

"Fine," the duty officer said.

Within minutes, heavily armed and masked Serb police units occupied the federal police building without firing a shot. They quickly proceeded to oust and lock out all employees. Having cleared the building, they systematically removed all secret police files and hauled them to the Serbian Interior Ministry.

The speed, secrecy, and efficiency of the operation were overwhelming.

Cosic and Panic were in Geneva that day, attending negotiations on the war in Bosnia. Once again Milosevic had successfully resorted to force.

Panic's Boeing 727 touched down at Belgrade airport shortly before midnight that Saturday and he immediately knew something was wrong. The security people were missing. Only three members of his government were on hand to greet him.

When a security escort reached the federal policy ministry by cellular phone, he was told cryptically that the Serbian police had taken over the building and would not allow anyone to enter it.

Where are the government limousines for the prime minister's entourage?

They were all "requisitioned" by the Serbian government, came the answer.

"Funny thing, we didn't immediately notice that there were not enough cars around for everybody," Foreign Minister Ilija Djukic recalled later. "Was this a coup?" Nobody knew the answer.

The party moved to the airport's VIP lounge and began working the phones. Scanlan called Robert Rachmales, the American chargé d'affaires, at his home. A drowsy Rachmales, already in bed, said he was not aware of anything unusual in the city.

Panic tried unsuccessfully to locate the interior minister. He reached General Zivota Panic, the chief of general staff, at home. The general sounded surprised and professed not to know anything. He said he would immediately check things out and meet the prime minister at his residence.

The entire Panic party rushed to the prime minister's office in a four-car motorcade.

The situation in the prime minister's office was surreal. "We began to think out loud what it all meant: is the government next?" the foreign minister recalled. "Panic was on the phone. So were some of his aides. We just sat there, and as we waited, I joked that it was a shame we did not have cards to play."

Finally, the interior minister, Pavle Bulatovic, was located. A proud Montenegrin, who undoubtedly saw the seizure of his office as a blow to his own prestige and manhood, he asked the prime minister to issue an order immediately to the federal police and the army to retake the building.

Panic vacillated, fearing confrontation. This seems to have been one time in his life when he lost his nerve. He would make a decision, he said, after conferring face to face with General Panic. Privately, he was no longer sure about his tennis partner. They had exchanged confidences. They had discussed the possibility of using the army to remove Milosevic from power and the general was ready. That had been two months earlier.

Reaching his residence, Panic found the general waiting. Yes, the general said, the federal building had been taken over by the Serbian police. But the whole thing seemed to him like "a tempest in a teapot." He advised against the use of the army. This was not the occasion for a confrontation with Milosevic, he added.

Panic agreed. "Let's follow the legal route," he said.

The next morning Panic was downplaying the incident and talking about political and legal means to fight Milosevic. Scanlan disagreed. "We are making a serious tactical error," he said. "I think the general is lying to you."

A forceful response was necessary, Scanlan said. "You've got to confront this, Milan. You cannot avoid it. This is the ultimate challenge. Of course it is a tempest in a teapot as far as the building is concerned, but the image of Milosevic blatantly using his police with impunity to seize a federal ministry, and particularly the federal police ministry, will be seen both domestically and internationally as an indication of Milosevic's power and authority vis-à-vis you." Panic, unwilling to risk civil war, decided to stick with the legal route.

Milosevic's bold and brazen action shocked and impressed the bureaucracy. Panic's failure to assert himself and defend his prerogatives only reinforced the perception that Milosevic had regained his bearings and that he was the ultimate arbiter in Serbia.

A few days later, Panic's main political ally, Dobrica Cosic, chose to assert himself in an entirely unpredictable way. Pleading poor health, Cosic announced that he would not run against Milosevic in the December elections after all.

Cosic's change of heart caused consternation in opposition circles; he was widely considered a candidate who could easily defeat Milosevic. Panic pleaded with him to reconsider, but without success. One possible explanation for the decision was that Cosic was intimidated by Milosevic's show of force; another was raised by his critics, who ascribed it to his vanity and cunning ambition. A Cosic ally said later that he believed "Cosic began to like the trappings of being president of Yugoslavia"—and expected Milosevic to retain him in the largely ceremonial post.

Instead, Cosic urged Panic to run himself against Milosevic.

But here was another Byzantine maneuver in a convoluted Balkan intrigue, with the ever present Kosovo obsession weighing on the mind of an otherwise kind, grandfatherly writer. It ultimately amounted to a repudiation of Panic and a split in the opposition ranks.

While presenting a friendly face and promises of support, Cosic suffered acute anxiety over Panic's policy toward Kosovo, his can-do attitude and pragmatism in dealing with the ethnic Albanians. The writer had reached the conclusion that Panic had outlived his usefulness, especially since he had failed to change the views of the American administration.

"Cosic told us he thought Panic was not enough of a Serb to be able to win against Milosevic," said David Owen, the European Union peace envoy. "He was suspicious of Panic's Serbianness! He said he could never give him his full backing. On this issue—he is too crude, you know—it was his visceral reaction, instinct. Panic stood for a different world from his."

Indeed, Owen and Cyrus Vance, the former U.S. secretary of state who was now a UN peace negotiator, read the new cards being dealt and quickly abandoned Panic for Milosevic. As co-chairmen of the permanent International Conference on the Former Yugoslavia, Vance and Owen were in the position to influence Western policy makers. Owen, in particular, believed strongly that the key to the resolution of the crisis in Bosnia lay with Milosevic.

"Vance and I wanted him [Panic] to do well, but we didn't believe he could win, and we had to somehow keep open the lines of communications to Milosevic. While Cosic was there, we were ready to sacrifice the relationship with Milosevic. Once Cosic bowed out, we had to deal with him."

Milosevic quickly grasped the situation. All the propaganda vitriol was now focused on Panic while the media treated Cosic with the respect accorded a political ally.

Cosic responded in kind. He never came out openly and unequivocally in support of Panic and he declined to authorize a campaign spot showing Panic and Cosic holding hands. He also demanded that Panic fire Scanlan, something Cosic later denied, saying he had only urged that the former U.S. ambassador be sent "on vacation or something."

But Cosic was evasive in his explanations. "I invited Milosevic on two occasions in September [of 1992] and urged him not to run [in the December elections]. I told him I was talking to him like his father—I emphasized the differences in age and experience. Milosevic said he would not run for reelection if I decided to run."

"I'm sure Milosevic would not have run had I decided to run," he added.

But what, then, was the reason for his decision against running? "I thought the situation was odd," Cosic replied. "I was president of Yugoslavia and I would have to resign to run for the presidency of Serbia. It didn't make sense." Milosevic couldn't have put it better himself.

The December 1992 elections were the only truly serious electoral challenge Milosevic faced in his life.

Finding himself under great pressure to jump into the fray, Panic summoned his American friends—among them former Senator Birch Bayh, California Democratic Party operatives Bill Press and Tom Hayden, and Democratic pollster Douglas Schoen—for consultations. Schoen carried out polling and analyzed Serbian polls as well. His results showed that Panic could beat Milosevic.

"He convinced me too," Scanlan said later. He quoted Schoen as telling them: "I'm a professional, I know how to analyze these things. I have talked to everybody else, I have analyzed other polls. There is no question in my mind. I can say that if it were an honest vote you would beat Milosevic. I can't address how the political situation is going to work in Yugoslavia."

Panic decided to run barely forty-eight hours before the filing deadline. In order to get his name on the ballot, Panic had to submit a list of at least ten thousand signatures of citizens endorsing his candidacy.

Milosevic's Electoral Commission provided Panic's office with a set of forms with enough space for a total of twenty-eight signatures.

His American staff rose to the occasion. David Calef, veteran of many California political campaigns, turned everyone into campaign mode. Xerox machines were put into high gear. University student volunteers worked round the clock and succeeded in collecting more than thirty thousand signatures before the deadline.

Milosevic threw up every delaying tactic and roadblock he and his men could think of. A law was rushed through the Serb parliament raising the residency requirement. Panic's American citizenship was also raised as an issue, but nine days later the Supreme Court of Serbia overruled the Electoral Commission on both points.

Rumors were floated that ultra-nationalist groups were planning to assassinate Panic. And there was some truth behind these rumors. Goran Hadzic, Milosevic's proconsul in the Krajina region of Croatia, was quoted in the official press as vowing to bring his gunmen to Belgrade to kill Panic.

But Panic's main problem was access to television. Not once was Panic given access to Radio Television Belgrade. He announced his candidacy on a local Belgrade station, saying: "Milosevic has not kept his promises. Our economy is in shambles. Unemployment is skyrocketing. Inflation is out of control. Our children have no future. Under Milosevic we have become isolated internationally as well as victims of the cripling sanctions. The [Bosnian] war is raging out of control. All that Milosevic has to offer is fear, division, and confrontation."

But his speech was heard only in Belgrade. National television, moreover, refused to accept Panic's ads. Serb television journalists who saw them said later that had they been aired, Milosevic would have been defeated.

"The ads were slick, professional, but not provocative," David Calef said later. "All that was needed was to contrast the gush of Milosevic optimism with the grim reality. The first one had Milosevic's face and the slogan THEY PROMISED. They refused to run it. They said you can't have that; it's provocative. We went back and blew up the image so all you could see were Milosevic's lips. People would recognize his lips, he's always scowling, right? They came back, saying no.

"We had to go through three rounds of censorship and editing, which of course emasculated the ad. Another commercial showing a burning match stick with the slogan THE LAST MATCH FOR A BRIGHTER FUTURE, FOR WARMER HOMES, SO THAT WE HAVE LIGHT. VOTE FOR PANIC. NOW OR NEVER. It was also declared provocative. Yet another ad showed Milosevic with the caption OFFERING OUR CHILDREN: WAR, POVERTY, UNEMPLOYMENT, FOODLINES. VOTE FOR PROSPEROUS AND DEMOCRATIC SERBIA."

Schoen produced an ad which featured a picture of Milosevic and asked the question whether he had improved the quality of life and the economy. The answer was a series of shots of ordinary people with looks of desperation amid the shabby reality of Belgrade with its bread lines and gasoline lines. TV officials refused to put it on the air because it was too critical. Schoen asked technicians to remove whatever could be considered objectionable, and they cut out all the references to Milosevic. The TV officials again refused.

No matter what Schoen, Calef, and others did, Panic's ads were barred. He was present on television only as an object of contempt and ridicule, while Scanlan was portrayed as the sinister "dark figure" carrying the virus of American treachery. Several ultranationalist Serb Americans led by an aggressively hysterical university lecturer named Radmila Milentijevic denounced Panic on the air as an unscrupulous adventurer who was bankrolled by the CIA; some produced forged documents to prove that Panic was a CIA agent.

Slander and fabrications, like an acid rain of scorn, descended on Panic daily. A huge rally in front of St. Mark's Church in Belgrade, when Panic and his wife, Sally, were mobbed by well-wishers trying to shake their hand or just touch them, was presented in a twenty-second-long voice-over report on the evening news as a protest against the traitor to the Serbian people.

This type of propaganda may have been counterproductive in Belgrade, which Milosevic knew he would lose anyway, but it was designed for the rest of the country where more than 75 percent of the Serbian population lived.

Despite unremitting attacks, Schoen's polls showed Panic well ahead of Milosevic. Anecdotal evidence supported Schoen. The warmth, the hope for change, the flicker of recognition in people's eyes that there was a different way to do things, all provided his entourage with an emotional high. In the southern city of Nis, which was a Milosevic stronghold, Panic received a thunderous welcome even though the city's mayor had asked him not to come and civic leaders and factory managers had announced they would not receive him. But when Panic's car pulled into the main square, he found a crowd of twenty-five thousand chanting his name.

With events rushing toward their climax, Panic moved around at breakneck speed from one town to another, but in different vehicles, constantly changing his route, and taking other precautions. With ever more frequent rumors that he would be gunned down, Panic's security people took no chances; nobody knew for sure whether these threats were real or merely Milosevic's ploys to slow down the challenger.

Panic asked a number of Western figures for international observers to monitor the elections. The Serbian people needed their support, he told them. "They need to know that they are not being punished for Milosevic's policies; they need to know that they would be welcomed into the international community if they reject the dictatorship; they need to know that sanctions would be eased."

With the 1992 American presidential election over, Panic and his advisers felt that the outgoing Bush administration would no longer feel constrained in endorsing Serbia's democratic challenge to dictatorship, if not Panic's personal candidacy. Birch Bayh and Bill Press also sought to convince President-elect Clinton to issue a statement of support. "But Clinton would not do it even though he liked Milan," Press said later. "He was too new, too green, and did not want to take any chances."

There was thus no foreign support for the Panic experiment, which turned into a great lost cause.

Milosevic prepared for the elections as if for war. The word went out to the old Communist Party machinery: they were to quietly purge from the rolls all voters who had not participated in an election the previous spring—an election that had been boycotted by the opposition parties. A cumbersome and time-consuming procedure was devised for those who wanted to be reinstated. Most significant, Milosevic decreed that the ballot boxes were not to be sent from precincts directly to the Central Election Board but to newly created county electoral boards, an interposition that would give Milosevic's people sole control of the ballot boxes. Fraud took place at that level before the boxes were forwarded to the Central Election Board.

On election day, university students—who supported Panic—were to be required to register for subsidized housing and pick up stipends for the following semester, which meant that they would have difficulties in reaching their hometowns and villages to vote. Milosevic also ordered that border crossings be shut on election day to prevent citizens, in particular members of ethnic minorities who were working in neighboring countries, from voting.

One of Milosevic's aides, Sveta Babic, was now confident of victory in the days before the election. Forgotten was Babic's furtive attempt in August to meet with John Scanlan and offer his services to Panic when Milosevic looked weak. "Remember Stalin's immortal principle," he said, laughing broadly. "It doesn't matter how they vote, it's how the vote is counted that matters."

The last hysterical hours of the campaign played on people's feelings of insecurity, and portrayed Milosevic as the sole person strong enough to stand up to foreign pressure. His final address was brimming with nationalist fervor. "Serbia will never be brought on her knees," he vowed before a national television audience and a crowd of about four thousand party faithful in the controlled setting of a large convention center.

By contrast, Panic was denied television coverage when he addressed more than 150,000 people in front of the parliament building, many carrying lighted candles on a balmy December evening. Milosevic, Panic said, "is the force of darkness" leading Serbia into catastrophe. "Milosevic's Serbia is an outcast, isolated, humiliated, and wounded by sanctions."

The absence of international pressure encouraged Milosevic to delay the arrival of European election observers until after the campaigning had ended. When a few observers finally showed up, their capacity to monitor electoral practices was pathetically limited.

December 20, 1992, was a warm, sunny day with a blue sky of near-Alpine clarity. Voter turnout was heavy. Reports of fraud, intimidation, and other shenanigans were numerous, particularly in villages and small towns where the local police chiefs and the old Communist machinery controlled things. The same was true of outlying districts of Belgrade; one American reporter who covered a suburban polling station reported that five out of the first six people who showed up were not permitted to enter, even though they were on the rolls. Schoen's exit polls of 1,371 voters selected at random at 60 polling places showed Panic and Milosevic tied at 47 percent. But in the capital, more than 80 percent of the voters polled said they had voted for Panic.

Yet when the results began coming in that evening, it was apparent that the election had been rigged. In one Belgrade precinct, Zemun, Panic received zero votes. In the end, with a 69 percent voter turnout, Milosevic gained 56 percent of the vote and Panic 34 percent.

The next few days passed in analysis and recrimination. Milosevic's men in parliament raised demands for the arrest of Panic and other Americans. Panic, alarmed, asked all American citizens on his staff to leave the country as soon as possible, but to do so quietly. "The situation's dangerous and you have to leave," he told them. "You are in jeopardy."

Almost unnoticed in the midst of Belgrade's political turmoil was President Bush's letter dated December 25, 1992, and delivered to Milosevic the following day. The president announced a new American policy toward Kosovo in sternest terms, warning Milosevic that the United States would intervene militarily if the Kosovo crisis escalated into violence:

> In the event of a conflict caused by Serbian action, the United States will be prepared to employ military force against the Serbians in Kosovo and in Serbia proper.

By all indications, the warning seemed to have been ignored and received no attention in the media.

On December 29, the parliament adopted a no-confidence motion against the Panic government. Panic was to remain the head of a caretaker government until his successor could be named as prime minister of Yugoslavia.

The next day, as he was preparing to set off for a trip to California and wanted to make last-minute calls, Panic told a servant in the residence to instruct the driver that he would be leaving in fifteen minutes.

"Mr. Panic, the chauffeur is not here, nor is the car."

"What do you mean not here?"

"Nobody checked in this morning."

Panic looked out the window from his residence. The official Mercedes 600 was not there.

Milosevic inflicted a final humiliation on Panic when the caretaker prime minister returned to Belgrade in late January 1993 to wind up his affairs.

When Panic and his entourage reached the Yugoslav border

with Hungary at Horgos, they were detained by police, their documents confiscated. As the prime minister was being held for five hours at a police station, Cosic, still the titular head of state, urgently called Milosevic.

"Slobodan, what's happening? Is it true that Panic was arrested?"

"He has not been arrested yet, but we will arrest him and shave his head and then you can pardon him!"

Cosic, who thought that Milosevic had indeed planned to carry out his vengeance, asserted himself vigorously until Milosevic relented.

"Okay, okay, I'm going to give him to you," Milosevic said and proceeded to order Panic's release.

Four months later, it would be Cosic's turn to be dispatched unceremoniously into political oblivion.

# 8

# A Question of Loyalty

In the spring of 1993, Slobodan Milosevic was in his fifty-second year and beginning to be worn down with frustration.

The December 1992 meeting of the International Conference on the Former Yugoslavia had adopted a proposal for the establishment of an international tribunal in the Hague to try crimes against humanity committed during the wars in Bosnia and Croatia. U.S. Secretary of State Lawrence Eagleburger, who attended the December meeting in Geneva, publicly threw America's backing behind the court and named Milosevic, his Bosnian ally Radovan Karadzic, and others as potential war criminals who should be brought before the Hague tribunal.

Milosevic chose to ignore the threat, while Karadzic dismissed it as a public relations gimmick. But Eagleburger's warning remained in their minds.

Some months later, Karadzic quietly approached the famed Harvard law professor Alan Dershowitz to inquire whether he would represent him should Karadzic ever have to appear before the Hague court.

Dershowitz turned him down.

Publicly, Milosevic was silent on the issue, but one of his frequent foreign visitors noted that references to war crimes were only a marginally less neuralgic point for him than Kosovo. His standard explanation was that in wartime, atrocities are invariably carried out by small groups of paramilitaries. Any mention of Karadzic's role was immediately countered by the assertion that Alija Izetbegovic, the Bosnian Muslim leader, was equally guilty. In Milosevic's view, Karadzic and Izetbegovic were political leaders who knew nothing about crimes committed by individual soldiers. There was never any suggestion that he shared in the guilt for having started the Yugoslav wars.

Even so, Eagleburger's warning remained in his mind. He decided that he had to change his tactics: he had to extricate himself from the Bosnian mess and salvage anything he could from the ruins of his Bosnia policy. Not only was Serbia suffocating under the crushing weight of UN economic sanctions, but a new package of crippling financial sanctions was being prepared in the UN Security Council. Even though a final vote had been delayed until after the April 27 referendum in Russia on a new constitution—the delay designed to help Boris Yeltsin's campaign against a pro-Serb coalition of Russian nationalists and Communists—Milosevic knew that its adoption was inevitable. His overwhelming objective was to have the economic sanctions lifted and he definitely did not want additional financial sanctions imposed. Under his leadership, Serbia had regressed into a shabby, impoverished Balkan backwater. Inflation had reached astronomical levels.

The economic misery fed continued social unrest that seemed more dangerous to Milosevic now that he no longer had the support of nationalist intellectuals. He set about calming the unrest and settling scores with editors and intellectuals who had criticized him the previous year, when he had appeared to be on his way out. Once again, Radical leader Vojislav Seselj and his paramilitaries were assigned the task of intimidating critics. Seselj himself publicly humiliated Cosic. At a meeting of party leaders shortly before the president of Yugoslavia was removed from office, when Cosic's

Slobodan Milosevic, after assuming the presidency of the truncated Yugoslavia in 1997; his wife, Mira, is in the background. (Reuters/Peter Kujundzik/Archive Photos)

Slobodan Milosevic and wife, Mira Markovic, after voting in the November 3, 1996, federal and local elections. (Vreme Photo Archives)

Josip Broz Tito, the charismatic Communist guerrilla leader who seized power in Belgrade in 1944 and ruled Yugoslavia until his death in 1980. (Vreme Photo Archives)

Former Serbian president Ivan Stambolic, Milosevic's friend and patron, photographed in 1998. (Vreme Photo Archives)

Patriarch Pavle, head of the Serbian Orthodox Church. (ICN)

Dobrica Cosic, the nationalist writer who served as Yugoslavia's president from 1992 to 1993. (Reuters/Emil Vas/ Archive Photos)

Milan Panic, the Belgrade-born California millionaire who served as prime minister of Yugoslavia from 1992 to 1993, mounted the most coherent challenge to Milosevic's dictatorship, but he was outmaneuvered. (ICN)

Acting Secretary of State Lawrence Eagleburger, left, during a luncheon in Washington, D.C., with Yugoslav prime minister Milan Panic in September 1992. (ICN)

Bosnian Serb leader Radovan Karadzic, escorted by his bodyguards in July 1994 at Pale, in the suburbs of Sarajevo. (Reuters/Peter Kujundzik/Archive Photos)

One of the most notorious Serb paramilitary leaders, Arkan (Zeljko Raznjatovic), reviewing his troops at his military base in Erdut, Eastern Slavonia, in 1992. (Vreme Photo Archives)

President Franjo Tudjman of Croatia, at Dayton, Ohio, where a Bosnian peace agreement was initiated on November 21, 1995. (Reuters/Neal C. Lauron/Archive Photos)

President Alija Izetbegovic, the leader of the Muslims in Bosnia-Herzegovina, at the Dayton peace talks in 1995. (Reuters/Neal C. Lauron/Archive Photos)

Vuk Draskovic, the nationalist writer who emerged as the main opposition leader when he openly challenged Milosevic in 1991, shown here during a news conference in that year. (ICN)

Vojislav Seselj, leader of the ultra-nationalist Radical Party and Milosevic's political ally, brandishes a pistol inside the parliament building in early 1993. (Vreme Photo Archives)

Milosevic addresses a news conference during the NATO bombings of Yugoslavia in April 1999. (Reuters/Emil Vas/Archive Photos)

A side view shows the destroyed Belgrade residence of Slobodan Milosevic, April 1999. (Reuters/Pool/Archive Photos)

press secretary proffered his hand, Seselj shouted: "I know you, and I have no intentions of meeting you or shaking your hand. I've come here to arrest you!"

"You don't say," the press secretary replied. "You certainly must have a revolver on you."

"I don't need a revolver! I'll choke you with my bare hands!"

Cosic had managed to utter only one sentence before he was interrupted by Seselj's tirade of threats and ridicule.

"Call the security, have them take him away," shouted another presidential aide.

"Let me see what security is going to remove me from here," Seselj shouted, glaring at Cosic and his aides. "Who's this fool? What does this fool want?" The presidential consultations were turned into a street brawl; the representative of the ruling Socialist Party, Milomir Minic, joined Seselj in criticizing the president. Seselj later told journalists that he had "carefully prepared" his outburst in order to destroy Cosic's public standing.

Milosevic, by contrast, carefully observed public decorum.

But it was foreign affairs—specifically his mishandling of the Western allies—that needed his immediate attention. He decided to mend fences by making a dramatic U-turn in his foreign policy and endorsing a comprehensive peace plan for Bosnia that he had previously criticized as unacceptable.

The plan, developed by Cyrus Vance and David Owen, was perhaps the most rational proposal to keep Bosnia united. It divided Bosnia into ten cantons: three with a Serb majority, two with a Croat majority, three with a Muslim majority, and one mixed Muslim-Croat. Sarajevo, the capital, would be the tenth canton, patterned on the District of Columbia, with all three ethnic groups sharing power and accorded the same influence and privileges. The plan envisaged a central government that would control foreign policy and borders while leaving economic matters to the cantons. The Bosnian Serbs would have to relinquish roughly 20 percent of the territory under their control; this was a swath of territory that they had seized at the beginning of the war and had "cleansed" of its Muslim majority, most significantly in the Drina River valley.

Milan Panic had endorsed the plan even before it was publicly advanced. Milosevic and his Bosnian proxies rejected it; the distribution of territory in essence would deprive the Bosnian Serbs of their gains and leave their pockets of territory without secure communication links.

The Vance-Owen plan had been covertly backed by the Bush administration. "The United States will not officially embrace your proposal," Eagleburger told Vance and Owen in December 1992. "But neither will it attack it. If you can make it work, we would back you."

When the negotiators made the plan public in January 1993, only the Bosnian Croats were happy; the map gave them a block of territory adjoining Croatia proper. The Serbs rejected it, for the map denied them the unified territory they had created by the force of arms. The Muslims too were unhappy because they saw the map as confirming the ethnic partition; however, they came around to accepting it because, by their own admission, they felt sure the Serbs' rejection would kill the project anyway.

Milosevic also felt he had to distance himself from the Bosnian Serbs' string of wholly destructive violence and atrocities. The cold-blooded execution of Hakija Turajlic, a deputy prime minister of the Muslim-dominated Bosnian government, in January 1993 provoked worldwide condemnation. The Muslim official was being escorted by French UN troops from the Sarajevo airport into the city when their armored personnel carrier was halted at a Serbian roadblock; over the ineffectual protests of French officers, Serb soldiers opened the doors of the vehicle and shot dead the Muslim official.

In April 1993, Milosevic publicly embraced the Vance-Owen plan. In his discussions with Owen during the previous two months, Milosevic had received "clarification" about interim constitutional arrangements for Bosnia which in practice gave the Bosnian Serbs veto power; they could sign the agreement without having to implement it.

But in reality it was Milosevic's instinct for self-preservation that asserted itself.

From the moment Vance and Owen had been appointed mediators in the Balkan conflict, they had regarded Milosevic as the key player in the unfolding drama. The former U.S. secretary of state, Owen told journalists, had "always been clear that we must never ostracize him [Milosevic]; we never did. Cy's relationship with him is a very important one. There is trust there, at a level of man to man."

Owen too established a similar relationship, especially after he publicly criticized Eagleburger's Geneva outburst in which he had called Milosevic a war criminal. He was, he told journalists, puzzled by Eagleburger's action. "Why call someone a war criminal and then negotiate with him?"

Milosevic had also convinced himself that he would be betraying Serbia's holy cause by shirking from decisive action. Short-term concessions, in his view, would bring long-term benefits. He understood that the Vance-Owen plan was unworkable because it depended on cooperation between the ethnic groups. He believed it could be easily subverted once the international outcry against the Serbs died down, but that it would provide him with an exit strategy from the impasse in which he had found himself. This change in his views brought him into a conflict with the Bosnian Serbs—a rift he could have prevented had he brought Karadzic along, gently and diplomatically, by explaining his own failure to anticipate the adverse turn of events. But Milosevic was no diplomat, and saw no need to be one in dealings with his underlings.

In his meetings with foreign envoys, Milosevic now showed the kind of charm and tact that he found impossible to replicate in his dealings with his subordinates because, like so many powerful men of action, he believed he was entitled to automatic obedience. It was not his nature to share information and deep insights with his associates. These personal failings lay at the root of what was now to become a deep rift with Karadzic. Milosevic made no sustained effort to win Karadzic over because he could not be bothered to argue a case he knew to be right. Having organized and financed the Bosnian Serb war effort, he expected them to take his judgment without questioning.

Milosevic certainly never gave the Bosnian Serbs the full picture at his disposal. In his book *Balkan Odyssey,* David Owen provides a glimpse into Milosevic's need-to-know information system. At one point Owen briefed Milosevic and Cosic about the full extent of the Yugoslav Army's activities in the Bosnian war. Owen observed that Cosic, who as president was the army's commander in chief, "was quite shaken and had possibly not known the full extent of their involvement, but Milosevic batted not an eyelid for I told him facts of which I am sure he was fully informed, probably having authorized every aspect of the military relationship."

Karadzic and his associates were given basic details in the form of instruction. When they asked questions, Milosevic shouted at them. When they raised objections, he threatened them. It was sufficient for them to know that he had made a decision.

When Karadzic injected that it was important that a final accord include a clear statement that the Serbs in Bosnia were a "constituent unit" equal to the other two ethnic groups, Milosevic exploded: "Fuck you and your constituent unit!"

Witnesses have reported other insults, epithets, and threats an agitated Milosevic would hurl on the "Bosnian knuckleheads," as he referred to Karadzic and his aides, in emotional outbursts that did not address the substantive aspects of their objections.

"You can't hold Serbia hostage to your stupidities," Milosevic shouted once.

Karadzic and his people tolerated these outbursts of bad temper and publicly treated Milosevic with the respect due to the Serb national leader. But on key issues, no matter what his demands and threats, they would now not budge an inch.

The rift between them that spring was real and deepened over time, although Western diplomats never quite grasped this and thought it another diabolical Milosevic ploy designed to deceive them.

Milosevic seemed absolutely confident that he would have his way when on April 25 he told Owen: "Okay, I'll go along with the plan. You have convinced us. We'll invite the Bosnian Serbs to listen to your explanation."

Milosevic was in an expansive mood when late lunch was served following the session at the government villa in Dedinje. Stretching his arms over his head, he leaned back in his chair and said, "I can live with this decision."

That same afternoon, Karadzic and other key Bosnian Serbs were summoned to the villa to hear details of the plan from Owen himself. Owen felt he had achieved a breakthrough, which, he recalled, "left us all a little light-headed and, as it turned out, over-confident." The Bosnian Serb assembly, meeting that evening in the border town of Bijeljina, about an hour's drive from Belgrade, was to put the final seal of approval of the Vance-Owen plan.

Owen delayed his departure from Belgrade awaiting the final go-ahead. Milosevic, Owen added, "showed no sign of being in any doubt" about the outcome.

In the early evening of April 25, Milosevic was alerted that things in Bijeljina were now moving according to his plan, and that some Bosnian Serb deputies were voicing sharp criticism of the Vance-Owen plan.

He promptly summoned Cosic and Momir Bulatovic, his proconsul in Montenegro, to the same government villa for consultations, proposing a stern letter to the assembly. A two-thousand-word letter was drafted over the next two hours; its high-handed tone reflected Milosevic's arrogance, his boundless self-confidence, and was composed (according to Cosic) without much deliberation. It criticized Bosnian deputies for their "irresponsible statements" and said:

> Now is not the right time for us to compete in patriotism. It is the right time for a courageous, considered and far-reaching decision. You have no right to expose ten million citizens of Yugoslavia to danger and international sanctions merely because of the remaining open issues which are of far less importance than the results achieved so far. We simply wish to tell you that you must be measured in your demands.

The letter then detailed guarantees and clarifications which meant that "the danger of the Serb people being separated and divided has been eliminated."

> In other words, we do not expect that the procedure envisaged by the plan would be used to pass decisions highly detrimental to Serb interests, not merely because this would be illegal and unfair but also because . . . all decisions would be passed by consensus of the Serb side and because without the agreement of the Serb side Bosnia-Herzegovina would not be able to function at all. We feel entitled to the same rights as you to pass decisions of significance for the Serb nation and insist that you heed our categorical stand and accept the plan. This is an issue of war or peace and we are opting for peace, an honorable peace with guarantees of your equality and freedom. The other option is an unnecessary war which . . . will bring nothing but adversity, suffering and violence to you and others.

Milosevic raised his foreign minister, Vladislav Jovanovic, out of bed shortly before midnight and immediately dispatched him by helicopter to Bijeljina to read Milosevic's letter to the Bosnian Serb Assembly.

It was another miscalculation which the Bosnian Serbs interpreted as a slight. Jovanovic received a hostile reception. "Who is this Jovanovic?" the hawkish Bosnian Serb vice president Biljana Plavsic demanded, setting the tone. "Who is this Milosevic, this Bulatovic, this Cosic? Did this nation elect them? No, it didn't."

The assembly rejected Milosevic's argument in the predawn hours. The deputies, Karadzic announced, could not return to their constituencies if they accepted the Vance-Owen plan as presented to them. "We hope that the entire Serb nation will mobilize all its forces to survive," Karadzic added.

That night, Western diplomats realized that the Serbs were divided and that Karadzic was no longer obeying unconditionally his master's voice. From that point on, the objective of Western policy was to keep the Serbs divided, isolating Karadzic and his associates and forcing their submission.

When asked to accept the Vance-Owen plan, Karadzic saw no reason for Milosevic's cautious (craven, it seemed to Karadzic) scaling down of the Serb national agenda. Having once absolutely rejected the legitimacy of the Muslims' interest in Bosnia, Karadzic could not understand, as Milosevic reluctantly understood, that their original plans could not be carried to fruition in the face of implacable opposition from the only superpower in the world.

At that point, Milosevic and Owen enlisted the support of the Greek prime minister, Constantine Mitsotakis, perhaps the only foreign leader who had influence on Karadzic and his people. Greek public opinion was strongly supportive of the Bosnian Serbs, providing various forms of aid, including summer holidays for Bosnian Serb children. Mitsotakis offered to host a summit conference in Athens on May 1–2, 1993. Karadzic agreed to attend.

With the help of Mitsotakis, Milosevic laid a trap for Karadzic. In an all-night session, the Bosnian Serb leader was subjected to threats, cajoling, browbeating, and other types of pressure from his counterpart in Belgrade. (Karadzic said later that even the Greek waiters who were serving him cup after cup of thick Turkish coffee were trying to persuade him to sign.) Realizing that he would not be allowed to leave Athens until he had agreed to sign the Vance-Owen plan, Karadzic finally said yes, provided that his signature would be valid only if his assembly ratified the plan. At that very moment, by prearranged signal, Mitsotakis appeared with a photographer, proffering his pen to Karadzic to sign. Milosevic handed him a copy of the Vance-Owen document he had kept for the occasion.

Owen was triumphant, announcing a "bright sunny day in the Balkans. Peace in Yugoslavia is within our grasp."

By this time, Owen and the other Western players had developed a vested interest in Milosevic as part of the solution to the Bosnian war. After contemptuously dismissing the importance of the Bosnian Serbs' opposition, Owen told journalists: "Believe me, I have been in politics a long time, I know that Milosevic is on board and that is what counts."

It was, in fact, merely another of many diplomatic "breakthroughs" to pop up on the front pages of the world press over the years that were not breakthroughs at all. Cyrus Vance chose this moment to resign his post as UN Special Envoy to the former Yugoslavia; he was replaced by the former Norwegian foreign minister, Thorvald Stoltenberg.

From Athens, Milosevic, Mitsotakis, and others traveled to the Heavenly Valley Hotel at the Olympic ski complex outside Sarajevo where the Bosnian Serb Assembly was due to meet. Milosevic was confident that their presence would help sway the vote. But there was a mood of defiance in Bosnia—a mood summed up in a popular song that echoed in villages through which the motorcade of black limousines was passing:

*Goodbye, Slobo the pretty one,*
*we are no longer blind.*

On the eve of the session, the best-known Bosnian Serb journalist, Risto Djogo, famed for his sense of humor, foreshadowed the outcome. He appeared on the Bosnian Serb evening TV news, staring at a blank piece of paper. Then he signed it, took a pistol, and committed a mock suicide on the scene. Just to make sure his pantomime was understood by all, Djogo said: "The Serbs of Bosnia are not about to commit suicide."

As the motorcade approached the Heavenly Valley Hotel, two U.S. F-16 jets swooped low over the Jahorina Mountain on a reconnaissance mission. They were greeted by large white slogans in English—FUCK YOU F-16—which the Serbs had painted on the rooftops.

Immediately upon arrival, Milosevic knew he was in trouble. Shaking hands with the Bosnian leaders in a reception line, he proffered his hand to Vice President Plavsic, but she refused to accept it.

Throughout the night, the word "suicide" was repeatedly invoked before the motley collection of deputies—men in full battle-dress, bearded Orthodox priests with flowing beards, and professional politicians in sharkskin suits—by the proponents of the plan, as well as by those who insisted on its rejection. Even though he had signed the plan in Athens, Karadzic offered only a halfhearted recommendation.

A potent infusion of Kosovo mythology marked most of the speeches. The memory of Milos Obilic, the bravest fighter of the Serb epics, hung in the air. One delegate reminded the assembly that Milos Obilic had known that the Serbs would be defeated by the more numerous Turkish Army. He told his comrades on the eve of the 1389 battle that "If all of us were turned into salt that wouldn't be enough to season a Turkish dinner." Yet he had led the troops into battle and personally killed the Turkish Sultan at the Field of Blackbirds. Obilic certainly would have had nothing but contempt for Milosevic's concern about economic sanctions, the assembly was told.

A more enlightened deputy, the Shakespearean scholar Nikola Koljevic, saw the Milos Obilic story differently, arguing that "we should not risk a desperate battle with the greatest superpower on earth."

Milosevic addressed the assembly several times, employing all manner of arguments to persuade them to endorse the plan and openly hinting that he would punish them if they failed to do so. Seated next to Karadzic, he at one point said that the Bosnian Serbs must not gamble everything like "a drunken poker player," only to lose it all; he was plainly attacking Karadzic, whose fondness for Belgrade casinos was widely known. "One can sacrifice for one's nation everything except the nation itself," Milosevic said. "If you do not accept the Vance-Owen plan, you are going to sacrifice your people."

Mitsotakis and Cosic also urged the assembly to approve the plan. Multi-ethnic Bosnia had been destroyed, Cosic told them. The Muslims would never have a state. "In places where a Serb house and Serb land exist and where the Serbian language is spoken, there will be a Serb state," he said. Cosic was in effect saying that they should accept the Vance-Owen plan as a tactical gesture.

The Bosnian Serb military commander, General Ratko Mladic, offered a strictly military analysis of the situation, and his maps ultimately proved decisive. Mladic was a talented, efficient, and ruthless soldier, much loved by his troops, whom he had personally led into a number of most dangerous battles. Mladic's father had been one of Tito's Partisans and had died in a battle with Ustashe and German forces when Mladic was only two years old. He was a lifelong Communist and had graduated at the top of his class from the Yugoslav military academy. His phobia against Germany and Ustashe Croats led him to switch allegiance to the Serb nationalist cause. He was not a politician, and could not see the larger picture, but he inspired loyalty and returned it to his troops.

At the time of the Croatian war in 1991, Mladic was the commanding officer of the Yugoslav Army garrison in Krajina and had helped organize, train, and arm the rebel Krajina Army of about forty thousand troops. Milosevic had personally selected him in early May 1992 as commander of the new Bosnian Serb Army and had promoted him to the rank of general. He was indeed a compelling presence, but in a negative sort of way. As the war dragged on, Mladic became intoxicated with his success and press attention; he was given to making martial noises of the most menacing kind, such as his absurd threats that Vienna and Trieste might become targets of his missiles and planes, which turned him into a perfect villain straight out of central casting.

Mladic's first map showed the existing front lines. His second map, which he superimposed on the first, showed the cantons proposed by the Vance-Owen plan. The Bosnian Serbs were asked to give up their gains while at the same time leaving some Serb communities isolated. But what may have had the most impact on the delegates was Mladic's bragging. He and his men, he said, could repel any Western intervention.

In the final hour of the sixteen-hour session, the assembly booed a humiliated Milosevic, who sat glowering silently, unable to grasp what was happening. One delegate bluntly told him: "You are no longer what you used to be!" By a vote of 51–2 (with 12 abstentions), the assembly refused to ratify the Vance-Owen plan.

It was Milosevic's first public defeat as Serbia's leader. Plavsic berated him before the assembly journalists: "He was not normal. This could be seen on his face and on his hands. . . . He did not know how to behave himself in parliament because he never attended parliamentary sessions."

A humiliated Milosevic and an exhausted Mitsotakis left at 5:00 A.M. on May 6 for the long ride to Belgrade. Milosevic also phoned David Owen in London. He was "angry, fed up and tired," Owen recalled. He said that "Mladic had intervened in the small hours against acceptance of the plan to considerable effect." Mladic had done so even though the previous day, during a meeting with senior Yugoslav generals, he had been warned that supplies and other help would be halted if the plan was rejected. Milosevic was not so much angry at Mladic as at Karadzic and other Bosnian Serb politicians.

Milosevic told Owen he was sure that his "technology of power"—a term he used jokingly or semi-jokingly to describe an array of pressures he could bring to bear on the Bosnian Serbs—would soon bring them to the negotiating table. "Those who have crossed me have not long survived," Milosevic said.

That same day, he announced that Serbia was cutting off all aid to the Bosnian Serbs, the only exceptions being food and medicine. The first time Plavsic attempted to cross the border into Serbia to visit her mother, who lived in Belgrade, she was refused entry. Some months later, Risto Djogo was murdered at a motel near the border town of Zvornik where he had attended a concert by the folk singer Ceca, Arkan's paramour and future wife. It was rumored that the journalist was gunned down by Arkan's men acting on orders from the Serbian security service.

To be sure, Milosevic continued to have influence on the Bosnian Serbs, but this influence was nowhere as significant as Western diplomats believed. True, Mladic and his officers were on Belgrade's payroll; the Yugoslav Army was providing Mladic's army with spare parts and maintenance service. Milosevic, for his part, could not reveal the extent of his frustrations with the Bosnian

Serbs because it was his perceived ability to influence Bosnia's events that had made him a major player in the Balkans.

Milosevic set about transforming his image from warmonger to peacemaker, a process that was slow and methodical. In addition to accepting the Vance-Owen plan, he moved to reinforce his image as peacemaker by entering into a dialogue with Croatian president Franjo Tudjman in April 1993, with an eye toward restarting talks between the rebel Serbs in Croatia and the Croatian government. The rebels had consolidated their control over the Krajina, as well as over large parts of eastern Slavonia, the flat, fertile land that stretches along the Danube River valley. The presence of UN peacekeepers along the front lines had stabilized the situation, but Tudjman wanted to recover the territories by force, if necessary, and was forging a strong army with American help. Milosevic offered a deal that would restore Croatian sovereignty in the rebel region in exchange for political autonomy for the rebels. He and Tudjman also laid grounds for an exchange of diplomatic offices in their respective capitals.

But just when the fighting on all fronts appeared to be winding down, the Clinton administration pulled the rug from under the Vance-Owen plan. At a May 23 meeting in Washington, D.C., the United States, Russia, France, Britain, and Spain issued a Washington Declaration which called for the creation of six safe areas around the besieged Muslim enclaves in Bosnia—and an effective acceptance of the Bosnian Serb territorial gains.

Owen was furious. "I was being deliberately kept in the dark" about this maneuver, he recalled. "I was hearing the death knell of the VOPP [Vance-Owen peace plan] wrapped up in diplomatic language."

Karadzic and his allies were jubilant, while Izetbegovic derisively rejected the initiative, saying it would allow the Serbs to keep the territory wrested by force and turn the "safe areas" into reservations.

Milosevic was in one of his periodic moods of deep depression and indecision. The Vance-Owen plan, in which he had invested so much of his prestige and energy, had been ditched. He was suddenly vulnerable to charges by Karadzic and Radical Party leader Vojislav Seselj that he was caving in to the Americans and abandoning the Serbs of Bosnia and Krajina.

On May 25, Milosevic instructed his proxies in Krajina to abandon their negotiations with the Croatian government. Milosevic's own police and security services had a high percentage of Serbs from Kosovo, Bosnia, and Krajina. Perhaps the most telling sign was the replacement of a special unit in charge of his personal security (composed exclusively of Krajina Serbs) with a unit staffed with officers from Serbia proper.

By the end of May, then, Milosevic had established himself in the eyes of the international community as a peacemaker, a man capable of making concessions, who had almost brought the Vance-Owen plan to life.

He used this newfound international respect to help solidify his power base at home. Stung by Milan Panic and Dobrica Cosic, Milosevic would never again endorse anyone with a mind of his own to hold a senior position in his regime.

On May 31, Milosevic flew to Lake Ohrid, in the newly independent Macedonia, for secret talks with the Macedonian leaders. He and Mitsotakis had considered dismembering Macedonia the previous year, dividing it between Greece and Serbia, but Mitsotakis had felt constrained by Greece's membership in NATO and the European Union. The Clinton administration, in order to make sure that the two conspirators would not proceed with their plan, deployed seven hundred U.S. troops in Macedonia in early 1993 as the bulk of a UN observation force; these were the first U.S. troops to be deployed on the territory of the former Yugoslavia.

For Milosevic, Macedonia was a vital route for secret shipments of oil and other goods in violation of the UN sanctions. Moreover, he believed that the Macedonians would eventually join his Yugoslav federation and he wanted to test the mood of the Macedonian leaders. They were polite but firm in their intention to create their own state, despite serious internal problems caused by ethnic Albanians, who accounted for almost one-third of Macedonia's 2 million population and who were agitating for independence. Precisely what the two sides said to one another is not known, but a Macedonian account said the talks ended with Milosevic's warning: "Mark my words, we'll meet again over the Albanians."

On June 1, 1993, the day after Cosic had been ousted from the presidency of Yugoslavia, Milosevic started settling scores with another potential rival, the leading opposition politician Vuk Draskovic. Milosevic's tactics were so brutal and ruthless that in the eyes of his countrymen he became not just Serbia's despot but also its chief gendarme. But this was of marginal concern to Western politicians, who desperately sought a way to end the Bosnian war and saw Milosevic as a key ally in the process.

June 1 was also marked by a new public protest, one touched off by an incident in the Serbian parliament. One of the opposition deputies was knocked unconscious by a political ally of Milosevic's, Radical deputy Branislav Vakic, a former boxer with links to the underworld. (As a teenager, Vakic once hijacked a bus on the Nis-Leskovac route and collected money from passengers.) Shortly before attacking the deputy, Vakic had told him in the corridor: "I've cut the throats of many people, so it's not going to be a problem to cut yours too."

The severely injured opposition deputy was taken out on a stretcher and the event was shown on television. Soon the parliament building was besieged by opposition supporters who pelted it with stones, breaking many windows. The arrival of Vuk Draskovic and his wife, Danica, emboldened the crowd, which attempted to break into the building.

Draskovic, a Rasputin-like figure with a long black beard and piercing eyes, has a charismatic hold on many Serbs. A former journalist and novelist, he had burst onto the scene as a rabid nationalist in 1990, when he founded the Serbian Renewal Movement, which called for a Greater Serbia and accused Milosevic of failing to deliver the nationalist dream on which he had ridden to power. Draskovic even formed paramilitary units to fight in Croatia, but he quickly turned against the war, trimmed his beard, toned down his emotional, flowery rhetoric, and began calling for a more constructive sort of nationalism. His power to bring crowds to the streets frightened Milosevic, who saw Draskovic as his most dangerous potential opponent. In private, Milosevic was given to bouts of raging invective against Draskovic and at least on one occasion, while receiving a senior foreign diplomat, he spent a good deal of time raving about "that psychopath Draskovic who should be locked up."

This time, Draskovic made no particularly inflammatory pronouncements. Yet, as is usual in these situations, scuffles broke out as the protest gained strength in numbers. Suddenly a policeman was reported seriously wounded; he died shortly afterward in the hospital. The demonstrators insisted that the policeman was shot by a regime agent to provoke retaliation; the regime accused the protesters of insurgency.

Draskovic and his wife had left the demonstrations when two thousand riot police arrived at the scene, pummeling protesters. Police also arrived at his party headquarters after midnight. Draskovic was beaten unconscious in the elevator. He was revived and then savagely beaten again as he ran a gauntlet from the building into a police van; policemen kicked the opposition leader and his wife as they lay on the street, yelling at Madame Draskovic—"We have been waiting for you, you whore!"—so loudly the whole neighborhood could hear.

For Milosevic, the incident took on aspects of a personal inquisition that continued for thirty-eight days. Whereas in the past he would distance himself from such incidents, leaving them ostensibly to the relevant authorities and intervening only to show clemency, Milosevic personally directed the violence and humiliation administered to the man he despised and feared. By the time it was over, he had established his ruthlessness in the minds of his subjects. If the leader of the legal political opposition could be so badly mistreated, what was an ordinary citizen to expect?

Draskovic later recalled those moments in which "they kept pulling me by my hair so that my body would accelerate and my head would hit the wall with greater force." He thought that that was the end, but his tormentors revived him with buckets of water and slaps on his face, asking him, "Leader, was this hard enough?"

"I said no, and then they repeated the whole thing. When I recovered consciousness, the question was popped, 'Was this hard enough?' and I said with some impudence, 'You are not strong enough to do it properly so that I'd feel pain.' I don't remember anything after that."

Because of serious head injuries, he was taken to the Neurological Clinic for treatment, then moved back to prison.

To Milosevic, the brutal treatment of Draskovic was intended to be an object lesson for anyone who contemplated open resistance to his rule. It differed from the innumerable brutalities, covert assassinations, and other criminal acts of the past that remained shrouded in mystery. This time everything was in the open and the opposition was the target to be destroyed. Having established himself as a peacemaker, Milosevic could afford to ignore appeals from the leaders of France, Britain, the United States, and Greece, as well as scores of prominent international figures.

The joker in the pack was Draskovic himself. He was forty-seven years old. After more than three weeks in jail, he began a hunger strike. He had decided to die, he later recalled. He stopped drinking water and set a date for himself.

Draskovic's only act of contrition was an appeal to Milosevic's wife, Mira Markovic, asking that his wife, Danica, be released from jail: "For me, she is my wife and my child, and my entire family. While she remains in jail, my entire family is in jail. Help her, Madame Markovic, and you'll be helping me too. I would be eternally grateful to you until the end of my life." Danica was indeed released.

Draskovic's hunger strike changed the balance of power in a test of wills between the dictator and his prisoner. Foreign pressures escalated. Danielle Mitterrand, wife of the French president, flew to Belgrade to plead the case and to visit Draskovic in jail. David Owen also felt compelled to visit the prisoner, and then similarly raised his case with Milosevic.

The patriarch of the Orthodox Church three times went to prison to urge Draskovic to abandon his hunger strike. This was, the patriarch said, "an anti-Christian act."

Draskovic, who had become a devout Christian even though in his youth he had been a Communist Party member, replied that he was not committing suicide "since the rope is not in my hands."

The patriarch could not accept this explanation.

On the tenth day of the strike, public opinion in Belgrade suddenly turned ugly. Forty-two people, including twenty opposition members of parliament, began a hunger strike in Belgrade's central square. The opposition called for mass protests. The whole affair suddenly appeared to threaten Milosevic's hold on power. Draskovic's imminent death in prison posed a clear and present danger, for it could touch off a popular revolt. On that same day, Milosevic issued a presidential pardon.

Milosevic's image was, in short, awful. Inside Serbia itself, the year 1994 was marked by renewed discontent and lack of direction. With the regime's political program in shambles, the drift that began with the crackdown on the opposition in the summer of 1993 showed no signs of abating. It was accelerated by the bad news from Bosnia, where the Serb siege of Sarajevo provided an endless stream of adverse publicity for the entire Serb nation. Nightly newscasts in America and around the world carried footage of the plight of people trapped in Sarajevo and pounded by mortars and sniper fire. The Serbs were seen as heartless monsters.

It was at this point that Mira Markovic emerged once again from the shadows. From the end of 1993, her role became more public and assertive. Like other power couples before them—Louis XVI and Marie Antoinette, Nicholas and Alexandra, Juan and Eva Perón, Ferdinand and Imelda Marcos, Nicolae and Elena Ceausescu—Slobo and Mira became joint rulers in the public mind.

The woman who had long told friends that she was the driving force behind her less able husband gradually became a public and political figure.

"She has always claimed she is more competent than he is," a former Milosevic aide said. "She believes, and says quite openly, that she made her husband what he is." In the male world of Balkan politics, though, she had pushed him forward, not herself. She had helped orchestrate the coup against Ivan Stambolic, who himself described it as "a conjugal undertaking," and then she surrounded Milosevic with her own friends, who were as loyal to her as to him.

From the time they met as teenagers, those who knew them described the two as a self-contained unit. She was the more forceful partner, dictating their tastes in everything from movies (avoiding war movies and preferring happy endings) to music (they are said to like 1960s America pop). Though she once said she would have preferred to be a writer, with Slobodan an architect, their main, joint preoccupation was reaching and remaining in power.

Milosevic had tried to bring his wife into the inner leadership of the party in the 1980s, but was rebuffed by Stambolic. In hindsight, Stambolic reflected that the start of the rift between them dated to his refusal of Milosevic's request.

In the dynamics of their relationship, she filled his emotional life completely. The only photograph in his office is of her. She, by contrast, has pictures of Lenin and Tito alongside photographs of her husband and children. Though that would seem to reflect a committed ideologue, it is not hard to detect another, personal dimension. In her own mind, Mira is continuing the romanticized ideals of her executed Partisan mother. It is a way for her to rehabilitate her mother and at the same time overcome her father's rejection.

In the process, she ignores reality as she insists that communism is the way of the future even though the world may not be quite ready for it. In interviews she repeatedly returns to her central theme, predicting communism's rebirth. Her articles have such titles as "Socialism Has Raised the Oppressed from Their Knees" and "The Left Will Rise, You'll See."

Milosevic is ferociously protective of his wife and unforgiving of those who insult her. This protectiveness led to an unprecedented incident in parliament on June 22, 1994, when an opposition deputy attacked Mira and would not be stopped; a frightened Speaker urgently summoned police. Soon some fifty policemen burst in and forcibly removed the critic from the chamber.

Emotionally bruised and self-absorbed, the Milosevics—he taking her lead—are lax parents who romanticize and indulge their children. "I always knew I would give birth to Marija and that she would be intrepid and beautiful," Mira said of her daughter, born in 1965. "Ever since she was born she has been the object of my great love."

She wanted both Marija and Marko—born eleven years later—to "become attached to the ideals of freedom and justice for which my mother died and for which I have lived. In my opinion, a family passes on a certain system of values—aesthetic, ethical, political. That is how my family is."

But that was hardly the case. Marko did not attend classes during his last high school years; it was his decision, Marko explained, because it was impossible "to have a good time and be a regular student at the same time." After graduating in 1992, he became a racing car enthusiast and was involved in numerous accidents. "I had about twenty car accidents," he explained later. "Dad was angry over the first fifteen busted cars, but after that number he no longer paid attention."

He and Marija were rumored to have become quite rich using daddy's connections. Marko owns Madona, which he describes as the largest discotheque in the Balkans, a radio station, and a theme park in Pozarevac. The theme park named "Bambipark" was opened shortly after the end of the Kosovo war; Marko told reporters he had not let NATO bombardments interfere with the preparation for his latest business venture, which, he explained, symbolized "the proof of care for the young generations." During the war, the entrepreneur playboy was pictured walking around Pozarevac in fatigues and carrying a gun, but he was not thought to be in any military unit.

Marija was given a Belgrade pop radio station, Koshava, to run and gained a reputation for constantly changing boyfriends. She married and moved to Japan in the 1980s but soon returned. She was also accredited as a foreign correspondent for an English-language weekly, *Balkan News International & East European Report,* published in Athens.

Mira never went to public receptions and was rarely seen in public with her husband during his first years in power. She dressed conservatively, though she used to wear a plastic flower in her hair because she had seen a photo of her mother wearing one. (She later said she stopped because it attracted too much attention.)

Those who know her say she often bristles with resentment, which she disguises—though she always eventually takes revenge when someone crosses her. She always resented her stepmother, for example, feeling she was the reason behind her father's rejection of her. "If I had been in her place, I would have behaved differently," she wrote. After his death in 1992, she fought a long and nasty legal battle with her stepmother and half sisters over the rather meager inheritance. "I would not wish such a brother-in-law and sister-in-law on my worst enemies," her brother-in-law, the writer Momcilo Selic, said of Slobo and Mira.

It was always Mira—not her husband—who most jealously guarded access to the Milosevic home. They would frequently change their phone number, giving it out only to their friends. The possession of the right phone number for the Milosevics was the litmus test for high officials: it determined who was in the magic circle and who was out of favor. She trusted nobody and believed the worst of anyone who thought to influence her husband. She would make and break ministers, chief editors, generals on his behalf. When the directors of the newspaper *Politika* and Radio Television Serbia were suddenly fired and replaced by her friends, the deputy chairman of the ruling Socialist Party, Borisav Jovic, was asked for comment. "What's there to comment on?" Jovic said, noting that nobody in the party leadership had discussed the changes. "This is a matter of relations within a single family."

As the deepening Bosnia crisis in 1993 pushed Milosevic into a new bout of depression and procrastination, Mira apparently felt that only she could save him. She began by writing a regular column in the fashionable biweekly magazine *Duga*. Her first aim was to humanize her husband: she frequently complained that his people did not know him well enough.

Mira's column depicted a different Milosevic from the man who had used Serb nationalism to grab power. He was, she said, a loving, family man "who has never been a nationalist." She defended his Communist-style economic policy and described politicians who advocated genuine privatization of the economy as "lunatics who instead of being in an asylum are sitting in their so-called political parties and who, instead of taking medicine, are making pronouncements."

The more Mira wrote, the more her sense of her own power and importance seemed to grow. She began commenting on Serbia's political life and personalities, weaving in bizarre details about her own habits or observations, fulfilling her youthful ambition to be a writer. She wrote, for example, that she had always worn her hair in the same style, but would never let her husband see her brushing it. Or she would wax lyrical about nature: "I have never had the opportunity to watch birds and clouds as I had this summer"; "the winter is so beautiful, with white trees, bluish mist and the pale light of distant lonely stars."

Since Milosevic himself rarely made pronouncements and never talked to journalists, the column was read avidly for signs of what he might be thinking or do next.

It was perhaps natural that wags in the capital took to calling her column "The Horoscope," particularly since Mira admitted that she loved astrology. "I say often," she wrote, "with a mixture of sadness and irony, that things that some governments or some ministries cannot resolve, may be resolved by the stars."

Unlike most columnists—or astrologers—she had the power to make her predictions come true. After a trip to China, on which she was accompanied by Belgrade University professor Slobodan Unkovic, Mira casually remarked before a group of journalists that "Unkovic would make a terrific ambassador to Beijing." He was soon appointed. An attack on Serbian officials in her column usually foreshadowed their dismissal. At other times, she simply marked out who were enemies of the ruling couple or defined their relationship to Serb politicians outside Serb proper.

In one column, she lashed out at the prime minister of neighboring Montenegro, Milo Djukanovic, who had openly criticized her husband. Djukanovic, she asserted, was a black marketeer and should be jailed. But the attack only helped sharpen conflicts within Montenegro itself. Ever since Montenegro had joined Yugoslavia in 1918, its policies were marked by a division between the Greens, who believe that Montenegro would be better off as an independent state, and the Whites, who favor union with Serbia. A beleaguered Djukanovic now identified himself with the Greens, whose numbers have been increasing as a result of Milosevic's war policy and appalling economic conditions.

Mira's writings also prepared the ground for a hardening attitude toward the Bosnian Serbs, in particular toward Karadzic, who was emerging as a rival for her husband's mantle as leader of all the Serbs.

By 1994, Karadzic's standing was on the rise among the monarchists and nationalists within Serbia proper and within the Orthodox Church hierarchy; Vojislav Seselj had become his passionate advocate in Belgrade. Unlike Milosevic, who has only slightly changed the old Communist system, Karadzic had begun openly to advocate a monarchist revival and the supreme role of the church in national life. He stood for everything Milosevic no longer did. "God is going to help us," he kept saying, "because God is a Serb."

In popular songs, Karadzic was now compared to Karadjordje, the leader of the 1804 Serbian insurrection against the Turks, as he marched off to negotiations in Switzerland.

*Radovan, you man of iron and*
*first leader after Karadjordje,*
*protect our freedom and faith*
*on the shores of Lake Geneva.*

Milosevic and his wife were particularly concerned about the church's support for Karadzic. In a meeting with Patriarch Pavle,

Milosevic sounded like a believer: "So help me God, Your Beatitude, I am talking to you sincerely, like a son to his father." He proceeded to point out that a number of senior bishops had made warlike statements that seemed at odds with Christian thinking, but that suggested strong backing for Karadzic and his struggle. The patriarch remained noncommittal.

Mira attacked Karadzic as a gambler, a war profiteer, and an egotist. She dismissed Karadzic's arguments about the plight of the Serbs in Bosnia prior to the Bosnian war by saying that "of all the innumerable absurdities and untruths that have been uttered, this statement truly takes the cake." She assailed Karadzic's vice president, Biljana Plavsic, as a "psychopath," and compared her to the infamous Nazi doctor, Joseph Mengele.

On August 4, 1994, urged on by his wife, Milosevic declared an open war against the Bosnian Serb leadership, charging that their refusal to accept various peace proposals was a "crime against the Serb nation" and a "betrayal of Serb national interests." The Yugoslav government therefore had decided to "break off all political and economic relations" with the Bosnian Serb state and to "prohibit the presence of members of the Bosnian Serb leadership" on Yugoslav soil.

Few people expected such a drastic turn of events. A year earlier—after he had been humiliated by the Bosnian Serb Assembly—Milosevic had angrily announced that he was terminating all aid to Karadzic's government; but that was an impetuous action that he abandoned a few weeks later. Not so this time. Telephone contacts were cut off. The border with Bosnia was closed. The Serbian media unleashed a campaign against Bosnian Serb "war profiteers and criminals." Zoran Lilic, a political yes-man installed by Milosevic to replace Cosic as president of Yugoslavia, described Karadzic as an "ordinary liar" who was responsible for ethnic cleansing of Bosnia and a variety of other crimes that were designed to get Serbia proper into war with the West. The Bosnian Serb leaders were blamed as the warmongers who had started the internecine war in Yugoslavia.

Milosevic, who had complained about "genocidal sanctions" imposed against his country by the United Nations, imposed far more rigorous sanctions against the Bosnian Serbs. In his struggle for survival, Milosevic had finally done something that secured him American support.

However, the Orthodox Church sided with Karadzic. On August 10, it issued a pronouncement obliquely denouncing Milosevic for succumbing to "powerful foreign powers." The church, it said, "will remain with the people." It used the image from the great Serb poet Njegos's "terrible warning" against the "cursed" leaders who are prepared to betray the Serb nation.

Mira then stepped out as a political figure in her own right, creating a powerful force out of her own political party. In her writings, she perhaps unconsciously gave the reason: "If one single woman is capable of destroying the best possible man and is capable . . . of mobilizing those better than herself to make a success of herself—even more of a success than he is—then such a woman deserves to enter the new century as its ruler." Elsewhere she wrote that it was time for the end of male domination and that men should "pass the baton" to women.

Her Yugoslav United Left (YUL) Party united twenty-three small leftist parties. It had been little more than a nostalgic organization of old Communists when it was founded in 1990. Now, it became a real force. YUL's core was a party of unreconstructed Communists—former generals, intelligence officers, bureaucrats. Like Communist parties in different times, it was a reflection of its leader's personality.

The flavor and stamp of Mira's character came through when she addressed its congress on July 24, 1994. Noting that *Yul* also means "July" in Serbo-Croatian, she talked of the month as "symbolizing life, the sun and energy," with "longest days and shortest nights" and the time of the year when "the stars are closest to man." This was said by way of expressing optimism in the party's political future. YUL gradually began sharing power with Milosevic's Socialists on his orders. It gave Milosevic an ideological way out, a return to Titoist communism and multi-ethnicity which Mira said that she—and he—had never abandoned.

YUL people began taking charge of the economy. It was in a mess. In the course of 1993, the economic situation had reached catastrophic proportions. Inflation began to edge over 200 percent per month in February; by July, it was over 400 percent; in August, it reached 1,880 percent. Specialists calculated that at an annualized rate, this was 363 quadrillion percent. Milosevic responded by flooding the country with notes in dinar denominations of 1 million; 5 million; 10 million; 100 million; 500 million; 1 billion; 10 billion. The November rate went over 20,000 percent, escalating the process to the monthly rate of 300 million percent at the end of the year—the annual rate at this point being beyond calculation. The largest bank note issued in December had a face value of 50 billion. The dinar was no longer the currency of the country; it was replaced by the Deutschemark. The average monthly salary plunged below $10. The country's economy stopped functioning. Corruption and economic crime flourished.

In January 1994, Milosevic devalued the dinar by wiping all zeroes from the one-billion-dinar note and announced its convertibility. One new dinar was worth one Deutschemark. Milosevic also produced a new governor of the Central Bank, an economist and retired World Bank official, Dragoslav Avramovic, who announced that he would never permit uncontrolled printing of money.

The results were little short of amazing. The inflation was kept in check; in 1994, for the first time since the outbreak of the Yugoslav wars, the Serbian economy grew by 6.5 percent; in 1995, the growth was 6 percent, but Avramovic had to devalue the dinar slightly and the annual inflation rate was a relatively modest 119 percent.

By 1995, YUL had developed into the corporate wing of Milosevic's Socialist Party. It had also become a haven for a new class of rich businessmen who needed political protection. One of the YUL vice presidents, Nenad Djordjevic, had become a multimillionaire during Serbia's economic chaos of the 1990s (he publicly estimated his net worth at about $80 million). When workers from one of Djordjevic's factories approached Mira to complain about low wages, she replied: "He is my party comrade, but I do not know what he is doing outside the party."

But though she claimed never to have given up on communism—it was men, not the system that had failed, she said—her ideas were muddled.

Indeed, Mira's former professor Mihajlo Markovic (no relation to her), who was the chief ideologue of the ruling Socialist Party, publicly criticized people in her party "who pose as leftists but are just war profiteers and criminals." He reprimanded Mira for deviation. While denouncing capitalism, he said, Mira has been welcoming large financial contributions from the newly rich businessmen who were corrupt and who manipulated the closed Yugoslav market.

She was unfazed. "Friedrich Engels was an industrialist," she replied, referring to Karl Marx's co-author, "but he was also a communist."

Mira's articles were collected and published in a book, *Night and Day,* that was selected as the 1994 book of the year at the annual Belgrade Book Fair by a jury that described it as a "first class literary and philosophical text that enriches the Serbian literature." Critical acclaim was immediate. A review in *Politika* claimed that Mira's were "the most frequently quoted books in the world" and "the favorite reading matter of American President Bill Clinton."

There were dissenting voices in the literary establishment, but they were almost unnoticed. One literary critic called Mira's work a "mixture of hallucination and marketplace philosophizing of a vain woman, a mixture of sickness and kitsch." Professor Svetlana Slapsak, an author herself, wrote a review saying that "it is difficult to imagine a more false and amoral book." Under normal conditions, Slapsak added, "this book would be scandalous, perhaps it could bring down [Milosevic], but in any case would be used for hilarious jokes."

But the state-run media dominated. Mira's book was translated into eighteen languages. She was thrilled. At the launching party, Milosevic gave a rare public display of his affection for her. "Kitten," he said, raising his glass, "to your book—and that you may always love me."

Mira also became Milosevic's special envoy, someone to carry out the most sensitive missions. In early 1995, Milosevic wanted to repair relations with Vuk Draskovic, whom he now saw as a potential ally. The vicious beating two years earlier appeared to have softened Vuk (whose name means "wolf" in Serbian), so much so that police czar Radmilo Bogdanovic joked around the capital that he had "turned a wolf into a sheep."

On March 8, Mira met with Vuk and Danica for two and a half hours of pleasant conversation. Draskovic arrived with a bouquet of flowers for Mira, and kissed her hand loftily as if assuring her that he would let bygones be bygones if she would do the same.

It was a surreal situation. The two women had fought a vicious war of words, Mira using her *Duga* column, Danica her party paper, *Srpska Rec*. Danica had asserted that "it would be impossible to find a physician in Serbia or in the world who could certify that the [Milosevic] couple are normal," adding that Mira was "schizophrenic" and "the bastard product of wild partisan orgies in the woods." Mira had accused Danica of "hysteria" and called her "an unfulfilled woman who has the mannerisms of half-wild cattle herdsmen and highwaymen who steal baggage and kidnap children."

On this occasion, however, both sides spent an enjoyable afternoon discussing the situation in Serbia and the Balkans and the overall political strategy of their parties. They professed to be in complete agreement with respect to the war in Bosnia and the eventual settlement of the Yugoslav crisis.

"Why not have someone from the opposition take a diplomatic posting?" Mira observed, leaving the question hanging. Draskovic was not quite sure whether this was an offer or not. The ubiquitous Dusan Mitevic, who organized the meeting, suggested a dinner on another occasion that would also be attended by Milosevic.

Milosevic sought to use Draskovic for his purposes and was prepared to reward him, but Draskovic would not accept a second-rate position. He saw himself as an alternative to Milosevic and presented himself as such to foreign diplomats. "I'm Mike Tyson," he told a visiting foreign minister, "but what can Tyson do if his hands and feet are tied?"

While her husband never sought to establish a cult of personality, Mira by contrast encouraged publicity and adulation. Serbs began calling her "the Red Queen" or "the Red Witch." Her activities were given wide coverage and she was treated as a high government official when she traveled abroad. In Hungary, an official communiqué was issued after her meeting with the president of the ruling Socialist Party in 1995. She was given a warm reception in Russia and elected to the Academy of Sciences—the first non-Russian woman accorded that honor. The patriarch of the Russian Orthodox Church, Alexei II, presented her with the icon of St. Nicholas with a gold leaf after she told him that Nicholas was her mother's patron saint.

Her frequent exposure to television cameras and foreign audiences made her more conscious of her looks: in the summer of 1996, two Italian plastic surgeons, engaged by the Yugoslav ambassador to the Vatican, Dojcilo Maslarovic, performed a face-lift on Mira at the Military Medical Academy Hospital in Belgrade.

But she sometimes faced obstacles from the least likely quarters. Her membership in the Russian Academy was almost blocked by her former professor Danilo Markovic (no relation), the Yugoslav ambassador to Moscow. Markovic had been Mira's mentor at the University of Nis, where she had defended her doctoral dissertation, "Sociological Aspects of Education in [the System of] Self-Management." At the time, he had given a positive assessment of her work; she had rewarded him by engineering his appointments as Serbia's minister of education, deputy prime minister, and finally ambassador to Moscow. But when the ambassador heard that his former student was to be elected to the Russian Academy, some professional envy must have led him to try to block the move; in a diplomatic note to the president of the academy, the ambassador warned that the decision "could have negative consequences." The

Russians took the warning seriously; two days before her scheduled departure for Moscow, they announced that the matter was being postponed indefinitely. Other Milosevic agents quickly moved in to straighten out the confusion and Milosevic personally phoned the ambassador. Nobody knows what Milosevic told Markovic, but the ambassador cried at Moscow airport, seeking Mira's forgiveness. Mira was touched at the sight of her former mentor; but Dusan Mitevic, who accompanied Mira on the trip, told her succinctly: "It's better that he cries, rather than us." The ambassador was soon asked to resign.

Mira's colleagues at Belgrade University were incensed over her membership in the Russian Academy of Sciences. "Did you ever attend a meeting of our sociological society and present a report?" another of her former professors, Mihajlo Popovic, asked in an open letter to her. "Did you ever publish some professional contribution?"

Mira's reply to such criticism was sharp. Its authors, she said, were inferior people with "certain endocrinological" problems. They envied a successful intellectual like herself; she was determined to enjoy it.

Serbs got something to enjoy in 1995, too. After three years of complete isolation, sanctions against Yugoslavia's participation in international sporting events were lifted in recognition of Milosevic's constructive approach toward Bosnia. The Serb nation followed apprehensively as their national basketball team fought its way to the finals of the European championship in Athens. When, on July 2, Yugoslavia won the European crown, the entire nation plunged into delirious festivities; the sounds of gunfire lasted long into the night as a degraded and impoverished nation experienced pride and joy that had been denied it for three years. Slobodan Milosevic for the first time personally congratulated the players and tens of thousands gathered in central Belgrade to give them a hero's welcome.

# 9

# The Most Expensive Cease-fire in History

The Bosnian war dragged on. Month after month, year in year out, peace negotiators raised hopes that major breakthroughs had been achieved. But the people of Bosnia continued to die; many more were left homeless. The world had become impervious to the daily Serb shellings of Sarajevo; it blamed UN generals and international bureaucrats for their prevarications, indeed stigmatized them as men with feet of clay, hearts of stone, and heads of wood. In reality this merely obscured the unwillingness of top Western leaders to get embroiled in the Yugoslav mess.

There were echoes of nineteenth-century great power politics, when Bosnian Christian rebellions against Muslim misrule shook European peace. When Bosnian uprisings began in 1875, King Milan in Serbia had tried to resist demands for a national crusade. For almost three years the powers indulged themselves in frantic diplomacy to broker a peaceful resolution, but all along remained at loggerheads among themselves.

The Bosnia crisis of the 1990s was the other way around, touched off by Christian atrocities against the Muslims. In the Muslim world there was an immediate outcry. A number of Muslim nations—Turkey, Iran, Malaysia, Pakistan, and Saudi Arabia among them—promptly extended material and diplomatic support to the Bosnian Muslims. Muslim volunteers recruited in Jeddah and Teheran—including fierce Afghan mujahedeen—formed the backbone of a Bosnian Muslim army, injecting both fanaticism and more brutality.

The five powers which took upon themselves in 1993 the task of dictating the future of the former Yugoslavia—the United States, Russia, Britain, France, and Germany—had no common strategy. There was a basic split between France and Britain, on the one hand, and America and Germany on the other as to how to achieve stability in the region. The Franco-British view was that Serbia was the key; the Americans and Germans insisted that Serbia must be weakened and neutralized. Russia spoke with two voices: Boris Yeltsin no longer stood in undisputed control over his own foreign policy because pro-Serb sympathizers had penetrated the highest levels of the Russian Army and the bureaucracy, not to speak of the nationalists and the Communists.

The consequence of this allowed the protagonists in the Bosnian drama to exploit divisions within the five-power "Contact Group." Milosevic, while cooperating with the Contact Group and with Lord Owen, the lead negotiator, vigorously lobbied his sympathizers in Moscow. The Bosnian Muslim government's central goal was to get the United States involved militarily. The Bosnian Serbs played the Orthodox card, which meant courting popular opinion in Russia, Serbia, Greece, and other Orthodox nations. The five powers themselves, wishing the problem would go away by itself, placed the entire matter into the cumbersome UN machinery. Air strikes—the holy grail of Clinton administration policy—had been tried several times without effect on the course of the war.

Owen and other international diplomats insisted that everything depended on Milosevic. Only he could stop the war.

Milosevic encouraged such attention, for it was his path to rehabilitation. He had indeed repeatedly tried to break Karadzic's hold on the Bosnian Serb government through a series of punitive measures—cutting off relations, imposing economic embargos—but it was Milosevic's links to the Bosnian Serb security service that, like a tentacle, allowed him to receive intelligence and apply pressure. In early 1995, Karadzic claimed to have discovered that a number of senior officials in his security services were linked to Belgrade and were planning a covert action to depose him. Scores of agents, including the security service chief, were arrested for their role in the operation code-named "Typhoon" which was planned in Belgrade. Karadzic completely reorganized his police; his paranoia had led him to travel little and to surround himself with dozens of bodyguards. From Milosevic's standpoint, the exposure of Karadzic and his allies was all good politics: Karadzic was a convenient scapegoat for the steep price the Serb nation was paying for Milosevic's own misjudgments.

But he could not go further. It was within his capabilities to order the assassination of Karadzic; even after the "Typhoon" operation was broken, Milosevic still retained some agents under deep cover within the Bosnian Serb security. But deep down Milosevic was a prisoner of his background. He could not afford to be seen as a traitor to the Serb nation, a latter-day Vuk Brankovic whom Serb mythology blames for the loss of the 1389 battle of Kosovo.

Instead, his strategy was to wear Karadzic down. Salacious stories were floated in the Serbian press about videos showing Karadzic in compromising sexual situations; other leaks detailed Karadzic's corruption and profiteering, including gambling losses of thousands of dollars a night in Belgrade's casinos and his wife's extravagant shopping sprees while accompanying Karadzic on negotiations in Geneva and New York. Milosevic's personal bitterness was reflected in an assertion he made to Special U.S. Envoy Robert Frasure: "Those who have crossed me have not long survived."

Milosevic's influence on the Bosnian Serbs remained considerable—the Serbian government paid the salaries of Bosnian Serb Army officers, and he tried to advance General Ratko Mladic as an alternative to Karadzic. However, Mladic's large ego and arrogance grew progressively with each press interview, as did his conflicts with Karadzic and other politicians. Milosevic had encouraged this split without realizing the destructive capacity of a man such as Mladic who was single-mindedly devoted to a military solution of a complex ethnic conflict. But it became apparent to Milosevic in the course of numerous twists and turns of the Bosnian war. Mladic, he told Dusan Mitevic, was an "unguided missile" he could not rely upon. This added to Milosevic's frustrations; he had no one to work with in Bosnia. Richard Holbrooke has quoted Milosevic as describing the general as "clinically mad."

Here was a game of Balkan deception and intrigue few outsiders could quite comprehend. In the Western press, each Milosevic move was automatically branded a Machiavellian maneuver to hoodwink the "international community." This was also the view of Madeleine Albright, America's UN ambassador and one of Milosevic's fiercest critics.

Frasure, who had negotiated extensively with Milosevic during the first part of 1995, came to the conclusion that Milosevic had indeed parted ways with the Bosnian Serbs and was prepared to undercut them. Frasure and Milosevic reached an agreement to this effect, after spending three days together in Tito's old hunting lodge in Karadjordjevo. The deal committed Milosevic to formally recognize Bosnia's international borders in exchange for the suspension of sanctions on non-strategic goods, including oil imports to meet Serbia's non-military needs. Frasure returned to the U.S. Embassy in Belgrade on May 18 and reported to Holbrooke in Washington. Holbrooke approved the arrangement.

But over the weekend, internal struggles in Washington caused the deal to unravel. According to Frasure, Madeleine Albright had opposed it most vigorously, and she was supported by Vice President Albert Gore and some other key players, who felt Milosevic should be pushed much harder.

Albright, in particular, had taken the whole matter very personally. For her, Milosevic and his rule combined all the main themes of the twentieth century: Fascist racial supremacy, Communist terror, and the newly reemerging rampant super-nationalism. She had understood Milosevic earlier than most. She viewed his cynical program in the destruction of Yugoslavia through the tragic prism of her own life—a life marked by the Nazi genocide and Communist conquests. Milosevic became for Albright a metaphor for the same evil that had forced her family to twice flee their native Czechoslovakia: after Munich in 1938 and again after the Communist coup in Prague in 1948. As early as August 1993, she had written a memo to President Clinton arguing that only a bombing campaign could force the Serbs to negotiate the end of the Bosnian war. She had lived in Belgrade with her diplomat father, and she felt that she understood the role of coercion in Serb society. But while her influence on the administration in 1993 was peripheral, by 1995 Albright had gained in stature as America's forceful UN ambassador. She viewed Frasure's deal with Milosevic as merely a twist in the West's policy of inaction and evenhanded hypocrisy, the same sort of approach that allowed Hitler to dismember Czechoslovakia in 1938 and helped Stalin take over the Prague government in 1948.

Milosevic had understood early on the context of this unusually personal confrontation, which would eventually culminate in the eleven-week war over Kosovo, and his media had cast Albright as a congenital "Serb hater." Already in 1993, one of the most poisonous snakes in the Belgrade zoo was officially named "Madeleine Albright," accompanied by a chorus of approving media comments. But Milosevic probably never entertained the idea that Albright could rise higher in the ranks of the Clinton administration to become secretary of state and, as such, someone directly responsible for U.S. policy in the Balkans.

When Frasure called on Milosevic on Monday to relay the bad news and outline new American conditions, the Serb leader was angry and hurt. He had thought, he told Frasure, that he was dealing with a presidential envoy authorized to negotiate. He had been expecting to announce the deal and had even had the leader of the ultranationalist Radical Party, Vojislav Seselj, arrested in anticipation.

Some time after Frasure's departure, Milosevic decided he would try to restart his talks with the Americans and offered a token of conciliation. On June 8, he summoned the U.S. chargé d'affaires Rudolph Perina to inform him that a five-year custody dispute involving two American children had been resolved.

It concerned a California woman whose former husband, a Serb immigrant, had kidnapped the couple's two young children in 1990 in violation of a custody agreement and brought them to his hometown of Nis, in southern Serbia. The mother flew to Belgrade and fought the case in Serbian court; she was awarded custody of her children by the Supreme Court of Serbia. When the police refused to enforce the court decision, senior U.S. officials, including Secretary of State James Baker and a number of U.S. senators, raised the issue with Milosevic.

Milosevic insisted that he could do nothing about the matter, which was outside his jurisdiction. The American woman, who is Jewish, took up residence in Belgrade and continued her fight. One day before the UN economic sanctions went into effect on May 31, 1992, Milosevic summoned the anguished mother to his office. He held her hand, telling her he felt like her father and was most concerned about her children. His secret police had just located the little boy and girl, he said—they were with their father in a hotel in the town of Dachau, famous as the site of a Nazi concentration camp. If she hurried there, she would find them. But that was a lie. The children were in Nis, where they were dropped off at school every day by her former husband in a car with California license plates.

Three years later, when Milosevic wanted to curry favor with the United States, he had the children delivered to the U.S. Embassy.

In Bosnia, the ground war had been static for more than two years. In April 1993, NATO had begun enforcing a "no-fly zone" over Bosnia and the United Nations had declared several Muslim enclaves, among them the town of Srebrenica, as "UN safe areas."

The first event to foreshadow a change in the military balance occurred in neighboring Croatia, but it had an immediate impact on Western policies in Bosnia. On May 1, 1995, U.S.-trained Croatian Army troops, encouraged by the Clinton administration, swept past UN peacekeeping troops to seize a Serb-held territory known as Western Slavonia. They burned down Serb homes and took no prisoners.

The Serb rebel army, under the command of a Yugoslav general handpicked by Milosevic, watched from across the river as the Croats "cleansed" the region with methodical cruelty. The Serb rebels fired a handful of surface-to-surface missiles on the Croatian capital of Zagreb, killing seven people and wounding forty others. However, the missile attack captured more publicity than the death of thousands of Serbs in Western Slavonia.

The most significant aspect of the whole operation was that Serbia's population had no inkling of what the Croats had done. Milosevic-controlled Radio Television Belgrade did not interrupt its regular programming. In towns and villages across Serbia, people enjoyed the May Day holiday, eating roast lamb and drinking beer, oblivious to the fact that one-third of the Serb mini-state inside Croatia, which Milosevic had once told them was an integral part of his Greater Serbia, had disappeared from the map.

Only an alarmed Patriarch Pavle telephoned Milosevic to demand an urgent meeting. What is happening? the old man asked, wondering whether Milosevic had already strayed from the narrow path of total solidarity with the Serbs of Bosnia and Croatia. Will Serbia help its brethren in need?

"Everything is going according to plan," Milosevic replied.

When Bishop Amphilohije, a member of the Holy Synod, heard about the exchange, he quietly implored the patriarch, "Your Beatitude, what is his plan? That man is anti-Christ!"

That quick conquest of Western Slavonia was a prelude to Milosevic's final settlement with Croatia as well as a precursor of more unrest in Serbia proper. Milosevic showed his true colors, abandoning the national dream that had once stirred his people when he realized that it was an impediment to his rule. Rather than protecting the Serbs who had placed their trust in him, he gave the final shove in their brutal eviction from the Serb enclave inside Croatia.

He did so by instructing General Mile Mrksic, the commander of Krajina's well-equipped army of fifty thousand, to abandon the enclave the moment the Croats made a grab for it.

Milosevic, who knew his people were not prepared to fight a war in Krajina, was in no position to throw his weight about or make any demands at all. Moreover, Krajina's political leaders had emerged as Karadzic's supporters, which made a settlement with Tudjman of greater importance to Milosevic's own political future.

The Croat success reinforced U.S. strategists' conviction that the use of massive force—air strikes as far as the United States was concerned—would break the Bosnian stalemate.

In May 1995, NATO planes finally mounted what was billed as a severe and sustained bombing campaign, hitting strategic targets and blowing up two ammunition dumps close to Mladic's headquarters near Han Pijesak, in eastern Bosnia.

But Karadzic and Mladic would not be intimidated; they took 375 UN peacekeepers hostage, manacled them to various potential targets in the Bosnian mountains, then showed the grim sight on Bosnian Serb television. The arresting spectacle of helpless young soldiers—British, French, and Canadian—being chained to telegraph poles and repeatedly shown on TV screens symbolized the utter humiliation of the international community.

The air strikes stopped.

Even the nationalists in Serbia proper were shocked and repelled by this action, not to mention the rest of the world. Milosevic saw it as a monumental public relations catastrophe that could rebound against him. As the worldwide outcry against the Serbs gained momentum and Milosevic was bombarded by Western pleas for help, he secretly dispatched his secret service chief Jovica Stanisic to Pale, the Bosnian Serb capital, with the following message for Karadzic: "I will have you killed if you do not release the hostages! You know I can do it."

Allied governments indeed were in dire straits and hard-pressed to obtain the release of the hostages. Their protracted and complicated dealings with Mladic seemed confused—at times flattering and coaxing, at times threatening, at times issuing vague promises.

In the end, it was Milosevic who obtained their release. This was the moment when Milosevic's new image finally took hold in the minds of Western politicians and the moment when they became indebted to him. He indeed seemed like a genuine convert to peacemaking.

He had to pay a price, however, something which made him furious at Mladic, Karadzic, and their accomplices. In exchange for releasing the hostages, Mladic insisted that Serbia urgently provide military spare parts. The secret haggling over what had to be delivered to Mladic and when was the real reason the hostages were freed in batches over a period of three weeks.

There was an incident following the release of the first batch of prisoners which provides a glimpse into Milosevic's motives. At that point, the Greek ministers of defense and foreign affairs dramatically surfaced in Pale. Milosevic was furious. He did not want to share credit with anyone and he blamed the Greeks for the delay in the release of the rest of the hostages. The Greeks were friends, of course, he remarked acidly, but they were "not a nation but a profession."

Karadzic and his accomplices saw the Western responses to the hostage-taking as more evidence of weakness. They decided to make a daring move: take over the remaining Muslim enclaves along the Drina River, including the town of Srebrenica.

The collapse of Western Slavonia had alarmed the Serbs of Bosnia and Krajina and galvanized the ultra-nationalist forces of Vojislav Seselj into action. Amid charges of sellout and treason, Seselj began organizing anti-Milosevic rallies in Kosovo, the mainstay of his support.

Already in 1994 he had been arrested over his vocal opposition to Milosevic's Bosnia policy and hauled before a judge even though he enjoyed parliamentary immunity.

"Judge, if you have no objections I'd like to immediately make my statement to the court."

"Just go ahead," the judge said.

"Slobodan Milosevic is the greatest criminal in Serbia. This is all I have to say in my defense."

Seselj was given twenty days in jail on charges of provoking clashes with the police.

In June 1995, Seselj was arrested in Kosovo and jailed for three months for organizing anti-government protests. The woman judge in the Kosovo town of Gnjilane at first released Seselj on his demand because he enjoyed immunity as a member of parliament, though she burst into tears and said, "I'll lose my job for this." Seselj walked from the courtroom into the arms of waiting police, who put him in jail while they awaited a fax from Belgrade revoking his immunity.

Seselj, a former professor of political science, had been a dissident during the rule of Marshal Tito. He had endured years of solitary confinement and been placed on Amnesty International's list of prisoners of conscience. His doctoral thesis dealt with the methods and structure of Hitler's Nazi Party. He drew on his research when setting up his ultra-nationalist Radical Party, which called for the creation of a Greater Serbia and the expulsion of all non-Serbs from Serbian lands. His paramilitary forces, wearing flowing beards and three-cornered Serb hats, fought their first battles in Croatia and Bosnia. Seselj became known as "the Red Duke," a name reflecting links to the royalist tradition as well as his subservience to Milosevic.

Strictly speaking, Seselj was a creation of Milosevic. For two years leading up to the December 1992 Serbian presidential elections, Milosevic had used Seselj and his paramilitaries to stage disruptions at opposition rallies and to wage wars in Croatia and Bosnia. Milosevic rewarded him in a July 1991 by-election, engineering his election to parliament. Seselj, Milosevic said the next year, was the politician he "admired most."

Their relationship changed as Seselj's Radicals, who continued to preach Serb nationalism, captured 27 percent of the votes in the December elections: Milosevic's Socialists saw their share of the vote drop sharply, to 40 percent. Milosevic's subsequent U-turn on

Bosnia ended their relationship. Milosevic branded Seselj a war criminal and disbanded his paramilitary force in November 1993. He used the occasion to blame the forces under Seselj's command for the atrocities committed in Croatia and Bosnia. According to the Yugoslav Army periodical *Vojska,* they were involved in "murdering, raping, slaughtering people and even playing soccer with chopped-off heads."

By 1995, Seselj had firmly sided with Karadzic in what had become a grudge match between the Bosnian Serb leader and Milosevic, the president of Serbia. Karadzic was now openly aspiring to be leader of the Serbs, and was obsessed with his struggle with Milosevic. The Bosnian Serb leader also drew closer to Seselj's coarse brand of nationalist extremism, especially after he and Mladic were formally named as war crimes suspects by the Hague tribunal on April 24, 1995. (Judge Richard Goldstone of the International War Crimes Tribunal in the Hague issued arrest warrants for Karadzic and Mladic on charges of crimes against humanity three months later.)

In July 1995, an entirely new and horrific event in Bosnia dramatically changed political and military dynamics in the former Yugoslavia.

On July 12, Mladic's troops seized the Muslim enclave of Srebrenica in the Drina River valley and massacred more than six thousand people, mostly men and boys. It was the worst single massacre in Europe since World War II.

During the preceding three days of Serb shelling, the enclave was abandoned by the UN garrison, which was supposed to protect it. When news of the massacre reached Western capitals, any remaining reticence about getting involved in Bosnia turned into an explosion of revulsion against the Bosnian Serbs—revulsion that was heightened by feelings of guilt that the West for so long had ignored the manifest barbarism in the Balkans. This feeling was summed up by Vice President Al Gore, who at the July 17 meeting of top American leaders said to President Clinton, pointing to a new photo of a refugee woman who had committed suicide by hanging herself from a tree: "My 21-year-old daughter asked me about that picture. What am I supposed to tell her? Why is this happening and we're not doing anything? . . . My daughter is surprised the world is allowing this to happen. I am too."

This is not the place to dwell upon the complex and endlessly shifting attitudes of American and European policy makers. UN peacekeepers were in Bosnia, supposedly protecting Muslim areas. But they had a weak mandate, allowed to fire only in self-defense. American forces were not included. Even before Srebrenica showed up their powerlessness, France's newly elected president, Jacques Chirac, had visited Washington and told President Clinton that France would withdraw its peacekeeping troops by September. A similar British message had been relayed through diplomatic channels. Without British and French involvement, the UN peacekeeping operation in Bosnia would collapse, and everybody anticipated the withdrawal would turn into a bloody affair. The United States was in a bind: it had reluctantly committed itself to sending twenty thousand U.S. combat troops as part of a previously agreed NATO strategy. But, with an eye on the 1996 presidential elections, Clinton was unwilling to send U.S. troops into a combat whose outcome was uncertain.

Instead, Clinton decided to abandon the "nickel and dime approach" that had been the hallmark of his policy toward the former Yugoslavia. At the same time, Western diplomatic assessments reported that Milosevic was unlikely to have sanctioned the massacre, even though he may have known about—or perhaps approved—the move to seize Srebrenica and other enclaves.

Clinton decided he could send troops not to fight in Bosnia but rather to enforce peace after the fighting died down. It involved Milosevic's tacit complicity, the deployment of proxy ground forces to fight Mladic's army, and a massive use of cruise missiles and airpower to force the Bosnian Serb leadership to accept peace terms dictated by the United States.

U.S. Department of Defense officials had developed contingency plans to use the U.S.-trained Croatian Army against the Bosnian Serbs. The Croats were thirsting for revenge. Their key goal was to rid themselves of their Serb minority in Krajina. The

Croats needed no prodding to join the Bosnian war, provided that Washington agreed to their conquest of Krajina.

Determined to lift the problem out of the slow-moving machinery of government, Clinton appointed Richard Holbrooke as his personal envoy with full powers to settle the war. Holbrooke was to report directly to national security adviser Anthony Lake, and through him, to the president.

The choice of the ambitious and forceful Holbrooke was fortuitous. By temperament, he was not a team player, which in this situation proved to be an asset. Nor was he burdened by too detailed a knowledge of the area and its history. Previous joint mediation efforts had invariably bogged down in Contact Group squabbles. This, by contrast, was an American show. Moreover, Holbrooke did not have to look over his shoulder all the time; for all practical purposes, Clinton and Lake were his desk officers.

Much depended on Milosevic. Should he decide to throw Serbia's support behind his Serb brethren in Krajina and Bosnia, a Balkan-wide conflict seemed inevitable. But President Tudjman of Croatia knew better. Milosevic had telegraphed four years earlier at their secret Karadjordjevo hunting lodge meeting that he did not consider Krajina and its 240,000 Serbs as Serbia's vital interest. There was also a feeling of optimism among U.S. diplomats, although nobody could be absolutely sure.

The entire assault was publicly portrayed as a purely Croat initiative, even though it was an essential ingredient of Clinton's endgame strategy. "The Croats kept coming to us and asking for clearance to use the military against rebel Serbs in Krajina," a senior U.S. official recalled. "First we said no. Then we gave them a yellow light to move on Western Slavonia. That was in May. Then they came back to us in June talking about a 'limited operation' in the Bihac pocket [in northwestern Bosnia] and so on. We said no. Then they came back to us after Srebrenica with the same argument. Now we gave the Croats a green light."

The moment the Croatian Army attacked Krajina in the first week of August, Serb general Mrksic ordered an immediate withdrawal. More than three hundred tanks led the way, joined by heavy artillery pieces and other equipment, moving east to Serb-held Bosnia and toward Serbia proper. They were followed by about 170,000 men, women, and children jammed in cars, trucks, tractors, or walking on foot—heading to Serbia.

Krajina's political leader, Milan Martic, accused Serbia of betrayal. "It is quite clear that this was a shameful and ugly ploy, which was planned by Belgrade, to have the army retreat and simply relinquish the territory to Croatia," he said, after fleeing and finding refuge with Karadzic's forces in Bosnia. General Mrksic and other Yugoslav officers had not even informed the Krajina leaders that the Croatian attack had started. "They simply took off," Martic said.

Milosevic and Mira were spending a weekend with the Belgrade banker Bogoljub Karic at a Black Peak Mountain villa south of the capital when they were informed by telephone that the Krajina was being overrun by the Croats.

Milosevic expressed surprise. "Look, these idiots are withdrawing!" he was quoted as saying.

Once again the programming on Belgrade Television was not interrupted; the screen was dominated by a live transmission from Monte Carlo, where the finals of a circus festival were underway. Patriarch Pavle dispatched a letter to the television director Milorad Vucelic, in which he noted with "sadness" that the television had not informed the population about the collapse of Krajina, adding, "Your responsibility before God and history is enormous." The main headline in *Politika* the next morning read: "Serbs Withdraw; Military Command Moved to Reserve Positions."

What ensued in Serbia, however, was a typical Milosevic maneuver to confuse the population and advance conflicting interpretations designed to deflect criticism by blaming others. The next day, Milosevic summoned his army chiefs, key editors, and top propagandists of the Socialist Party to his government villa in Dedinje. He blamed Martic and Karadzic for the fall of Krajina. Editors were instructed to make sure that their reporters assigned to interview Krajina refugees "blame Martic and Karadzic." Mira's YUL Party issued a statement emphasizing that "the most important interest of

Yugoslavia is to secure peace." In her *Duga* column, Mira blamed the Krajina refugees for their plight. "Why didn't they stay and defend their hearth? Why did they come here at all?"

More than 200,000 Krajina Serbs were expelled or forced to leave Croatia, where they had lived for four centuries. Most of them were descendants of those Serbs who fled from Turkish rule in the seventeenth century and settled along the borders of what was then the Habsburg Empire.

What are we going to do with the refugees? Dusan Mitevic asked his friend.

"Send them to Kosovo," Milosevic replied. "We need more Serbs in Kosovo, don't we?"

Yugoslav prime minister Radoje Kontic invited two of his close friends to visit him in his office on August 7. "I invited you so we all can get drunk," he said, pointing at a bottle of French Cognac on his table. "I don't know how you feel, but I, as a Montenegrin, feel ashamed. This morning my kids told me, 'We piss on your premiership!' What could I tell them? I had to keep silent."

In Bosnia, Mladic suddenly and wholly unexpectedly faced a strong enemy along a 150-mile front that was completely defenseless following the collapse of Krajina. The bulk of his forces were deployed in eastern Bosnia.

In the second week of August, the Croats moved into Bosnia, pushing toward Banja Luka (the largest Bosnian Serb city) after producing a humanitarian tragedy in Krajina whose scope was obscured by a massive public relations effort and American acquiescence. The ethnic cleansing carried out by the Croatian Army was ruthlessly efficient: all Serb villages were burned to the ground and the few thousand Serbs who had remained in Krajina were slaughtered.

Holbrooke, in his memoir, produces the following note written by Robert Frasure during a lunch with Tudjman on August 17 at which the scope of the Croatian operations inside Krajina and Bosnia was discussed:

Dick: We "hired" these guys as our junkyard dogs because we were desperate. We need to try to "control" them. But this is no time to get squeamish about things. This is the first time the Serb wave has been reversed. That is essential for us to get stability, so we can get out.

The Croat troops, aided by some element of the Muslim army, rapidly reached the outskirts of Banja Luka. The inevitable fall of the city was prevented by a "red light" from Washington, as the Croats were ordered to pull back their forces.

Holbrooke, shuttling between Belgrade and other Balkan capitals, established a good rapport with Milosevic. The two seemed to enjoy each other's rough sense of humor and brutal frankness. The man Holbrooke described in 1992 as "the bloodiest tyrant in Europe" now struck the American envoy as a reasonable, charming person who, in different circumstances, he quoted a colleague as saying, "would have been a successful politician in a democratic system."

Each man boosted the other. Holbrooke's help was necessary for Milosevic to finally reinvent himself as the "guarantor" of peace in Bosnia while at the same time delivering his country from crippling economic sanctions. The deal with Milosevic would ensure that Holbrooke was described in glowing terms, hailed in *The New Yorker* as "the superdiplomat in the central crisis of the age."

Once Mladic's army was defeated by the Croats, Holbrooke asked for massive air strikes against Bosnian Serb positions. On August 30, NATO launched the largest military action in its history on the already defeated Bosnian Serbs; cruise missiles and some 3,400 air sorties destroyed much of their military potential and infrastructure.

Five days earlier, Milosevic had convened a secret meeting with all top Bosnian Serb leaders and all Serb and Montenegrin officials in the presence of Patriarch Pavle. At that meeting, Karadzic and his colleagues surrendered to Milosevic's blandishments: they agreed to grant him full authority to negotiate the future of the Bosnian Serb republic.

On August 28, when the same cast was reconvened to make the final decision, Karadzic and his accomplices formally capitulated. They signed a document placing the fate of Bosnian Serbs into Milosevic's hands; it formally empowered Milosevic to negotiate on their behalf at any future peace talks. Milosevic's use of the old patriarch was a brilliant move; Pavle signed the document along with all others, but added the sign of the Orthodox cross for good measure. (The patriarch later withdrew his support for the document when his nationalist bishops realized what he had done; by then, it was too late.)

Milosevic displayed the paper to Holbrooke and other Americans when they called on him on August 30. "And this document has been witnessed by Patriarch Pavle, the head of the Serbian Orthodox Church. Look here," Milosevic said.

The Americans were ecstatic. The Patriarch Paper meant that real peace talks could soon begin. Indeed, Milosevic himself had proposed convening an international peace conference immediately.

When Holbrooke asked him about the attitude of his Bosnian Serb "friends," Milosevic exploded: "They are not my friends. They are not my colleagues. It is awful just to be in the same room with them for so long. They are shit."

Milosevic brought Holbrooke together with Mladic and Karadzic some days later as details of the proposed cease-fire and the future map of Bosnia were discussed. When discussions reached a stalemate, Holbrooke recalled, Karadzic said, "If we can't get anything done here, I will call President Carter. I am in regular contact with him." After Holbrooke replied that Jimmy Carter was only a private citizen and "We take orders only from President Clinton," Karadzic was on his best behavior for the rest of the meeting.

"You know, that was smart, what you said about Jimmy Carter," Milosevic later told Holbrooke. "Those guys are so cut off from the world they think Carter still determines American policy."

The peace conference to end the Bosnian war was convened on November 1, 1995, at the Wright-Patterson Air Force Base outside Dayton, Ohio. Richard Holbrooke later described his strategy as the Big Bang approach to negotiations: lock up the warring parties until they reach agreement.

Before going to Dayton, Milosevic told the Serb nation, "I hope it is sufficiently and finally clear to our public why, in the interest of the entire people, we had to come out so sharply against the leadership in Pale." His delegation included three Bosnian Serbs, but not Karadzic and Mladic, who had been charged with war crimes by the Hague tribunal and could not travel abroad without risking arrest.

Milosevic sought to provide himself with political cover for his ultimate acceptance of the Serb defeat. He insisted that the peace conference should be held in the United States. It was to be modeled on the 1978 Camp David talks when President Carter helped forge the historic agreement between Egypt and Israel; Milosevic was hoping that Camp David would be the venue here as well, but the Clinton administration selected Dayton instead.

"What, are you going to keep me locked up in Dayton, Ohio?" Milosevic protested. "I am not a priest, you know."

He was determined to present a new and gentler face to the world, reasonable and friendly. He sang "Tenderly" with the piano player at the Officer's Club; he was fascinated by Pentagon computers and spent time playing with the joystick. He was prepared to compromise or seek imaginative ways out of an impasse. In contrast to the dour Muslim leader Alija Izetbegovic and Croatia's Franjo Tudjman, Milosevic charmed his hosts with his outgoing manner and his constructive approach. He ignored the three representatives of the Karadzic regime, treating them with open contempt. In fact, they had to ask the Americans what was going on at the conference. "Pay no attention to those guys," Milosevic told Holbrooke. "I'll make sure they accept the final agreement."

Milosevic agreed to Tudjman's demand to regain full control over the Serb-occupied Eastern Slavonia region of Croatia within twelve months, telling Secretary of State Warren Christopher that he "needed a few days to work this out so that it looks like the issue was determined by the local leaders in Eastern Slavonia."

The agreement was to give the Bosnian Serbs 49 percent of the territory of Bosnia-Herzegovina, while the Muslims and the Croats would get 51 percent. The three weeks of haggling at Dayton involved details, and Milosevic accepted the various Muslim demands—including a corridor from Sarajevo to their enclaves in eastern Bosnia—but he insisted on keeping parts of Sarajevo in Serb hands.

The breakthrough came at the eleventh hour, when failure seemed inevitable. It involved the Bosnian capital. The American proposal was that the problem should be resolved on the basis of the District of Columbia model—all three communities sharing the city and taking part in its administration. Endless haggling went on over how the city should be divided; in the end it became quite clear that the Muslims wanted the whole of Sarajevo and that they were prepared to return home without an agreement at all if they didn't get it.

Milosevic was desperate to have an agreement. At that point, he stunned everybody even more by offering the whole of Sarajevo to the Muslims as a "gift."

"You deserve Sarajevo because you've fought for it," Milosevic told Bosnian Muslim prime minister Haris Silajdzic. "Accordingly, since you deserve Sarajevo I am going to give it to you."

A surprised Silajdzic took Milosevic's hand and the deal was done. Warren Christopher opened a bottle of his favorite wine to celebrate. Silajdzic, in a euphoric mood, left the room to get Izetbegovic.

The Muslim leader, looking sleepy and annoyed, appeared in his pajamas and began to study the map. Then he stunned everyone by asserting that he could not accept the agreement.

"What did you say?" Christopher asked incredulously.

"I cannot accept this agreement," Izetbegovic replied in English.

Failure now appeared certain. Izetbegovic wanted control of Brcko, the border town which was the site of a two-mile-wide corridor linking the two parts of the Bosnian Serb republic.

Christopher, after consulting Clinton, decided to close down the conference unless the agreement was accepted. He angrily castigated Izetbegovic, adding: "We must have your answer in one hour. If you say no, we will announce in the morning that the Dayton peace talks have been closed down. Not suspended—closed down. In one hour."

The Americans went to Milosevic to inform him of the failure shortly before midnight. Milosevic was in a jovial mood and offered everybody drinks, but when told that the conference would be closed the next morning, he became visibly agitated. "You can't do that," he said. "We've got this agreement almost done, you can't let this happen." They talked until 2:00 A.M., with the Americans prodding Milosevic to "save" the negotiation. It was up to him, they said.

At dawn next morning, the Bosnian Muslims leaked the story that the conference had failed. They had been given an ultimatum and they had refused.

Milosevic met with Christopher and Holbrooke before breakfast.

"Something has to be done to prevent failure," he said. "I suggest that Tudjman and I sign the agreement, and have Izetbegovic sign it later."

"We cannot have an agreement that is not signed by everyone," Christopher replied. "It is not a viable contract."

"Okay," said Milosevic. "Then I will walk the final mile for peace. I will agree to [international] arbitration for Brcko one year from now, and you can make the decision yourself, Mr. Christopher."

The Dayton negotiations were saved. Later that day, November 21, 1995, it was signed by all parties in the presence of Clinton and other high officials.

The three Bosnian Serb delegates had no idea what had been agreed upon. Milosevic showed them the final maps only ten minutes before the signing ceremony. Karadzic's deputy, Momcilo Krajisnik, fainted when he saw the map and refused to initial the accord. Keeping Sarajevo had been a Holy Grail for the Bosnian Serbs.

The Americans were insistent that the Bosnian Serbs sign. "Why are you making such a big thing of such bullshit," Milosevic told Holbrooke. "I guarantee you that I will have their signatures within twenty-two hours of my return to Belgrade."

He did.

The Clinton White House sold the Dayton agreement to the

American people as a great triumph of U.S. diplomacy—an undertaking to turn Bosnia into a multicultural European society, a "single state" with a central government, a central bank, and a single currency. This was to be done within a short period of time—a year or two. A twelve-month deadline was set for U.S. troop presence in Bosnia.

Izetbegovic thought that Dayton would turn into "the most expensive cease-fire in history," a rather poignant comment given the fact that four years later American and other foreign troops were continuing to keep peace between the three parties. "It is not a just peace, but my people need peace," he said.

Milosevic sold Dayton to the Serb nation as a personal diplomatic triumph. Newspaper headlines read: "Milosevic—The Man of Peace" . . . "Decisive Role of the Serbian President." The propaganda machine shifted into high gear to generate peace euphoria. The Socialists from the city of Nis proposed Milosevic for a Nobel Peace Prize: he had, they said, "united the Serb nation with the aim of realizing their national interests." A brand-new gas station in downtown Belgrade was christened Dayton by the parliament president to commemorate the lifting of the UN embargo. A cabinet member, Dragan Kostic, who happened to be visiting a snowbound Moscow at the time, topped all accolades by insisting that to him it appeared that "the snow was joyful, the snow seemed less cold" as a result of Milosevic's success.

Dayton, in fact, sounded the death knell to the cherished concept of a multicultural Bosnia. "I knew that the moment Milosevic gave all of Sarajevo to the Muslims," a key aide to Holbrooke told us. Insofar as Bosnia was ever a multinational state rather than a state comprising several nations, Sarajevo was its truest fragment, the place where multiculturalism stood its best chance to be carried out in practice. Izetbegovic's first public statement about the future of Sarajevo's Serbs was ominous: "Women and children are fine, but men shall be investigated for war crimes."

More than 100,000 Serbs who were still in Sarajevo quickly left the districts given to the Muslims; they carried everything, including the bones of their ancestors. At the time of Dayton, according to

CIA calculations, more than half of Bosnia's prewar population of 4,365,000 had either fled the country, been displaced within Bosnia, or been killed.

Despite the regime-induced euphoria, Milosevic was wounded. The majority of Serbs saw Dayton as a great defeat.

One issue that the leaders of Yugoslavia's successor states did not address at Dayton was Kosovo.

Milosevic had the opportunity, in the immediate post-Dayton period, to put his domestic policy on a different course. But he felt betrayed. Holbrooke had "double-crossed" him, he said. He had been promised full normalization and had seen instead an "outer wall of sanctions" erected. Dayton did not mean instant readmission of Yugoslavia into the world community nor access to foreign credits and international financial institutions. The new sanctions seemed to him linked more to his domestic problems than his international behavior.

His immediate instinct was toward strengthening his hold on power and moving the country toward self-isolation.

Shortly after returning from Dayton, Milosevic purged his closest collaborators from his party's leadership, among them his chief ideologue Mihajlo Markovic and Borisav Jovic, Milosevic's onetime factotum who had helped plan the Yugoslav wars. Mira's column in *Duga* had foreshadowed all these personnel changes by a few months. Jovic, a narrow-minded apparatchik whom Milosevic had promoted to the top, had published a personal diary about the final days of Yugoslavia. Mira had not mentioned Jovic by name, but everyone knew who she had in mind when talking about intriguers whose "recollections are full of lies"; "the poison in their memoirs is destroying the lives of their contemporaries and will continue to destroy the lives of yet unborn generations."

Jovic learned about his removal from a reporter for the student Radio B92, Milica Kuburovic, who phoned him at home for a comment.

"Good morning," the reporter said.

"Good morning."

"I'm wondering if you have any comment?"

"Comment about what?"

"About your resignation."

"Resignation? Has it been announced?" Jovic sounded surprised.

"Does that mean you didn't know about it?"

"No, no, I didn't know. Nobody told me."

The party congress in early 1996 was held in the same spirit. The delegates celebrated "the victory of peace" and "the entry into the twenty-first century." People were led to believe that things were bound to take a turn for the better with the sanctions being lifted and Serbia's isolation finally coming to an end. Comrade Mira—she insisted on being addressed as "Comrade" rather than "Madame"—pushed Milosevic to look toward the East, the models being China, North Korea, and Cuba. The Socialists gave the warmest welcome to the Cuban delegation attending their congress. Milosevic was reelected party leader with 99.88 percent of the votes (1 vote against, 1 not valid).

By all indications, Slobo and Mira were turning the Socialist Party back to its Communist roots. Some critics suggested that YUL—which did not have a single deputy in parliament—had swallowed Serbia's largest party. After Dayton, members of Mira's party were increasingly placed in positions of influence and economic management that would have normally gone to the members of Slobo's Socialist Party. This was more than a partnership in power. The removal of Milorad Vucelic, the director of Radio Television Serbia, was done at Mira's insistence; Milosevic liked Vucelic, who was also a leading figure in the Serb parliament, and wanted to compensate him and send him as ambassador "to any country I chose," Vucelic recalled later. Vucelic declined, however.

Mira's neo-Communists slowly injected the Communist management style into a country still under UN sanctions; while most of them were lifted after Dayton, an "outer wall of sanctions" remained in place, barring Belgrade's access to the international credit markets. Mira's argument was that the regime had to reestablish order and discipline after several years of black marketeering and corruption during the chaotic years of the Croatia and Bosnia wars. According to opposition critics, the war profiteers had moved more than $2.5 billion into various foreign accounts, many of them in Cyprus. The identities of the account owners have never been disclosed, nor has Milosevic ever ordered an investigation into the matter. There is no evidence that Slobo and Mira have enriched themselves, however, even though this was within their power.

She gave him a way out, a new credo—a return to Tito's communism, brotherhood, and unity—as he climbed back from nationalism. But Mira was later to become a liability when voters in 1996 trounced her party and staged demonstrations against the Red Queen.

Throughout 1996 and 1997, Milosevic's power base kept shifting to the left. Mira used "usurpation and blackmail" to infiltrate YUL operatives into leading positions in all state institutions, including the military. General Momcilo Perisic, the chief of staff, later said that the ruling couple had turned the high command "into a party cell" of their leftist coalition. They removed the sole source of competence in the economic establishment by dismissing the governor of the Central Bank, Dragoslav Avramovic, the retired World Bank economist. The much-respected Avramovic, already in his late seventies and affectionately referred to as "Grandpa" by most Serbs, had been the architect of Serbia's economic recovery from the Weimar Republic–like conditions of 1993–94.

Milosevic also cracked down on what was left of the independent media. The regime took over the opposition daily *Nasa Borba* and the independent local TV station Studio B, and closed down the Belgrade offices of the Soros Foundation which had helped finance the independent sources of news.

The ensuing process of political polarization was dramatic, especially the growing militancy of Seselj's Radical Party and its supporters, who insisted that Milosevic was courting a hostile West whose demands impinged on Serb internal affairs and sovereignty. By 1997, according to senior Western diplomats, Milosevic was no longer prepared even to discuss Kosovo with them.

Some European nations, concerned by Milosevic's proven capacity for mischief making, contemplated a concerted effort to encourage pluralism through a program of democratization and autonomy for Kosovo in exchange for access to European institutions. But, according to one West European source, "the Americans were allergic to any joint initiative with the Europeans over Kosovo. They clearly felt sensitive to the Albanians' charge that their interests had been forgotten at Dayton." The Clinton administration had opened a U.S. Information Center in Pristina, which the Kosovar Albanians viewed as a prelude to an American embassy. Washington continued to issue rhetorical warnings, but that was all.

Once again, the people of Serbia turned against Milosevic. Protesters became more vocal prior to the November 1996 parliamentary and municipal elections. The voters were to elect members of the Yugoslav and municipal councils.

The elections for the federal parliament were important for Milosevic since his five-year term as president of Serbia was expiring in December 1997, and the constitution barred him from seeking another term. He had planned all along to assume the post of president of Yugoslavia, with the added advantage of avoiding the uncertainties and risks of another popular election. (Yugoslav presidents are elected by the federal parliament.)

In an effort to frustrate Milosevic's plan, the opposition parties, whose leaders normally could not overcome petty jealousies and outsized ambitions, agreed to form a coalition with a joint platform for the November 3 elections. They asked the dismissed Central Bank governor Avramovic to be leader of the five-party coalition: he resolved a rivalry between Vuk Draskovic of the Serbian Renewal Movement and Zoran Djindjic of the Democratic Party, the two largest members of the coalition. The popular and vigorous Grandpa, who had tried to impose fiscal discipline on the Milosevic regime, had openly criticized the widespread corruption and incompetence of "aggressive cowards" in the Serbian government. He had dismissed the federal Yugoslav government as a body that "did absolutely no work." Grandpa's dismissal came when he refused to print more dinars as Milosevic demanded.

Grandpa accepted the offer of the Zajedno ("Together") coalition, but a week later abruptly stepped down, citing medical reasons. Most people dismissed his explanation; Grandpa was rumored to have been blackmailed by one of Milosevic's men, Nikola Sainovic, who allegedly presented him with a police file in which there were a couple of instances of minor corruption, the most serious being the alleged use of his position to obtain an apartment for himself and another for his daughter.

Once the popular Avramovic was out of the way, Milosevic had paid little attention to the prospective vote. His wife, on the other hand, had thrown herself into the election campaign with complete enthusiasm. The propaganda machinery hummed smoothly; the campaign of lies was elevated to new heights. Parliament president Dragan Tomic told voters that Yugoslavia in 1997 would have the highest growth rate in Europe; deputy minister of health Dr. Zoran Kovacevic reported that "Yugoslavia is on the way to becoming the first country in the world to develop an effective drug against AIDS." Another medical specialist, Dr. Jovan Stirkovic, urged the nation to move politically to the left "because left is the dominant side of Homo sapiens."

On the election eve, Mira's new book, *Between East and West,* appeared at the Belgrade Book Fair, with a proud Milosevic attending the launch as speaker after speaker extolled the author. Mira said, modestly, that she wrote her book—a collection of her essays from *Duga*—"for my people." Bishop Irinej, a member of the Holy Synod of the Serbian Orthodox Church, phoned Mira to praise the contents and to apologize for failing to attend her book party.

It seemed from the tone of the public debate that the opposition was non-existent: Draskovic, Djindjic, and Vesna Pesic formed a collective leadership of the Zajedno coalition, but their campaign lacked a coherent and positive message. Milosevic did no campaigning himself. But the media was flooded by thousands of telegrams praising "the greatest Serb statesman" who had "successfully secured peace and the lives of our citizens" and who was a "noble and exceptionally humane" person.

Everything had gone according to schedule. The preliminary indications on November 3 were that the Zajedno coalition was doing poorly. Milosevic and Mira voted early near their home in the exclusive Dedinje section and television cameras captured the moment when the Serbian president was asked to show his ID card, while Mira chimes in: "You see, no favoritism here!" After the polls were closed, Milosevic and Mira visited the YUL campaign headquarters, then repaired to bed. The victory was resounding. Slobo and Mira's left coalition won 64 seats in the federal parliament; Zajedno 24; Seselj's Radicals 16. Milosevic was triumphant. (In the Serbian parliament, which was elected three years earlier, Milosevic's Socialists and Mira's YUL had 105 seats, Seselj's Radicals 81, and Draskovic's Serbian Renewal 45.)

But the results of the municipal elections were so close that another round was required.

The second round of local elections was held two weeks later. At nine in the evening, Milosevic received a telephone call with disturbing news: preliminary results showed Zajedno victories in thirty-four cities, including Belgrade. Opposition parties and their supporters were celebrating in the streets.

Initially, Milosevic was unfazed. In a phone conversation he told his Montenegrin ally, Momir Bulatovic, not to be alarmed. "It'll make the party do better in the next elections," Milosevic said. "The loss of the cities does not represent a problem for me, my position with respect to the outside world remains unchanged."

As the former Communist boss of Belgrade, Milosevic quickly understood the scope of the problem and promptly ordered that the results be reversed through the usual means—ballot box stuffing and other shenanigans. Throughout the night of November 18, covered by the brazen use of the legal system which they controlled, the Socialist operatives directed by Nikola Sainovic cooked the books, stuffed the boxes, changed the votes, while Socialist spokesmen cried fraud, charged major irregularities, and demanded that the results in Belgrade be annulled. (The Zajedno coalition won 70 of the 109 council seats.)

Denied victory, the opposition protested. For eleven frigid weeks, tens of thousands of Serbs marched daily through the streets of Belgrade, armed with whistles, drums, trumpets, cans filled with rocks, all sorts of noisemaking devices that unleashed deafening sounds Milosevic could not escape from. They pelted government buildings with eggs. Unflattering effigies of Slobo and Mira were dragged on floats through the city. Similar demonstrations were held simultaneously in thirty other cities.

When foreign ambassadors called on Milosevic, he insisted that in 96.5 percent of municipalities the election results were clear-cut and undisputed. "He painted a fantasy picture of Serbia as an advanced democracy," one envoy recalled.

Privately, however, Milosevic was in the blackest of moods, raving that he had no intention of living in a city run by his enemies. He couldn't escape the noise. Those who saw him frequently noticed that his whiskey intake had increased. He could, he said, crush the protesters at a stroke. His hard-core supporters in Kosovo asked to be allowed to come to Belgrade to mount counter-demonstrations, but he said no. Riot police were repeatedly sent into action in the capital and other cities.

The journalist Kati Marton, Richard Holbrooke's wife, concerned about the crackdown on the media, asked Milosevic what he thought about the demonstrations. Ah, he said, a "few thousand people" and students led by nationalist professors. "They are all Karadzic's soldiers who misled the children eager not to go to school." Marton noticed that Milosevic was smoking constantly; he had given up smoking before Dayton.

Increasingly, Milosevic sought counsel from men in his wife's circle. (She was on a brief visit to India at the time and could not provide real input.) Her friends proposed new elections. New balloting was ordered in all municipalities in which the Socialists had lost. They took place at various times in the last week of November; this time around, the Socialists won.

But this only provoked a new wave of popular anger. Vuk Draskovic appealed to God and the "international community," vowing he would challenge Milosevic to a duel. Two other Zajedno leaders—Zoran Djindjic and Vesna Pesic—provided the energy that turned Belgrade into a city of revolution. Much of the organized life—schools, universities, theaters—was halted. Professor Kosta

Cavoski, an otherwise soft-spoken and highly respected academic, addressed the protesting Novi Sad students with a warning to Milosevic: "The Greek philosopher Xenophanes said that a tyrant cannot be removed from power and remain alive. People say that one cannot kill a snake by grabbing her tail but by hitting her head. To resolve this [crisis], only one man is needed, a man with a sharp eye and a steady hand."

Even Milosevic's supporters were rebelling. Five members of the Supreme Court openly protested the use of the legal system to subvert the election results. Milosevic's minister of information, Aleksandar Tijanic, resigned in protest.

Tijanic, a friend of Mira's, went directly to the couple to tell them of his decision. The atmosphere was tense. Milosevic told Tijanic that his resignation was a cowardly act and a betrayal. "You know the Chinese proverb," Milosevic told the minister. "Cowards die thousands of deaths, a brave man dies once." Mira attempted to defend her friend, but her husband invoked an old Montenegrin saying to make his point: "Snow not merely covers the mountain, but also shows us the footprints of each wild animal."

But while the cities of Serbia were in an uproar, and police cordons surrounded the Dedinje district where Milosevic and other powerful people lived, television stations carried reports from distant places without ever mentioning what was happening in Serbia itself. The sole exception was the student-run Radio B92, which could be heard only in Belgrade. (By accident, a B92 reporter captured information on a police radio on November 25 when police operatives were reporting to their superior that they estimated 153,000 people were taking part in the protest in central Belgrade.) But even this tiny voice was then silenced.

The holiday season provided a grim reminder for most Serbs of their impoverished condition. On New Year's eve, most of the country found itself without electrical power when the generators at the Kolubara power plant broke down. In Belgrade, which was not affected by the breakdown, Milosevic and his wife were preparing to usher in the new year when they received a frantic call from their son. Marko complained that the New Year's party at his Madona disco in Pozarevac would turn into a commercial disaster if the electricity was not quickly restored. An extremely agitated Mira assailed her husband in the midst of the party, ranting and raving about "subversives and terrorists" whom she blamed for the power failure. Milosevic spent much of the night on the phone talking to senior officials; he was finally told that nothing could be done immediately because of the lack of spare parts. The power was restored a day later, but all key officials of the state power industry were dismissed a few weeks later.

Milosevic was convinced that he still had the support of Serbia's "silent majority," and his wife and her friends assured him that that was the case. They proposed a series of counterdemonstrations organized jointly by his Socialists and her YUL. The Socialists ferried party members from the provinces and provided them with a free lunch; Mira's newly rich supporters shut down their factories and told their workers that attendance at rallies was part of their job description. The theme of the counterdemonstration focused on a rather mild letter from Warren Christopher, the U.S. secretary of state, in which he told Milosevic that his country should honor the election results. The letter was interpreted by the official media as an insult to the "dignity" of the Serb nation. Milosevic, in his reply to Christopher, described the demonstrators as "vandals and political terrorists," whose actions were "not only undemocratic but are also not political and should not have the support of democratic and progressive individuals, institutions and governments in the world."

Milosevic announced that he had "asked the press" to publish both letters, and his propaganda machinery took on an anti-American tinge: "Serbia will never be ruled by a foreign hand" and "Serbia will never bow before anyone."

But Milosevic had reached a dead end. Pressures were coming from all sides: from Greece and the United States; from Patriarch Pavle, who led the largest religious procession Belgrade had ever seen.

On February 4, 1997, three months after the November 3 elections, Milosevic conceded defeat. The loss of Belgrade was particularly galling, but Milosevic privately assured his supporters that the opposition would rapidly demonstrate its political incompetence. "They have a plane but they don't have a pilot," he remarked scornfully.

The protests subsided. The opposition assumed elected offices. Zoran Djindjic, one of Zajedno's leaders, became the first non-Communist mayor of Belgrade since 1945.

But within months, the Zajedno coalition fell apart. Again the egos and rivalries of its leaders were exploited by Milosevic to sow dissension in their ranks. Milosevic was a master at promoting chaos and conflict among his enemies. He initiated a secret contact with Djindjic, then leaked the story. Djindjic was forced to admit after initial denials that he had indeed held a secret meeting with Milosevic. Draskovic and the other opposition politicians were furious.

By the summer of 1997, the opposition was in disarray and Milosevic had himself elected president of Yugoslavia in an adroit parliamentary maneuver, gaining a comfortable majority in the federal parliament. Opposition parties said the election was unconstitutional because their deputies had boycotted the session. In addition to taking Tito's title, Milosevic moved into Tito's palace, and traded his favorite BMW for Tito's Mercedes 600.

As Serbia was slowly dying, Mira's megalomania induced Slobodan to adopt the lifestyle of Tito and his royal predecessors and once again to resort to electoral fraud and brutal repression. But the partners in power were in for a shock: the crowds pelted their limousine with old shoes, a message that the couple were not fit for the shoes of the old dictator.

# 10

# The High Priest of Chaos

In the end, Kosovo was to become the field of Milosevic's greatest battle and another catastrophe for the Serb nation. In retrospect, this was inevitable since he was a politician who had been shaped by the events he appeared to master. There was no hard center to his rule; no strategy. He lived from day to day. The only discernable pattern was perpetual mayhem. Like a high priest of chaos, he caused mischief to exploit for his own purposes. Oblivious to misery and suffering, he promoted conflicts—in Slovenia, in Croatia, in Bosnia, in Serbia itself—to enlarge his power and to keep his own people distracted. Behind every war he masterminded there had been a parallel struggle against his opponents in Serbia itself. He existed in a sort of shining void between his presidential office and his palace, where no one questioned his judgment, his command of affairs, and where a steady stream of foreign visitors came to pay court to him. Although his country was too small and too poor to play a world role, he left a personal stamp on the age—indeed, a remarkable legacy of deliberate malevolence and destruction.

His lack of judgment, of instinctive balance, which had already manifested itself in a number of ways, ultimately led to the Kosovo war of 1999. That the leader of Serbia—its finances ruined, its economy in shambles, its diplomatic isolation virtually complete—should embark on that course with all its evident risks was sheer madness.

Early in 1996, just as the Dayton agreement was beginning to be implemented in Bosnia, Kosovo's sullen but still quiescent Albanian majority was mulling over the meaning of the accord. Though many of the province's writers, journalists, and professors stood behind Ibrahim Rugova's non-violent resistance, young people were restive. How long were they to give non-violence a chance? There were rumors of weapons coming from neighboring Albania. Violence was clearly coming to Kosovo.

In the fall of 1996, after student unrest in Pristina, Milosevic and Rugova reached an agreement about reopening Albanian schools, which had been closed for eight years, but nothing happened. Western officials who urged Milosevic to implement the agreement and proceed with political reforms were told that they had been misinformed. He said that he had restored order to Kosovo, which was now quiet. If outsiders did not meddle, it would remain so.

But only a few days in Kosovo made nonsense of his protestations. The province was indeed quiet, but it was the peace of the graveyard. The Albanian schools remained shut; there were no jobs; many people lived off remittances sent by relatives working abroad. Frustration and impatience with Serb police rule were on the rise. The situation, in short, was envenomed by neglect: neither Milosevic nor Rugova seemed to have exit strategies if it remained deadlocked. The mass anti-government demonstrations in Serbia in the winter of 1996–97 emboldened young ethnic Albanians in Kosovo, and student demonstrations gained momentum.

Furthermore, Rugova was undermined by Albanian president Sali Berisha, whose own family came from Kosovo. Berisha openly sided with the young Kosovar militants, telling Tirana Radio that "it is very clear for the Kosovo people that their freedom and rights will not come as a gift from anyone and their problems will not be solved in Tirana, Belgrade or Washington, London and Paris. They are solved and will be solved in Pristina and the towns and villages of Kosovo."

Milosevic, a master of tactical surprises, seemed paralyzed when it came to Kosovo. Having once stated his position many years earlier, he was to remain passive, reluctant to take risks and ultimately downright suicidal: as champion of the Serb national cause it was his fate to engineer its final destruction.

Western envoys who dealt with Milosevic on a regular basis felt a sense of frustration because countless rounds of talks about Kosovo never seemed to move the agenda along. Was his stonewalling a part of some clever strategy? Or did he sense that there was no halfway house between Serb and Albanian nationalism? In retrospect, the arrest of Kosovo's Communist leader Asem Vlassi and his colleagues back in 1989 had effectively severed all links between the two communities and left Milosevic without anyone on the Albanian side he could rely on. As the frequency of violent incidents in the province rose after Dayton, Milosevic was showing that he understood the need for conciliatory action by meeting Rugova; but he still did not perceive the need for speed or the potency of the protest cry, "Give us back our schools!"

In the fall of 1997, Milosevic was in an expansive but combative mood. He said student protests in Kosovo had been fanned from abroad. He saw outside interference in Montenegro, too, where his political enemy, Milo Djukanovic, had been elected president. He took almost perverse pleasure in reminding his visitors that two years after the Croat conquest of Krajina and the murder of so many civilians, nobody had been indicted by the Hague court. This, he added, even though Carl Bildt, the former Swedish prime minister who became Bosnia's political administrator after Dayton, had publicly blamed Tudjman for the atrocities. "After a couple of hours we broke off having made little or no impression on him [Milosevic]," one of the visitors said later.

Another election that fall, for the presidency of Serbia, lasted for more than two months before Milosevic could get his man elected.

Milosevic's ally Milan Milutinovic, and his opponents Vuk Draskovic and Vojislav Seselj, were in the running. Experts from the Organization for Security and Cooperation in Europe who monitored the vote and two runoffs described all three ballotings as "fundamentally flawed." All the standard Milosevic techniques—cooking the books, stuffing the boxes, changing the votes, denying television time to others—were employed to get Milutinovic elected. In the final runoff Milutinovic took 58 percent of the vote to Seselj's 38 percent. Milosevic's mastery over Yugoslavia and Serbia was assured.

But Milosevic's attention now focused on Kosovo, where the cancer of discontent that killed Yugoslavia had begun. Ever since 1989, his regime had tried to break the spirit of the Kosovo Albanians through constant pressure: raids on villages, perpetual searches and harassments, fiscal measures against Albanian shopowners, and outright plunder. How could Milosevic entice them into a dialogue? Rugova, perhaps because of his academic background, was more rigid than his political position permitted. He stuck to his guns even though his demand for independence had gained no foreign support. (The Western nations had agreed to follow the 1991 recommendation of a European Union panel of jurists under the chairmanship of Robert Badinter of France, which had said that the administrative borders of the six Yugoslav republics—which excluded Kosovo—should become international borders of those republics opting for independence.) A frustrated David Owen once described Rugova and his aides as total secessionists. "It's like talking to Scottish nationalists," Owen added. "These are not people you can do business with."

After Dayton, Rugova's dignified if futile persistence became an issue within the ethnic Albanian elite and one of his critics, Adem Demaqi, argued that Rugova's "single-minded ethnic nationalism" served Milosevic's purposes. Demaqi, a dynamic and forceful figure who had spent twenty-eight years in Communist jails for "nationalist agitation," was open to negotiations with Milosevic and repeatedly predicted a bloodbath in Kosovo if political progress was not made.

When impatient young Kosovars began to organize the Kosovo Liberation Army (KLA), they were effectively repudiating Rugova's policy. Their strategy was that the sooner they asserted themselves and struck at the Serbs, the better. In the winter of 1997–98, the KLA mounted isolated attacks on Serb police patrols that provoked swift retribution. They undoubtedly counted that retributions would heighten tensions and strengthen their cause.

That winter the peace of Kosovo was shattered—a circumstantial warning to Milosevic, at the very least, of the kind of trouble that was brewing. But instead of reaching out to the Kosovo Albanians and meeting at least their demands for school reopenings, Milosevic's obsessive single-mindedness led him in the opposite direction. Police reinforcements and army troops were dispatched to crush the rebellion with savage and exhibitionist violence.

The Kosovo rebellion began in February 1998, when Serb police killed fifty-three suspected KLA guerrillas and their families in retaliation for the killings of Serb policemen patrolling a lonely stretch of the road between Pristina and Podujevo. The massacre in the Drenica area touched off several days of violent demonstrations in Pristina, the regional capital.

The Serbs further inflamed the situation with the sight of bulldozers they used to bury the victims in a mass grave. The Albanians exhumed the mutilated bodies and buried them in Muslim tradition. Serb police, using helicopters and armored vehicles, continued their sweep against the KLA "terrorists" in the Drenica area. In Pristina, Albanians and Serbs alike staged protest marches and countermarches.

When the television pictures of the massacred Albanians reached Western audiences, they provoked revulsion as well as the specter of another Bosnia in the making. Madeleine Albright, now the U.S. secretary of state, publicly held Milosevic "responsible" for the atrocities and warned that "decisive and firm action" would be taken against Serbia if it continued its violent campaign in Kosovo. She dispatched Robert Gelbard, a senior U.S. diplomat, to Belgrade to confront Milosevic with photographic evidence of atrocities and mutilations.

Gelbard had initially described the KLA as "terrorists," but this time he bluntly told Milosevic that his policies were inflaming the province and could provoke an explosion that would affect the whole region. "You have done more than anyone to increase the membership of the KLA," Gelbard said, referring to the Drenica massacre.

Milosevic had never been spoken to like this before—let alone by a diplomat he barely knew. Holbrooke, whom he knew and liked, could have said such things, but not Gelbard.

Milosevic bluntly rejected all charges and refused to meet with Gelbard again. Gelbard traveled to Pristina, where he demanded that international forensic experts be allowed to examine the bodies of the victims.

At the end of March, the foreign ministers of six leading Western powers met in Berlin and called for an "urgent start" of negotiations between Belgrade and the Kosovo Albanians. Two days later, Milosevic again refused to meet with Gelbard and rejected offers of European mediation to help end the crisis.

Richard Holbrooke was subsequently pressed into service to try to bring Milosevic around.

With President Clinton consumed by an incendiary sex scandal in Washington, nobody in his inner circle focused on Kosovo. The matter was largely in the hands of Albright and the State Department bureaucracy. Albright pushed a resolution through the UN Security Council imposing an arms embargo on Yugoslavia. Only China abstained, insisting that the move would not help negotiations.

As the skirmishes in Kosovo intensified, Milosevic and Rugova met in Belgrade on May 15; Rugova, who was becoming increasingly marginalized in Kosovo, agreed to travel to Belgrade after he was promised a meeting with Clinton two weeks later.

Indeed, Rugova met briefly in the Oval Office on May 27 with Clinton and Vice President Gore, where he pleaded for direct American action to halt the escalating violence. Clinton made no concrete promises.

Meanwhile, the situation on the ground in Kosovo deteriorated day by day. Yugoslav special police detachments, ordered into action to "pacify" troublesome rebel strongholds, began shelling villages in the western areas of the province. Thousands of terrified villagers fled their homes and began a steady exodus across the border to Albania; this was the onset of a major demographic change planned by Milosevic.

On June 6, Foreign Minister Pascal Milo of Albania appealed for NATO intervention. The region, he said, was "on the brink of open war."

The next day, British prime minister Tony Blair phoned Clinton and Russian president Boris Yeltsin to discuss the possibility of using force in Kosovo. A week later, the Clinton administration froze Yugoslavia's assets in the United States and banned all U.S. investments in Yugoslavia. Western allies imposed a boycott on Yugoslav commercial flights. Public opinion in Washington, London, and Paris turned sour; there was less talk now of negotiations, far more of the military punishment needed to stop Milosevic. In Brussels, NATO defense ministers met to consider a range of options, but settled on the use of airpower. Albright led the war party by indicating that the United States would not seek UN endorsement for an attack on Milosevic. "A [Security Council] resolution may be desirable, but it is not required," she said on June 13.

Two days later, allied jet fighters staged a show of force along the Yugoslav border with Albania.

With mounting pressures from abroad and escalating violence in Kosovo itself, Milosevic had boxed himself into a position from which it was difficult to pull back. He went to Moscow on June 16 to talk to President Yeltsin, but their discussions seemed to make little headway even though the Russians publicly issued statements backing the Serb positions in Kosovo.

Did Milosevic see war coming? Or did the White House sex scandal and shaky foreign policy embolden him to be more defiant? We shall never know. But the Albanian leaders were deeply concerned, and Ibrahim Rugova issued an appeal, saying, "NATO should undertake all possible measures to prevent further massacres and protect the people of Kosovo."

NATO's secretary general, Javier Solana, responded by insisting that diplomats—not generals—should achieve a cease-fire in Kosovo. While he was negotiating with Richard Holbrooke, Milosevic ordered his forces to press their offensive against the KLA.

Milosevic had set his course. Once again he resorted to the Serb obsession with ancient myths to mobilize the nation for a holy mission and to co-opt his old enemies in the opposition: first Vojislav Seselj of the Radical Party, followed by Vuk Draskovic of the Serbian Renewal Movement. Both were named deputy prime ministers, as the protests and skirmishes of the previous years were conveniently forgotten.

He was finally unchallenged, the high priest of chaos using the threat of foreign intervention to smash every vestige of opposition to his rule.

By taking the Kosovo issue to NATO, Albright had slightly diluted America's position as formulated by President Bush in his 1992 Christmas warning to Milosevic that "in the event of a conflict caused by Serbian action, the United States will be prepared to employ military force against the Serbians in Kosovo and in Serbia proper." Bush's stand was reaffirmed by the Clinton administration on February 13, 1993, and Clinton felt the need to do so again on March 4, 1998.

But by June 1998, Clinton talked about authorizing and supporting "an accelerated planning process for NATO," making it clear that if there was to be a military operation in Kosovo, it would be carried out by NATO. What this meant in practice was that everything about the Kosovo affair was subject to decisions by an alliance that operated by consensus; yet, however cumbersome, this arrangement was preferable to the involvement of a far more cumbersome UN machinery.

The Western objectives were confused and opaque. They were articulated by Clinton: political autonomy for Kosovo within Serbia; no reconfiguration of international borders.

This fell short of the Kosovo Albanians' demand for independence, while deeply distressing Milosevic. As a result, the policy

NATO was trying to enforce did not enjoy the support of the majority of Kosovars and it was strenuously opposed by a majority of the Serbs. The KLA, which by the summer of 1998 had almost 40 percent of the province's territory under its control, was hell-bent on independence; autonomy was not an option even for their leader, Ibrahim Rugova.

Holbrooke, shuttling between Belgrade and Pristina, seemed at one point to be making some headway toward brokering talks. But his hopes were shot down by KLA spokesman Jacup Krasniqi, who ruled out KLA participation in negotiations with Milosevic.

American strategists at this stage made two assumptions which later turned out to be wholly wrong.

One was a serious misreading of Milosevic the man. "A lot of people said a few bombs would do it," several senior officials confided later. Albright accepted this assessment and publicly talked of Milosevic as a "schoolyard bully" who would immediately back down if challenged.

A more serious misreading was based on the belief that the American experience with Bosnia provided the road map for Kosovo. The men who cobbled together the Dayton accords argued that the same could be replicated—including Russia's cooperation—and that Kosovo would in effect be turned into an international protectorate policed by NATO troops.

It was difficult to concentrate minds on Kosovo. The president was too preoccupied to think about it—he was facing the prospect of impeachment. Midterm elections were approaching and few politicians showed any enthusiasm for a military venture in the Balkans. Milosevic understood this and ordered a major military offensive against the KLA. Serb artillery and tanks assailed scores of rebel-held villages as various diplomatic mediators desperately sought to arrange a cease-fire.

"Milosevic assured us that the military action has come to a halt," Austrian diplomat Albert Rohan said following a meeting between a European Union delegation and the Yugoslav president on July 30. But there was no halt in the fighting. The Serb forces were, of course, far stronger and better equipped than KLA guerrillas.

They moved vigorously to recapture the Drenica area, forcing thousands of Albanian civilians to seek security in the mountains. Christopher Hill, the U.S. ambassador in neighboring Macedonia, who was visiting Kosovo, reported on August 3 that the province was on the "verge of humanitarian catastrophe," with tens of thousands of people hiding in the woods.

Hopes flared a little when Hill announced that he had persuaded Rugova to enter new talks with the Serbs, but once again the KLA shot the effort down. The detailed story of the diplomatic maneuverings that summer and autumn is relevant here only insofar as it exposes the uncertainties, the anxieties, and the divisions of various Western capitals at a critical moment in the process that was to culminate in a European war in the last year of the century. It was clear that all diplomatic prevarications could not prevent Milosevic from reimposing his grip on Kosovo. It was an old story. The men with guns control events; the ordinary people suffer.

At the end of September 1998, another massacre of Albanians took place at Gornje Obrinje: sixteen people—ten of them women, children, and elderly—were found dead by gunshot wounds at close range. The Serbs also moved in force into the separatist stronghold of Malisevo and the surrounding mountains.

The latest massacre provoked another international outcry and the UN Security Council passed a resolution on September 23, demanding an immediate cease-fire, an end to attacks on civilians, withdrawal of special Serb police units, and the resumption of a political dialogue. By October, Albright and other advocates of the use of airpower against Milosevic had gained the upper hand, despite reservations expressed by military specialists: NATO warned Milosevic that it would launch air attacks on Serbia if he did not comply with UN demands. Clinton, in a letter to senior senators, revealed that NATO air strikes were to be massive and progressively expanding in scope.

Again, Holbrooke was dispatched to Belgrade to ask Milosevic to halt his military campaign in Kosovo. Holbrooke had no carrots, only the stick of air strikes. At the end of marathon negotiations—the talks lasted nine days—Milosevic agreed to withdraw the bulk of his forces, permit sixteen hundred unarmed international inspectors into Kosovo, and sanction overflights of NATO spy planes to monitor the accord. An additional "confidence building" measure was agreed: Yugoslav officers were to be sent to the U.S. base at Vicenza, Italy, while an equal number of NATO officers would be based within the Yugoslav Defense Ministry.

In exchange, however, Milosevic insisted on the lifting of the order giving NATO commanders the authority to launch strikes immediately. The significance of this seemingly opaque request to Milosevic was enormous: once the order was lifted, the Americans would have to seek new approval by political representatives in the NATO council.

The Western allies, however, refused to remove the order and instead agreed to "suspend" it, not a meaningful change from Milosevic's point of view. When Holbrooke informed him the next day about the decision, Milosevic was furious. He had been "double-crossed" once, at Dayton, he said. "Not again."

According to one American diplomat, Milosevic considered the NATO decision "a declaration of war."

Milosevic had reached a decision of his own, yet he did not tip his hand. Holbrooke and other Americans left the meeting speculating whether the Serb leader was playing for time or preparing for war. Their assessment was that it was the first: Milosevic needed time to create political cover for himself the way he had done before Dayton.

That was a misjudgment. It was at this point that the drift to war became irreversible. Milosevic realized that he was being asked to capitulate in Kosovo and that he could not do it. Instead of withdrawing forces, he ordered that reinforcements and equipment be quietly sent into Kosovo. He also ordered a buildup around Kosovo—Operation Horseshoe—which was quickly detected by allied intelligence.

A few days later, when NATO commander General Wesley K. Clark arrived in Belgrade to discuss implementing the accord, Milosevic was defiant, gravely genial, and easygoing.

"That was not agreed," he stated categorically when Clark pointed out which units had to be withdrawn from Kosovo. "We have no extra forces."

Clark mentioned the possibility of air strikes. "NATO must do what it must do," Milosevic replied.

This was a very odd statement to make. Yet Clark and other Americans believed Milosevic was still playing for time. Which he was, pretending to be reluctantly dragged in the direction of compromise. He allowed the unarmed international observers, headed by the American diplomat William G. Walker, into Kosovo; but that was his insurance policy against NATO attacks. The presence of observers allowed the completion of Operation Horseshoe before the air strikes began on March 24, 1999.

He also carried out a purge of the Yugoslav Army command, dismissing "unreliable" officers. Among those who incurred the wrath of this unforgiving man were the chief of staff, General Momcilo Perisic, who had expressed reservations about the confrontational course with the United States and NATO, and his internal security chief, Jovica Stanisic, and the military intelligence chief, General Alexander Dimitrijevic, who both had privately questioned Milosevic's Kosovo policy in general.

On the ground in Kosovo, the fighting escalated. On December 14, 1998, more than thirty Albanian guerrillas were killed in a five-hour-long battle near Malisevo. The next day, the guerrillas slaughtered six young Serbs in a bar in the town of Pec and killed three members of a Serb police patrol outside Pristina. The Serbs responded with a new offensive on December 20. The "October Agreement" was not holding.

And yet most intelligence assessments that reached Clinton and other top officials that winter suggested that Milosevic was "susceptible to outside pressure" and that he was prepared to make a deal on Kosovo, including the acceptance of a "provisional status, with the final resolution to be determined" later, "as long as he remained the undisputed leader in Belgrade." This was an unfortunate assumption, as later events would prove.

But while misreading Milosevic's calculations and the reality of his political standing in Serbia, intelligence analysts correctly interpreted the secret military buildup. Milosevic, the analysts predicted, was preparing to purge the province of its Albanian population. CIA director George Tenet, testifying before the Senate Armed Services Committee five weeks before the start of NATO air strikes on Yugoslavia, predicted heavier fighting in Kosovo in the spring, "which will result in another humanitarian crisis, possibly greater in scale than" in 1998—"which created 250,000 refugees."

The KLA held out, amazingly, until well into January 1999, notwithstanding Milosevic's self-confident October assertion that they were two weeks away from annihilation. The insurgents continued small-scale actions, descending from the mountains to attack the Serbs' rear or to cut off their supplies. Supported by an Albanian diaspora in North America, Switzerland, and Germany, they were buying weapons and improving their training. Moreover, the world's mightiest military alliance was on their side. To be fair to Milosevic, the KLA leaders had no interest in cease-fire agreements; it was their intention all along to keep the situation inflamed.

Milosevic troops once again moved in force to root out the KLA. Once again, a massacre of civilians provoked an outcry in a world of round-the-clock cable news television. On January 18, the bodies of forty-five men, women, and children were found in the village of Racak; witnesses said a small group of hooded men dressed in black had carried out the killings. Arriving at the scene the same day, William Walker blamed the Serbian government for the atrocities, which, he said, looked "like an execution."

Milosevic, who insisted the victims were "terrorists" killed in combat, was furious. He ordered Walker declared persona non grata. (A few days later, after an international outcry, Milosevic decided to "freeze" the expulsion order.)

Two days after the bodies were discovered, Albright dramatically changed the Milosevic-Holbrooke October Agreement. Milosevic was not only asked to capitulate in Kosovo but also to relinquish control of the province to NATO's military.

Pentagon chiefs were opposed to any deployment of American forces in Kosovo, but Albright prevailed, and the president accepted her recommendation. British prime minister Blair, who had insisted that a forceful action was required to stop Milosevic—ground troops if necessary—was comforted when Clinton informed him that the United States was prepared to deploy American ground troops to enforce peace once an agreement was reached. Privately, Blair had long expressed his frustration with Clinton's vacillations and lack of resolve. This was to be the pattern throughout the Kosovo crisis: Blair insisting that the allies stay the course and Clinton following his lead.

Milosevic's answer was to escalate military operations inside Kosovo. General Clark flew to Belgrade to urge Milosevic to extend the October cease-fire agreement, but was rebuffed. Milosevic, Clark said after seven hours of talks, "is determined to go his own way." Clark recounted a red-faced Milosevic's description of the Racak massacre as a provocation. "This is not a massacre," he said. "It was staged. These people were terrorists."

When Clark warned that he might soon be ordered "to move aircraft" against Serbia, Milosevic exploded. "You are a war criminal to be threatening Serbia," he told the NATO commander.

Albright called for immediate air strikes in January, but the British and the French demanded another diplomatic effort. Albright interpreted the Anglo-French move as the Europeans' desire to have a peace conference as their equivalent of Dayton.

The talks opened on February 6 at the former French royal hunting lodge at Rambouillet, outside Paris. The agenda, however, was set by Albright. The warring parties were invited to sign an accord hastily prepared under Albright's supervision—not to negotiate. She set a two-week deadline. But both sides refused to sign.

The Albanians insisted that the accord should include a clear statement that a referendum on independence would be held after three years of autonomy guaranteed by NATO troops. On this point,

KLA representatives—particularly Adem Demaqi, who had emerged as their leader—were unbending. Moreover, nobody seemed to consider the Serb demands with respect to the NATO troops in Kosovo; Milosevic had agreed to grant autonomy to Kosovo but would not agree to the presence of foreign troops on Yugoslav soil.

Rambouillet was a debacle for Albright. The Albanian refusal to sign left her with no reason to demand immediate air strikes on Serbia. After Rambouillet fell apart, a follow-up conference was called in Paris three weeks later.

Milosevic, who was a central figure at Dayton, did not even bother to attend Rambouillet. His mistrust of the West was now profound. The arrest in Britain on October 16, 1998, of Chile's former dictator, General Augusto Pinochet, on criminal charges brought before a magistrate in Spain, was a warning that he might be arrested one day for his actions as Serbia's leader. His propaganda machinery had already begun to prepare the population for the coming showdown, presenting the likely outcome at Rambouillet as the final loss of sacred Kosovo ground, made palatable by diplomatic niceties. Milosevic's case seemed strengthened by Albright's image as a Serbophobe from her days as America's UN ambassador. Amid the groundswell of patriotic euphoria, nobody asked how—or why—Serbia had come to the brink of war with the world's mightiest military alliance. Who was responsible?

The European Union envoy, Wolfgang Petritsch of Austria, was among a dozen diplomats who flew to Belgrade seeking to engage Milosevic in a dialogue that could break the impasse. Milosevic's reactions stunned Petritsch. "He only wants to believe what he wants to believe," the Austrian said later. "He is not ready in any way to engage even in a meaningful discussion about alternatives and what can be done. He never refers to any of the issues that are of real relevance."

In Washington, Clinton held a meeting in the Oval Office with the visiting Italian prime minister, Massimo D'Alema, in early March. With his impeachment travails finally over—he was acquitted by the Senate on February 12—Clinton could at last focus on the problem of Kosovo.

A skeptical D'Alema asked Clinton about the exit strategy if Milosevic remained unbending and NATO failed to bomb him into submission.

"What will happen then?"

Clinton's national security adviser Samuel Berger replied: NATO will keep bombing.

D'Alema later told Italian journalists, "They have no exit strategy."

On March 18 in Paris, four Kosovo Albanians signed the agreement they had refused to sign at Rambouillet. The unyielding Adem Demaqi had been replaced with a younger and more flexible KLA leader, Hashim Thaci.

The Serbs did not sign.

The brief ceremony at the International Conference Center in Paris committed the United States and NATO to war. Albright expressed satisfaction: she had gotten the Europeans to agree to the use of force and the Kosovo Albanians to accept her settlement proposal. However, the foreign ministers of Britain, France, and Germany—Robin Cook, Hubert Vedrine, and Joschka Fischer—immediately proposed to fly to Belgrade for a final appeal to Milosevic. Albright disagreed. They all agreed to send Holbrooke instead.

What dark thoughts were harbored by this man who had earned the reputation of being deadly treacherous and double-faced? In a battle for his very life, Milosevic's actions were shot through with contradictions and uncertainties, but nobody could be sure that this was not done deliberately to confuse everybody. He was aware of a discord within the new Contact Group (the United States, Britain, France, Russia, Germany, and Italy). The foreign ministers of Russia and Greece had called on him in mid-March, looking for grounds of possible compromise. Holbrooke and Christoper Hill saw him several times, as did various other envoys.

Hill was struck by the fatalism of the Serb leader as he knowingly led his nation into a catastrophe. "You are a superpower," Hill later quoted Milosevic as saying. "You can do what you want. If you want to say Sunday is Wednesday, you can. It is all up to you." When

Hill said he had personally observed Serb atrocities committed in Kosovo, including the burning of Albanian homes and shops, Milosevic seemed upset. "There is no excuse for that, even if the Serbs in Kosovo are very angry," Milosevic said, starting to pace around. "I accept responsibility. One of the most important tasks of a democracy is to protect its minorities."

What was remarkable in all these diplomatic dealings as well as in military actions in Kosovo was that one man, Milosevic, was holding all the threads of power in his hands, refusing to take his ministers and generals into his confidence, micromanaging the entire affair on the Serb side without any institutional or personal restraints. There was no one in his entourage, apart from Mira, who could tell him that his calculations were reckless and potentially fatal. General Perisic later described him as not living in reality, rejecting "competent opinions and proposals," and resorting to "fraud and lies . . . to change and shape the people's perception of reality."

Milosevic was surrounded, the general said, by two categories of people: loyal executors "without sufficient personal integrity," and "those who hold no office or position but who know and, unfortunately, can do everything," the latter being a pointed reference to Mira and her friends. Perisic was dismissed as chief of the general staff when he refused to blindly follow "sometimes imprudent and fatal decisions." Two other top officials who shared his views—the chiefs of the secret police and of military intelligence—were also summarily fired. How could such a man, not stupid and indeed quite cunning, disregard the information and advice of his three top security officials on a matter as grave as a war with NATO?

Milosevic did not need advice. He was sure of himself. He seemed to have convinced himself that NATO would not bomb Yugoslavia, that the West was bluffing. When Hill suggested that the bombing was a wholly realistic option if he refused to accept the American conditions, Milosevic retorted:

"Anyone who does that—bomb—is going to spend the rest of his life on a psychiatric couch."

Yet he had calculated all along that even if Yugoslavia were assailed from the air, the West could not sustain a bombing campaign for very long. Moreover, the Americans lacked the resolve for a ground invasion as well as the requisite tolerance for casualties. He thought he had several options for seizing the initiative.

There was always Bosnia as a potential source of trouble, even though the Bosnian Serb leaders were wary of Milosevic and their troops were demoralized. Another of his terrible options was to destabilize Macedonia, the tiny landlocked country between Serbia and Greece which was home to a sizable ethnic Albanian minority. This was a part of his calculations when he ordered Operation Horseshoe the previous October as the war loomed larger. An even more terrible scenario—which was within his reach—was to provoke a wider Balkan war through a severe simultaneous destabilization of both Macedonia and Bosnia.

Indeed, Macedonia played a significant role in Milosevic's calculations in the winter of 1999. Both he and his wife had always believed that, sooner or later, Macedonia would have to rejoin the Yugoslav federation. They had supported a strong and militant Serb minority in Macedonia that could be used for mischief making.

Initially, Milosevic had conspired with Greek premier Constantine Mitsotakis and other Greek politicians to divide Macedonia between the two countries. In 1992 he had publicly proposed a union between Serbia and Greece as a maneuver to that end. Without outside help, U.S. Ambassador Warren Zimmermann warned at the time, "Little Mac is doomed to be crushed between the two big hamburger buns of Greece and Serbia." The Greeks were restrained by their NATO and EU membership, and by President Clinton's decision in early 1993 to deploy some seven hundred U.S. ground troops in Macedonia as part of a UN observation force.

"Mark my words, we'll meet again over the Albanians," Milosevic had warned the Macedonian leaders during their May 1993 meeting on the banks of Lake Ohrid.

Macedonia indeed is Europe's most fragile country. It is the strategic hub of the Balkans, the only area of the peninsula that allows easy north-south and east-west access. Ever since the former Yugoslav republic proclaimed its independence in the fall of 1991, its neighbors have tried to thwart its progress. Bulgaria, to the east, has always insisted the Macedonians are not a nation but are rather ethnic Bulgarians. Serbia, to the north, regards Macedonians as "southern Serbs." Greece, to the south, had objected to Macedonia's very existence on grounds that the Macedonian Slavs had not only appropriated the name of an ancient Greek kingdom but had also hijacked the heritage of Alexander the Great. A Greek official summed up the contemptuous sentiment of Macedonia's neighbors in this way: "Why do the French call fruit cocktail a *macédoine de fruits*? Because it is a mishmash, a mixture of everything. Macedonia is a counterfeit nation."

But the real problem of Macedonia is its delicate ethnic balance. More than half of Macedonia's 2.1 million population are Slav Macedonians in whose hands political power is concentrated. But almost one-third are ethnic Albanians, who are concentrated in the west along the border with Albania and Kosovo. The Macedonian capital, Skopje, is the largest Albanian city in the world. And although the Macedonian government has had a more flexible attitude toward its Albanian citizens than did the Serbs in Kosovo—indeed, some Albanians are included in the administration—distrust between the two communities remains intense. The Macedonians regard their country as a Macedonian national state and do not welcome any influx of Albanian refugees that would change the delicate ethnic balance. Albanians in Macedonia had attempted to proclaim independence of their lands in western Macedonia in 1994; it was brutally crushed. Most of them are fervent KLA supporters.

A collapse of order in Macedonia would create a security vacuum and touch off a land grab that could provoke a larger war involving Greece and Turkey.

Precisely these fears have been at the heart of American policy toward Kosovo for a decade. They were behind President Bush's Christmas warning to Milosevic in 1992 as well as President Clinton's decision to start an air war against Yugoslavia over the Kosovo problem. Clinton's most convincing public argument—at least one that resonated with the public—was human suffering in Kosovo. But if there was a real American strategic interest in the territory of the former Yugoslavia, then that was the determination to prevent the wider Balkan conflagration that any forcible border changes would provoke by reviving various old territorial claims.

The last few days before the war began in March 1999 were confusing and hectic. The Yugoslav military intensified its attacks on KLA guerrillas in the eastern parts of Kosovo, sending thousands of Albanian refugees fleeing through the Djeneral Jankovic valley into Macedonia. International monitors of the Organization for Security and Cooperation in Europe evacuated Kosovo on March 19, and moved into neighboring Macedonia, also through Djeneral Jankovic.

On March 22, Milosevic flatly rejected Holbrooke's final warning. But while the two men were talking, the Yugoslav media made public Milosevic's letter to the foreign ministers of Britain and France, which said in part:

> You say that large movements of our security forces are a matter of great concern. If you think they are a matter of concern for the separatists who would like to take away part of the territory of Serbia and Yugoslavia, they of course should be concerned. If you have in mind some possible aggressors outside of Yugoslavia, this should be a matter of concern to them too. Is it really possible for a normal person to think that somebody who is being threatened will not show the intention to defend himself?

Lieutenant General Edward G. Anderson, the director of strategic plans and policy for the Joint Chiefs of Staff, accompanied Holbrooke and met separately with the new Yugoslav chief of staff, General Dragoljub Ojdanic. "It appears to me that there is a considerable amount of misunderstanding" in Belgrade, Anderson said. Later that day, Milosevic fired a senior general who had attended the meeting with Anderson.

Meanwhile, Western diplomats and their families were ordered to evacuate Yugoslavia. Only Italy and Greece kept their missions open with skeleton staffs. The Yugoslav government called up the reservists as part of its mass mobilization.

Holbrooke, after his final meeting with Milosevic on March 22, declared upon his return to Brussels: "It was Milosevic who deliberately and consciously chose to trigger the bombing of his own country."

In Belgrade, Milosevic was silent and kept himself out of sight. His Montenegrin ally, Prime Minister Momir Bulatovic, addressed the nation to proclaim a state of emergency. The war was imposed on the Serb nation, he said. Milosevic indeed did not start the war, but he was the main actor in creating the situation which made war possible—and his final misjudgments converted possibility into certainty.

Parliamentary deliberation, televised live and full of defiance and bravado, provoked a furious uproar of violent jingoism and patriotism on the part of some sections of Serbian society. Milosevic's ally, President Milan Milutinovic of Serbia, proclaimed his people "moral winners" in the coming war with the West. An anchorman on the main evening news program assailed Western media for broadcasting lies about the Kosovo violence; it quoted a government spokesman describing some thirty thousand fleeing Albanian refugees as "just people out for a walk." But most people were worried. Shoppers crowded into stores and markets in Belgrade and other cities to buy food and essential items. Lines of cars at gasoline stations stretched for blocks.

The next day, in Serbia's sister republic of Montenegro, the parliament rejected the state of emergency proclaimed by the federal government of Yugoslavia. It was a blunt rejection of Milosevic's war policy. President Milo Djukanovic, a longtime opponent of Milosevic, desperately sought to keep his republic out of the conflict.

Serbia and Montenegro were on a collision course.

On Wednesday, March 24, Russian prime minister Yevgeny Primakov was halfway across the Atlantic for a scheduled visit to Washington when he got word from Vice President Gore of the imminent attack on Yugoslavia. He ordered a midair change of course and returned to Moscow to dramatize Russia's opposition to NATO's air campaign.

A few hours before the attack started at 11:17 P.M. local time, the authorities ordered a change in television programming. A much-advertised comedy featuring Arnold Schwarzenegger was replaced by a Yugoslav-made epic about the first battle of Kosovo.

# 11

# The End of the Caravan of Dreams

The principal image of the war was one of traumatized and forlorn-looking Albanian refugees languishing in appalling conditions on a stretch of no-man's-land between Serbia and Macedonia: weary, demoralized, cold, hungry, abandoned.

As the first bombs and cruise missiles fell, all Serbian restraints vanished and the premonitory fears of Western analysts about Operation Horseshoe became a grim reality. Milosevic would later insist that "before the bombing there were no refugees" from Kosovo, that the Albanians had fled to escape NATO air strikes. The truth is that Milosevic ordered the Serbian Army to move in full force against the remnants of the KLA. And that meant the annihilation of Kosovo society.

"With the [NATO] bombs, the Serbs turned on the people," an Albanian resident of a town called Stimlje recalled. On the night of March 24, "they started to burn Stimlje and shoot with different weapons." They went from house to house and didn't check if anyone was inside—they just shot and burned, recalled Fehmi Baftiu, the representative of the Mother Teresa charity in the town. "For five days without stopping, every night they shot weapons and burned and beat people in the street, and the people ran until Stimlje was nearly empty. The earth was burning, from the ground and from the sky, and it seemed there was nowhere to hide." Much of the violence was done by local Serbs, he said. "I know the names and the faces." Other villages and towns were similarly attacked, their inhabitants murdered or sent into panicked flight abroad. Fierce NATO bombardments no doubt added to the plight of Kosovo civilians and prompted some of them to flee. But they were not the principal cause.

The most sensible policy for the Western alliance would have been to move decisively in a major way to prevent the suffering and bloodshed. But that did not happen. President Clinton had ruled out a ground invasion.

Milosevic felt he had no choice but to go to war against the strongest military alliance in the world. He calculated that if he was to survive, he would have to take action to divide the allies and destabilize the region.

The Western alliance calculated wrongly when it believed Milosevic would sue for peace after a few days of bombing. It was taken by surprise by the rising tide of Serb resistance: the air strikes, far from causing dissension, united the Serbs behind their Kosovo, their army, and their leader. The spirit of defiance and contempt was captured by a "target" logo which Serbs began drawing everywhere in a taunt to NATO's missiles.

Milosevic's calculations—the calculation behind Operation Horseshoe—also proved wrong: the tide of refugees neither destabilized Yugoslavia's fragile southern neighbors nor destroyed the unity of the alliance. The refugees were flown into Western Europe and North America, or settled in camps inside Albania and Macedonia.

Like their ancestors, who seized Kosovo from the Turks in 1912, Serbian troops indiscriminately shelled villages, while paramilitary vigilantes aided by Milosevic's special police units terrorized the population. Thousands of women, children, and old men were packed onto trains and ferried to the border. Hundreds of thousands of refugees reaching neighboring Albania, Macedonia, and Montenegro told tales of atrocities—of massacres, rape, and plunder that provoked worldwide revulsion. The town of Pec, the seat of the ancient Serbian Orthodox Patriarchate, was cleared of Albanian residents by paramilitaries wearing Australian bush hats and bright green camouflage uniforms and moving methodically from house to house. Refugees interviewed by international rescue workers said they had been given a few minutes to leave their homes. Many were stripped of all documents, which meant that they would find it difficult, if not impossible, to return to a Serb-controlled Kosovo. Once again, as in 1912, the province's ethnic balance had changed within several weeks: more than 800,000 ethnic Albanians had been driven out of the province; another 400,000 to 600,000 had fled into the mountains; and an estimated 10,000 people were killed.

Milosevic insisted that "the refugees were fleeing in panic because of the war against the [KLA] terrorists and also because of disinformation horror stories being spread by the terrorists, which then became a word of mouth and forced even more people to join the exodus."

He conceded in an interview that "bad things happened [in Kosovo] as they did with both sides during the Vietnam war, or any war for that matter." But he blamed the abuses on paramilitary irregulars. "We are not angels nor are we the devils you have made us out to be. Our regular forces are highly disciplined. The paramilitary irregular forces are a different story." He insisted that only individual houses were torched and "not whole villages as we saw on TV in Vietnam."

Milosevic tried every trick the imagination could conceive of, every subtle opening on the diplomatic stage, to weaken Western resolve and to bring about a pause in the air war, knowing that once the attacks were halted it would be very difficult to restart them. He was his own public relations general. He brought the longtime Kosovo Albanian leader Ibrahim Rugova to Belgrade to negotiate a new autonomy for Kosovo, advancing cosmetic concessions. He was prepared, he told foreign intermediaries, to pull his army from Kosovo and to accept an international presence under UN auspices, but adamantly ruled out NATO troops. His regime, he insisted, had never discriminated against the Muslims or any other ethnic minority. “It has been our philosophy from the very beginning. In Kosovo as well. Equality was the basic principle in Kosovo,” he kept repeating.

The downing on March 27 of an America F-117A stealth fighter, the most advanced in the U.S. arsenal, was the only opportunity for the Serb media to make a little inessential hay. (The pilot of the aircraft was rescued by an American team six hours later.) On March 31, the Serbs captured three American soldiers on the Macedonian border, displayed them on Belgrade Television, and threatened to put them on trial.

On April 6, Milosevic announced a unilateral cease-fire in Kosovo, but NATO responded by intensifying its aerial attacks. Four days later, he announced a “partial withdrawal” of troops and police from Kosovo, saying they had completed their operations against the Albanian secessionists. Clinton cautiously welcomed the announcement, saying, “I think we have to do better, but any little daylight, any little progress is better than it was the day before.” Albright publicly distanced herself from this view. “If ever there was a definition of a half-measure, this is it,” she said.

In the second half of April, Milosevic received two Americans with an eye to relaying his views to the American public. One of them was Dr. Ronald Hatchett, director of the Center for International Studies at the University of St. Thomas in Houston, Texas. His trip to Belgrade was arranged with the help of American Serbs. The other was the veteran journalist Arnaud de Borchgrave, editor in chief of United Press International.

De Borchgrave found Milosevic relaxed and pleasant. In the midst of their two-hour meeting in an ordinary-looking empty house in Belgrade, the piercing sound of sirens announced the coming of NATO planes.

“I guess we should go into a shelter,” de Borchgrave said.

"Good lord, no," Milosevic replied, laughing. "They don't know where I am."

"I've heard that you carry a cell phone, that they know precisely where you are located all the time," de Borchgrave said.

"I never carry a cell phone," Milosevic said. "It's the other guys who carry them."

Hatchett, who had his interview filmed, subsequently spent two hours with Milosevic and his wife in private conversation. He noted that Milosevic was slightly unbalanced and realized that his sugar level was extremely high. Hatchett gave him his own medication to bring the level down—both men suffer from the same type of diabetes. Hatchett also described the televised pictures of the plight of Kosovo refugees. Mira's eyes, Hatchett recalled, were filled with tears. Hatchett thought that Milosevic saw himself in an epic struggle in which, Milosevic insisted, justice was on his side.

In Milosevic's conversations, there were echoes of Prince Lazar's fatalism and of the unbending self-righteousness of the old myths. He asserted that he was waging a "life and death issue of national honor and sovereignty." The Rambouillet plan was an American "diktat." He had to turn it down because he could not accept "anything that looks like an occupation."

"We have never thought that we could defeat NATO, an alliance of some 700 million people armed with the most advanced and sophisticated weaponry in the world," Milosevic said. But he explained his calculation, addressing the American people directly: "You are not willing to sacrifice lives to achieve our surrender; but we are willing to die to defend our rights as an independent sovereign state."

The refusal of the U.S. House of Representatives to endorse the air war by its 213 to 213 vote on April 28 had raised his hopes that the allied unity would soon be fractured. It coincided with the visit to Belgrade of the Reverend Jesse Jackson, Congressman Rod Blagojevich (D-Ill.), and a group of American religious leaders seeking the release of the three American servicemen captured by the Serbs on the Macedonian border a month earlier.

Milosevic was calm and businesslike. When Blagojevich, a Serb American from Chicago's Northwest Side, greeted him in Serbian, Milosevic replied in English. The guests were given a history lesson. "There hasn't been a generation of Serb men in this century that has not fought a war," Milosevic said. He could not understand America and England acting as though they were violating a sacred space in the Serb epics and forgetting that only the Serbs, faithful to their history, had stood by the Western Allies in both world wars while the Croats, the Albanians, and the others fought on the side of the Germans. He was waging two wars, an air war and a media war in which he was portrayed as Satan.

Jackson responded that he could shed the Satan image by making a "bold move" and releasing the three American soldiers.

"You have it in your power to make a bold move," Jackson said.

"I'll think about this," Milosevic replied.

Jackson said that public support for the air war was weakening and pointed out the 213–213 House vote. His son, Representative Jesse Jackson Jr. (D-Ill.), had voted against the administration. "Your homeboy," Jackson said, pointing at Blagojevich, "he was the swing vote."

Milosevic did not understand the term "homeboy," and asked the interpreter for help. It suddenly dawned on him that Blagojevich could have defeated the Clinton administration had he voted, and he assumed the "homeboy's" vote would have been the "Serbian way."

"You missed the vote?" he asked, incredulously.

"I had to in order to come here to see you," the congressman replied, without volunteering that he had been a strong supporter of the administration's war effort and would not have voted "the Serbian way" anyway.

"We were there to get our soldiers freed," Blagojevich later recalled. "But from that point on I sensed complete disdain directed at me, and he turned away from me."

A former Cook County prosecutor, Blagojevich said Milosevic reminded him of "a defendant who had prepared himself never to admit to anything and who had repeated his version of events consistently so that he essentially came to believe in it." When the issue of rape of Albanian women in Kosovo was raised, Milosevic did not know the word "rape," but when it was translated he became enraged. "Serb men do not like Albanian women! This is not true."

After more than three hours of conversations, Blagojevich concluded in his own mind that Milosevic did not expect to lose the war. "He talked contemptuously of the air campaign, saying, 'They are not even scratching us in Kosovo, they are just hitting the civilians,' but I also sensed that beneath his outward calm he was quite stressed," Blagojevich recalled. "He seemed like a clever guy in a tactical sort of way, but he had no global view, no big picture that I could detect."

When the meeting adjourned, Milosevic and Jackson took a walk alone in the garden of the White Palace.

"How about me giving you just one guy," said Milosevic. "The one who has a wife and young child."

"You can't do that," replied Jackson. "He's white and it will be perceived as very cynical." The other two imprisoned soldiers were of Hispanic background. "The three of them came here together and all three should leave together."

Milosevic choreographed the prisoners' release so that it would achieve the maximum impact and preempt the Sunday morning news shows in the United States while leading the Sunday evening television news in Western Europe. The surreal moment was broadcast worldwide on May 2—the moment that revealed the full scope of his cynicism—when Milosevic, his eyes closed, stood in prayer with Jackson and the other clerics in his Belgrade office, holding hands as Jackson quoted lines from Isaiah about the lion laying down with the lamb. How could anyone compare Milosevic to Hitler, this man who was magnanimously releasing the three soldiers into the hands of the religious leaders, and who cast himself as an innocent lamb showing generosity toward the fierce lion? A triumphant Jackson, having obtained the soldiers' release, called for a temporary bombing halt to "give peace a chance."

Mira joined the public relations effort to personally defend her family against charges of corruption leveled by British foreign secretary Robin Cook, who had said that she and her children were not in Yugoslavia under bombs but instead hiding in one of five villas the family had acquired abroad. In an open letter to Cook, Mira stated that her children were patriotic and courageous and that her son was "in uniform." Ending her letter "very disrespectfully yours," she denied that she and her husband owned any property abroad.

In early May, Milosevic permitted Ibrahim Rugova, who had consistently opposed the bombing, to travel to Italy, apparently calculating that the pacifist Kosovo leader would speak out publicly against the NATO campaign. Milosevic's scheme was frustrated by Albright, who promptly warned Italian foreign minister Lamberto Dini that Rugova's pacifism could sunder Western unity if he became the focus of media attention. Dini assured her that he would urge Rugova to refrain from making public statements "at least until he has a conversation with Albright's representative," the U.S. ambassador to Macedonia, Christopher Hill.

The accidental NATO bombing on May 7 of the Chinese Embassy in Belgrade, which killed three people and injured eighteen others, suddenly focused Western minds on the civilian costs of the war. The Chinese rose up in anger against the United States, staging mass demonstrations outside the U.S. and British Embassies in Beijing. The German chancellor, Gerhard Schroeder, publicly challenged Washington's official explanation—that the strike was due to a faulty street map—by demanding a formal NATO inquiry.

But while his public relations effort appeared to be on the verge of producing results, Milosevic faced the first rumblings against his policy in Serbia. Vuk Draskovic, the deputy prime minister and the most liberal member of Milosevic's government, was critical of the manipulation of patriotism for the political advantage of ultranationalists and leftists. Draskovic was against the bombing, but he had become convinced that the government should shift course and negotiate peace.

Milosevic took a tough line against what he termed "defeatism and subversion." On April 11, the independent publisher Slavko Curuvija, whose newspaper had suspended publication under the draconian press law that went into effect March 24, was killed in front of his apartment by two men in black leather jackets. The publisher was opposed to the NATO bombing campaign but was also critical of Milosevic's suicidal policy.

The murder sent shivers down the spines of regime critics; it was seen as an execution. A few days earlier, Curuvija had been falsely accused by Belgrade Television and the newspaper *Ekspres* of backing NATO's bombing. *Ekspres* quoted the president's wife as criticizing "the owner of a Belgrade daily newspaper [who] said that he supports the United States in its desire to bomb Serbia." The writer of the article then continued, "This is, of course, Slavko Curuvija."

Two weeks later, in the midst of Milosevic's propaganda maneuvers, Draskovic suddenly broke ranks with the government and publicly urged a compromise with NATO. Serbia's leaders, he told a television audience, must "stop lying to the people and tell them the truth. The people should know that NATO is not facing a breakdown, that Russia will not help Yugoslavia militarily, and that the world public is against us.

"Our people must know reality and our small nation, very brave and very proud, must respect reality," he said. "We cannot defeat NATO. We must recognize the fact that the world today is often ruled by the rule of power, not by the rule of law." He urged that the government accept a compromise on Kosovo and UN troops, including some NATO forces, to enforce a political settlement. Draskovic was fired by fax the next day, even though he insisted that he was not positioning himself as an alternative to the Milosevic regime.

Milosevic refused to be daunted by his old enemy, whom he loathed and detested and referred to in private as "that lunatic." The war continued. So did the systematic destruction of Serbia.

Yet Draskovic's outburst reflected a swing from bombastic optimism to something like defeatism among a section of the population. By May, the Serbs were growing weary and there were the first anti-government demonstrations in the southern towns of Krusevac, Raska, and Aleksandrovac. Women demanded the return of their men from the Kosovo front. The already impoverished population was hit by the loss of water and electricity. War fatigue was setting in. Graffiti on a wall in the town of Pancevo expressed a mood of fatalism and despair: "NATO in the sky, Milosevic on the ground: Where is God?"

Yet the NATO bombing had done little to "degrade" Milosevic's military and police forces. On May 12, Lieutenant General Michael C. Short announced that the NATO air strikes were being expanded to non-military targets. "I also need to strike at the leadership and the people around Milosevic to compel them to change their behavior in Kosovo and accept the terms NATO has on the table," Short declared. The distress of the Serb population, he said, would undermine support for the Milosevic regime. The targets now included residential districts of Belgrade and other Serbian cities. A few days later, NATO bombs hit the Dragisa Misovic Hospital in the middle of Dedinje. NATO bombs damaged the embassies of Sweden, Switzerland, and Norway. The consequence of this policy was a growing number of civilian casualties and an erosion in public support in the West for the air war.

The swift and deliberate emptying of Kosovo of almost 800,000 people created a new reality on the ground. As anticipated, the refugees were not welcome in a Macedonia obsessed with its own precarious ethnic balance. Western pledges, made freely at a time when top Western officials expected that Milosevic would cut his losses after a few days of bombing, suddenly sounded empty.

The politics and diplomatic maneuverings of Western powers were indeterminate and shifting. Some NATO members—Germany, Greece, and Italy—faced growing domestic criticism over the civilian casualties. The allies now openly staked out different approaches to ending the war in Yugoslavia. Germany and Italy leaned toward a temporary bombing halt as a part of a new peace initiative; only Britain's Tony Blair continued to press for a ground invasion, articulating in emotive language a moral justification for an uncompromising solution to the conflict over Kosovo: "No compromise, no fudge, no half-baked deals." Behind the scenes, the disagreements were intense. In a ninety-minute transatlantic phone conversation, Clinton told Blair that he was fostering a dangerous appearance of disunity. Meanwhile Chancellor Schroeder rejected Blair's proposal for ground troops and stated categorically that Germany would veto it in NATO; the Green Party, a junior partner in Schroeder's coalition, was forcefully demanding an end to the bombing, threatening to bring down the government.

Clinton, who realized that his presidency was now at stake, maneuvered mightily to hold the alliance together, determined to go on bombing Yugoslavia until his basic conditions were met: Serbian forces out, Kosovo Albanian refugees back protected by an international peacekeeping force with NATO at its core. He had also approached the Russians to help broker a face-saving deal with Milosevic: in mid-April, President Boris Yeltsin responded by appointing the former Russian premier, Viktor S. Chernomyrdin, as his special envoy to the Balkans.

The Yugoslav president was operating in a pressure cooker atmosphere. It would be hard to find a national leader in history who has gone into battle at a point of his own choosing more certain of defeat. The allied assaults on Yugoslavia were on an altogether bigger scale than a small people—however capable of endurance—could possibly handle over the long term. The country was being destroyed. Milosevic's palatial residence suffered a direct hit, as did the headquarters of his Socialist Party, Radio Television Serbia, and the buildings housing the ministries of defense, interior, and foreign affairs. Cruise missiles destroyed virtually everything of any military use: government installations, airports, military bases, bridges, heating plants, railway lines, highways, power grids, drug, cigarette, shoe, chemical, car, and light aircraft factories. Serbia's economy, already crippled by eight years of sanctions, was totally ruined.

Milosevic, however, knew that he had no friends. He felt that Russia, Serbia's traditional ally, had behaved treacherously from the day when Yeltsin had agreed to the imposition of UN sanctions against Yugoslavia in May 1992. When Prime Minister Yevgeny Primakov arrived in Belgrade on March 29, cameras captured a significant gesture: Primakov was about to try to embrace Milosevic when the latter's arm stiffened to prevent it. By contrast, Milosevic embraced Alexander Lukashenko, the president of Belarus, whom he considered an ally.

Primakov's dramatic U-turn in the sky encouraged the Serbs to think that Russia would help them, but Milosevic knew well that the bravura show of solidarity was staged to appease the Russian public, driven to a frenzy by a pro-Serbian press and demanding strong action in support of their suffering Slav brethren. Alexander Solzhenitsyn saw no difference between Hitler and NATO and said that the bombing of Yugoslavia was to serve as "a terrible example" of how the United States and its allies intend to impose their order on the rest of the world. "Stellar Hour of Slobodan Milosevic," proclaimed the banner headline in the Moscow newspaper *Itogi* as the Serb leader vowed in early May he would not permit NATO soldiers on the soil of Yugoslavia.

The Russian government was in no position to throw its weight about or to risk relations with the West at a time when it desperately needed Western financial support. Moreover, Yeltsin had kept Milosevic at arm's length ever since the Serb leader had openly sided with the Kremlin hard-liners in the 1991 attempted coup against Mikhail Gorbachev; the only other world leaders who had welcomed the coup were Libya's Moammar Qaddafi and Iraq's Saddam Hussein.

Milosevic's brother, Borislav, the Yugoslav ambassador to Moscow, furiously lobbied Serbia's friends in Moscow, who kept pressing the Yeltsin government. The attack on Serbia had strained U.S.-Russian relations as public opinion in Russia was overwhelmingly on the side of the Serbs, including the Communists and nationalists in the Duma. Publicly, Yeltsin kept issuing menacing denunciations of NATO, demanding a halt in the bombing campaign; privately, the Russians were prepared to go along with the United States but to do so by reasserting themselves as a significant diplomatic player and also gaining access to additional credits. "Russia cannot identify with that guy [Milosevic]," Chernomyrdin told Western officials. But he could not afford to be seen as NATO's messenger who was compelling "that guy" to capitulate.

In May, a way out was suggested by the Russians, who needed to provide their envoy with political cover. This was a turning point in the war. NATO bombing had wrecked Serbia's economy and civilian infrastructure, but inflicted surprisingly little damage on Milosevic's police and military forces. Yeltsin's acceptance of NATO's conditions and a growing consensus in the West for considering a ground campaign to break the standoff over Kosovo convinced Milosevic by the end of the month that he had better back down. Indeed, Milosevic relented a few days after Washington and London had agreed on a plan for a massive ground invasion of Kosovo to start in the first week of September 1999. But it was Russia's subtle duplicity that probably had a much more decisive impact.

The Russian scheme was presented by Chernomyrdin at a Washington breakfast with senior American officials. It called for Chernomyrdin to team up with a diplomat from a neutral country. Chernomyrdin would negotiate broad principles with Milosevic, while the neutral diplomat would deliver unpleasant messages to Milosevic and demand unconditional capitulation. Implicit in Moscow's proposal was a reward expected from Washington in the form of debt reschedulings and the resumption of International Monetary Fund lending to Russia that had been frozen since the summer of 1998.

Albright immediately saw the value of Chernomyrdin's idea and praised him as being "very astute about how to make things happen." Both agreed on Martti Ahtisaari of Finland as Chernomyrdin's partner in the venture.

The scheme allowed Moscow to ditch Milosevic without being seen as doing so. In return, the Russians were able to soften the terms of the Rambouillet deal with largely cosmetic concessions to Milosevic, providing him with political cover to justify himself and his policy before the Serb nation. The document no longer mentioned a referendum in Kosovo after a period of three years; NATO was not given access to Serbia outside Kosovo; Serbia's sovereignty in Kosovo was recognized.

As time went on and the NATO alliance held firm, it became clear to Milosevic that he had failed. The months of bombing had devastated his country and there was little to be gained from continued intransigence. NATO bombs were now raining mainly on civilian targets. On May 26, Chernomyrdin flew to Belgrade and spent nine hours in talks with Milosevic; after his departure, the capital was subjected to one of the heaviest assaults of the war. On May 27, Milosevic suffered a most severe body blow when Judge Louise Arbour of Canada, the chief prosecutor of the UN-created war crimes tribunal in the Hague, formally issued a warrant for his arrest, charging him with crimes against humanity for his role in the atrocities and mass deportations carried out by the military forces under his command in Kosovo.

Arbour's indictment was based on "unusually sensitive intelligence information" about Kosovo developments that the governments of the United States and Britain had supplied to the tribunal. The indictment made Milosevic the first sitting head of state to be accused of war crimes.

Milosevic remained outwardly unperturbed by the court action and the continued destruction around him, carrying on his regular routine. He attended cabinet sessions and outlined reconstruction plans for the postwar period. Privately, he was beginning to crack, staging temper tantrums, screaming at aides, and throwing documents into the air. For a man who wanted so badly to be accepted and respected and who had refused to fight "dirty" before the onset of the war by grabbing American hostages—the course urged by Seselj and ultra-nationalists who argued that this was the way to prevent bombings—the indictment was a decisive setback: he was doomed to be a perpetual pariah. It certainly shattered Mira's dreams of their retirement years, which she once painted to an interviewer as vacationing abroad, at a Swiss resort, "the two of them in Lugano eating ice cream, Mira wearing a white dress and a flower in her hair."

We may never know for certain what transpired in the mind of this most impenetrable of dictators as he watched his country continue to be pulverized by thousands of NATO sorties. Did he ever really believe that by presenting NATO with a fait accompli in Kosovo, he would once again manage to con everybody? Or was the whole affair another aspect of the narcissistic centrality of his own self, his own power, which had distinguished his behavior since his university days? Again, he was the prisoner of his background, the man who always looked toward Russia and had not expected that Russia would help engineer his defeat.

If there was an ultimate aim in his mind, it was his own survival. He had clothed himself in the glory of the Kosovo myth and spun dreams of the Heavenly Empire, but unlike Lazar he was a cynical man who did not believe in Lazar's kingdom of truth and justice and who had misused the old legends to do harm not only to other people but to his own nation.

He did not expect to win—he had said so publicly—but if he could survive after being hit by the best-armed military alliance in history, then he would be the winner. He knew that if he had capitulated at Rambouillet, he would have been politically dead. Hence bowing to the inevitable after a massive campaign of violent accretion was an act of political pragmatism; he would stay on in his shrinking Yugoslavia.

In late May 1999, Milosevic made up his mind to cut his losses and began preparing public opinion for the inevitable capitulation. In a letter to the German government on June 1, he formally accepted the principles for a peace agreement set three weeks earlier by the Group of Seven industrialized nations and Russia.

When Chernomyrdin and Ahtisaari came to the White Palace on the evening of June 2, they found Milosevic "serious and calm," and not under the stress Chernomyrdin had noted during his previous visits. Ahtisaari read the two-page document aloud line by line while Chernomyrdin kept silent. Chernomyrdin's presence, Ahtisaari said later, was necessary to make Milosevic realize that Russia was behind the plan.

He asked the envoys whether there could be revisions in the document. No, Ahtisaari said, it was a take-it-or-leave-it deal; they were there only to explain it.

Milosevic said he would send the document to his parliament for approval, then proposed that Ahtisaari address the parliament. Ahtisaari declined. Milosevic offered the envoys a dinner, but Ahtisaari declined that as well. The Finn suggested the Milosevic "should use the time" to consult his own colleagues and different political leaders.

Late that evening, Milosevic assembled the leaders of all political parties in the White Palace to inform them of his decision. "A few things are not logical, but the main thing is, we have no choice," he said. "I personally think we should accept," he added in measured tones. The outcome was favorable because Yugoslavia would continue to exercise sovereignty, albeit symbolic, over Kosovo. He emphasized a central role for the United Nations, adding that "to reject the document means the destruction of our state and nation."

"This is not a surrender of the state but of a wrong policy," his wife, Mira, leader of YUL, said. Vuk Draskovic supported the accord. Only Vojislav Seselj staked out an uncompromising note: "This document means capitulation. It is a shameful document."

The parliament met the next morning in a closed session and approved Milosevic's decision by a vote of 136 to 74. Shortly after 1:00 P.M., Ahtisaari and Chernomyrdin arrived at the White Palace.

Ahtisaari immediately came to the point, asking what was the decision.

"We accept your terms," Milosevic said simply.

After enduring three months of bombing and thousands of deaths, he accepted NATO's key demand: to withdraw all military and police forces from Kosovo and allow fifty thousand foreign troops under NATO command to enforce peace in the province. Kosovo's Albanians were granted "substantial autonomy" within Yugoslavia, though Milosevic would be allowed later to deploy less than one thousand uniformed men to guard religious shrines and key border posts as a token of Serbia's sovereignty over Kosovo. But for all practical purposes, Kosovo in the future would have little to do with either Serbia or Yugoslavia.

Milosevic made no public statement, but his Socialist Party praised the accord as guaranteeing Yugoslavia's "integrity and sovereignty." His wife issued a statement saying, "We are proud of the heroic resistance of our people."

The two negotiators departed for Cologne after leaving the telephone numbers of high NATO military officers to be contacted by the Yugoslav military. That evening, General Wesley Clark received a phone call from a Yugoslav general, suggesting that the military negotiations on details of the Serbian withdrawal from Kosovo start on June 6.

Over the next few days, as NATO bombings continued, Milosevic sought to exploit the ambiguities in the plan to claw back some lost ground. In particular, he wanted a higher degree of UN control over the force that would go into Kosovo, including a strong Russian contingent to dilute the NATO character of the peacekeeping operation. He insisted that the entry into Kosovo be postponed until the UN Security Council approved the mission. "Milosevic needs an alibi for both international and internal public opinion," Bratislav Grubacic, the publisher of an English-language news bulletin in Belgrade, said. "He does not want to surrender to NATO but to the UN Security Council."

Under the NATO plan, Kosovo was divided into American, British, French, German, and Italian sectors, but there was to be no Russian sector. Milosevic wanted to have Russian troops deployed in Pristina and in northern Kosovo, which would in effect create a zone under a friendly protective force for the Kosovo Serbs in areas close to Serbia proper. The Russians, who saw this scheme as serving their interests, agreed to dispatch a Russian unit from Bosnia to seize the Pristina airport before NATO forces entered Kosovo.

The allied bombing ended on June 10, after an agreement on Serb withdrawals negotiated between Yugoslav and NATO generals was reached. As convoys of Yugoslav military vehicles began leaving the province, the UN Security Council quickly approved an already agreed upon resolution that endorsed the foreign peace-keeping mission in Kosovo to, in effect, establish an international protectorate, assist almost a million refugees to return home, and organize an interim civilian administration. At China's insistence, the language of the resolution was changed to state that the Security Council—rather than NATO—had the "primary responsibility" for maintaining peace and security in Kosovo.

That evening, in a televised address to the nation from his palace, Milosevic tapped into the Kosovo mythology by echoing his 1989 speech in which he talked of the Serb nation as "an army great, brave and proud, one of the few that in defeat stayed undefeated." He announced that "the aggression is over—happy peace to all of us." He said 462 soldiers and 114 police had been killed in the eleven-week-long war "for the defense of the fatherland in the struggle for freedom and dignity of our nation." (NATO estimates of Serb casualties were in the thousands, however.)

> Throughout the rallies in this past year in our country, one slogan was often heard: We will not give up Kosovo. We never gave up Kosovo. Today, the territorial integrity and sovereignty is guaranteed by the G-8 nations and the United Nations. Open questions regarding the possible independence of Kosovo in the time before the aggression have been sealed with the Belgrade agreement. The territorial integrity of our country can never be questioned again. We survived and we defended the country.

Milosevic stressed that by insisting on the UN role, "we have not only defended our country but have brought the UN back to the world stage." This, he said, "is our contribution to the world: to prevent the creation of a unipolar world, to prevent the acceptance of a world based on the diktat from one center." He had "defended the only multiethnic society left over as a remnant of the former Yugoslavia," he insisted.

> This is another great achievement of our defense. The entire people participated in this war, from babies in hospitals to intensive care patients to soldiers in air-defense positions and soldiers on the border. The people are the heroes of this war. This may be the shortest way to sum up this war.
>
> We shall begin rebuilding our bridges immediately, our factories, our roads. We have to restart a great development to reflect the vitality of all our citizens. The work ahead will require great mobilization. I wish all the citizens of Yugoslavia much joy and success in reconstruction of our country.

A banner headline in *Politika* the next morning read: "Confirmed: the Sovereignty and Territorial Integrity of Yugoslavia, and the Role of the UN." The paper's correspondents around the world reported accolades and expressions of gratitude to Milosevic the peacemaker.

The next day, June 11, as the West was celebrating victory, a column of two hundred Russian troops, which had been stationed in Bosnia as part of the peacekeeping contingent there, suddenly left for Kosovo and arrived in Pristina in the early hours of June 12 to the tumultuous welcome of its Serb residents. The surprise move of troops into the Kosovo capital a few hours before NATO forces entered Kosovo at dawn was a public relations coup for Moscow; they established themselves at the Pristina airport to stake their claim in the peacekeeping operation. It was the revival of the old story of great power maneuvering in the Balkans. It was set against the background of yet another demographic change in Kosovo, new calls for revenge, the exodus of Yugoslav troops and many Kosovo Serbs, and the return of ethnic Albanian refugees and confident KLA militants eager to take charge of the province.

The political future of Kosovo may seem vague in the agreement that ended the war, but independence down the road seems almost inevitable. Milosevic had insisted that Kosovo was "the heart of Serbia," but he had now placed that heart in a foreign body.

The horror of Kosovo was a new low point in the series of

dreadful events that have happened during more than a decade of Milosevic's police rule, a new extreme in the reawakening of the demons of the past. For more than six hundred years, when the poppies in Kosovo bloomed in May, the Serbs used to insist their redness came from the blood of their slain ancestors; next May, however, there would be no argument where their color came from. Milosevic has turned independence into a moral question for the Kosovo Albanians. Kosovo has already become cut off from Serbia: the Kosovars do not serve in the Yugoslav Army or pay Yugoslav taxes; the Western administrators are in the process of creating a new police force and judiciary without Serbian influence; the shrinking Serbian community is bound to shrink further as many remaining Serbs will move to Serbia proper.

The war may have provided Milosevic with a plausible alibi to explain the disastrous state of the economy. His plans for rebuilding the infrastructure are based on Tito's post–World War II mobilization of enthusiastic "volunteers" to work on infrastructure problems. But the rebuilding of technologically sophisticated automobile, aircraft, or machine tool industries would require outside investments and access to the international credit markets.

In the past, Milosevic has managed to turn defeats into personal victories, but this time he faces an encroaching and more volatile circle of danger. The church has ditched him. The country has been devastated. Millions of industrial workers have lost their jobs and prospects of gainful employment any time soon are minimal. Angry Serb refugees from Kosovo felt betrayed, as did the refugees from Krajina and Bosnia. All the signs point to the buildup of a new revolutionary situation.

It is worth remembering that, with the possible exception of the 1990 elections, when he was still riding the crest of the first nationalist wave, Milosevic has never won a free election in Serbia. Most Serbs have little or no affection for a man whom they associate with a decade of calamitous wars and defeats—in Croatia, in Bosnia, in Kosovo—and with a catastrophic decline in living standards. For years, Serbs have predicted that Milosevic and his wife, Mira, will be murdered by their people, in the same fashion as Romania's despotic Communist leader Nicolae Ceausescu and his wife, Elena, in 1989. "I think there is a 50 percent likelihood that will be their fate," said former U.S. ambassador Warren Zimmermann.

But a flurry of summertime protest rallies after Milosevic's defeat in Kosovo failed to attract sufficient public support. Their impact was muffled by personal rivalries among opposition leaders, and conflicting political conceptions precluded a unified opposition assault on the regime. Vuk Draskovic, the self-described king of street demonstrations, insisted that the time was not ripe to confront Milosevic; he insisted that the best way to remove Milosevic from power was to seduce him to resign with a promise of immunity from arrest or extradition. Zoran Djindjic, on the other hand, insisted that Milosevic should be promptly confronted, ousted, and handed over for trial in the Hague. Both Draskovic and Djindjic courted President Milo Djukanovic of Montenegro, whose solid power base and record of resistance to Milosevic's rule made him the most credible opposition politician. But considering the number of Yugoslav Army troops in Montenegro, Djukanovic was forced to tread cautiously. He had advanced demands for constitutional changes in Montenegro's dysfunctional relationship with Serbia that would give his tiny republic equality within the federation. He had also joined Djindjic and the former prime minister Milan Panic to form the Alliance for Change and advance a program for a post-Milosevic regime: a transitional government headed by Panic or the former National Bank governor Dragoslav Avramovic was to lead the truncated Yugoslavia to free elections and democracy.

Activities of this kind posed no immediate danger for Milosevic. No master of Serbia has ever been brought down by street demonstrations; with the exception of Tito and Peter I, they were either assassinated or forced to flee abroad to save their lives.

More threatening were spontaneous eruptions of discontent, showing a country that positively seethed with indignation and frustration. Demonstrations broke out in towns of southern Serbia that were once Milosevic's stronghold. The burning anger, augmented by economic misery and disgust at the conduct of the Kosovo war, seemed like a wave of resentment slowly closing in on

Milosevic. Not since the pro-Austrian King Alexander and Queen Draga were assassinated in 1903 had the Serbs regarded their masters with such bitter and ineradicable hatred. This mood was bound to produce a head-on collision between authority—resting on bayonets—and the people, which would prompt the dictator to invoke emergency measures but would not mean the end of his regime. But an increasing number of former senior figures in the Milosevic regime have begun talking openly about the pressing need to liberate the country from the dead hand of dictatorship, a trend that could lead to the tottering regime's self-destruction, a crumbling from within. Even Zoran Lilic, a Milosevic acolyte and former titular chief of state from 1993 to 1996, was openly putting a distance between himself and his former boss, whose ouster he favored. Rumors of plots circulated in Belgrade.

Milosevic still had a grip on his large police force and the media. But could he rely on the army?

In an extraordinary interview with the weekly *NIN* in July 1999, General Momcilo Perisic, the former chief of staff, called for a removal of Milosevic from office, accusing him of "incompetence" and abuse of power. Milosevic's learning curve was tilted downward, he said. He had led the Serbs from one catastrophe to another to the Kosovo debacle and "this will continue to happen as long as [his regime] remains in power." The subtext of his remarks amounted to an appeal to junior officers to mutiny. Milosevic had disgraced the army, he said. The outcome of the war was "even worse than capitulation."

"What are the limits of cynicism of the present authorities when they wage a war to protect Serbs and (Serb) territories and end it with a 'victory' which resulted in the deaths and exile of Serbs and the loss of territory?" the general asked.

What was particularly fascinating about his remarks was the general's effort to reassure the police—who stood accused of Kosovo atrocities along with the paramilitaries—that they were "not to blame that politics placed them in such a situation." The Hague court had issued international arrest warrants for the top military and police officials; other ranking officials may also be charged. But the army and police are made up of citizens, Perisic said. Only "sick minds and irresponsible individuals," he added, could speak of differences between them "in their attitude toward the nation."

Milosevic's former information minister Aleksandar Tijanic went even further by suggesting, in the event of a palace coup, that clemency be granted to those close Milosevic aides who joined the putative plotters. "It would be wise and useful for the state to forgive them, because the transitional government [would] bring in a new constitution, free elections and a psychological purification of Serbia that would be more precious than blind retribution," Tijanic wrote in a scathing pamphlet which circulated in Belgrade.

It has been frequently argued that Milosevic's hold on the police is so firm that it is impossible to dislodge him. But how strong is that loyalty against a profound popular revulsion toward a defeated dictator and his wife? And when there is the real prospect of a freezing winter and widespread shortages of energy and food? How long can Milosevic count on his rich business friends who, because of the new sanctions, no longer have access to their assets abroad? Bogoljub Karic, chairman of the Karic Brothers Bank and personal friend of the ruling couple, was turned back from Larnaca Airport by Cyprus authorities even though he owns property and a large bank on the island. Many other members of the Milosevic kleptocracy are in the same situation.

At the end of the century, Serbia was again approaching its problems of government in a traditional manner, as though it had made no advance from the conditions of dictatorship in the past hundred years.

In 1900, Serbia's finances were in ruins. Corruption and fraud were rampant. Army and government officials were irregularly paid. The people hated the king for his complete subservience to Austria, which collided with their mythology and tradition. King Alexander resorted to terrorism to defend his crown. In 1901, he imposed a military dictatorship.

The popular resentment of the king's capricious despotism grew as rapidly as a passionate hatred of his queen. Unrest spread. In April 1903, demonstrators were shot down in the streets of Belgrade before the king yielded to their demand for a general election. The elections were held in May, but their results were blatantly falsified by the king's agents.

On June 11, the military ruler General Cincar Markovic submitted his resignation. He told the king he could no longer run the government in the face of such strong public opposition.

That same night, Alexander and his wife were murdered in the palace, and their naked, mutilated bodies were thrown from their bedroom windows into the garden. The regicides were army officers; a total of eighty-six were in on the conspiracy. But only twenty-six took part in the assassination. They blew open the palace doors with a stick of dynamite, which cut off electricity, cut off telephone wires, then roamed around the dark palace for two hours looking for the king and queen. The couple, hiding inside a secret closet next to their bedroom, were finally discovered, shot, and slashed with swords before being thrown out the window. The king clung to life even when they thought him dead; his right hand gripped the railing, and he fell to the ground only after an officer severed his fingers with a sword.

Before killing the royal couple, the conspirators murdered General Cincar Markovic in his home, unaware that he had submitted his resignation a few hours earlier. A prince from the rival Karadjordjevic dynasty was brought to the throne after four decades of exile in Switzerland. King Peter was sixty, with no experience of statecraft; but this sober and modest man proved to be the finest liberal ruler Serbia had ever known.

Rebecca West, fascinated by the gruesome tale, concluded that "this is not a strictly moral universe, and it is not true that it is useless to kill a tyrant because a worse man will take his place."

There is in Idries Shah's *Caravan of Dreams* the idea that people cannot reform society, or deal with each other as reasonable people, unless they locate and allow for "the various patterns of coercive institutions, formal and also informal, which rule" them. No matter what reason says, the late Afghan writer insists, the people will always relapse into obedience to the coercive agency while these patterns are within individuals.

How else can one explain the behavior of the Serb nation along the blood-spattered timeline of Milosevic's misrule? What other explanation is there for the defiant bugle music which filled the air in the initial months of the war when the Serbs blindly joined him on a mission of national suicide? How does one account for the spontaneous groundswell of support for the man who led them from one fearful disaster into another? Why had the Serbian Orthodox Church, which called on Milosevic to resign after it was all over, been strangely silent during the preceding months of forced exodus of Kosovo's Albanians? And what about high officials in the Milosevic regime who later said, "We told him he could be a wise coward or a foolish hero [but] he would not listen"?

There are, of course, many explanations. Serbia's Kosovo obsession is one: a peculiar Serb psyche of nationalism that some liken to a malady and others ascribe to a rustic fatalism based on xenophobia, superstition, and a long history of humiliation.

Another explanation rests on Milosevic's almost total control over the flow of information. "The essence of Milosevic's system is that no one knows anything," said Zoran Djindjic, the leader of the pro-Western Democratic Party, adding that the same system allowed the Germans under Hitler to discount the evidence of the Holocaust. People try to explain to themselves information they are given, he surmised, and think "maybe the victims are guilty, somehow, and deserve what they get."

Others insist that many people had access to independent information about atrocities in Kosovo—there are more than 100,000 satellite dishes in the Serbian capital alone and even more Internet links—but that they had been traumatized to the point that they could only care about themselves. The destruction and suffering caused by the bombing had done what only God could do, said the historian Aleksa Djilas—unify the Serbs. "They have been united from heaven—but by the bombs, not by God."

The fact is that, apart from the kleptocracy and gangsters, Milosevic's militant irredentism had been supported by a substantial minority of Serbs. His own former information minister, Aleksandar Tijanic, has likened the policy of nationalist madness to Hitler's Germany. "For ten bloody years, Milosevic, his wife, their fascist supporters and a coterie of domestic traitors have engaged in deception, cynically inciting and justifying crimes, killing, stealing and lying." He invoked the names of the two great West German chancellors whose work has restored Germany's good name. "Serbia now needs a Konrad Adenauer to create a normal democratic state and a Willy Brandt to wash off its besmirched honor."

Sooner or later the Serb nation will have to confront the senseless savagery that was committed in its name and deal with an ugly legacy, the legacy of one warped and malevolent man. With Milosevic's ascent to power the dream of Kosovo, enacted again and again, had come back as a nightmare just at a point when Yugoslavia stood ready to join Europe. In resurrecting it as a political motif, he debased his nation and pushed it back into another, earlier age. But Milosevic was part of Serbia's problem; what ails the nation is deeper than one man. It is the psychosis of a nation that nurtured its epic poetry as history during a five-hundred-year night of captivity and then continued to do so for almost two centuries after that captivity had ended. Perhaps now, having been forced by Milosevic to live out the epic of Kosovo again, the Serbs will have a chance openly to reexamine their past. But that could happen only under a democratic government.

"When this is all over," predicted Zoran Djindjic, "Kosovo will no longer be an important political issue, but we will have hunger and social unrest. That will not be very good grounds for democracy. We could turn into a European Iraq."

# Notes

## Introduction

Most of the material comes from our own reporting. Many of the general sources we have used are translated from material published in Serbia, in particular the newspaper *Politika* and the weekly newsmagazines *Vreme* and *NIN*. Epic poetry quoted throughout the book is taken from the two volumes of *Narodna Knjizevnost Srba na Kosovu i Metohiji*, edited by Vladimir Boban, Jedinstvo, Pristina, 1989; the translations are ours. Richard Holbrooke quotes are taken from Elaine Sciolino and Ethan Bronner, *The New York Times*, April 18, 1999. Milosevic's speech in Kosovo in 1989 was reported by Peter Millar and is taken from his "Slobo's Shame," *Sunday Times* (London), July 4, 1993. Also see Slavoljub Djukic, *On, Ona i Mi*, Radio B92, Belgrade, 1997.

## I Cold Narcissus

Sir Gardner Wilkinson's recollections are from Rebecca West, *Black Lamb and Grey Falcon*, Viking, 1956; Milosevic's family history was reported in *Barske Novine*, Bar, Montenegro, March 1990. Mira's recollections about their courtship were reported in *Duga* on March 19, 1994, and April 2, 1994. Mira's father's recollections are from Moma Markovic, *Rat i Revolucija*, Knjizevna Zadruga, 1991. Mira's conversation with her cousin is taken from Slavoljub Djukic, *On, Ona i Mi*. The quote about Milosevic's mother's attitude toward Mira is from Steven Erlanger in *The New York Times,* May 31, 1999. Mira's accounts are contained in Mirjana Markovic, *Answer* and *Night and Day,* both Quarry Press, Kingston, Ontario, 1995. For Alexander Rankovic's fall from power, see Dusko Doder, *The Yugoslavs,* Random House, 1978. For a revisionist view of Rankovic, see Jovan Kesar and Pero Simic, *Leka: Oprostaj bez milosti,* Akvarijus, Belgrade, 1990. Milovan Djilas's quote is from his *Montenegro,* Methuen, 1964.

## 2 Faustian Bargain

Cosic's article appeared in the dissident Marxist journal *Praxis,* Zagreb, 1995, and is taken from Doder's *The Yugoslavs.* The text of the Memorandum of the Serbian Academy of Sciences and Arts, is taken from Tim Judah, *The Serbs: History, Myth and the Destruction of Yugoslavia,* Yale University Press, 1997. For the use of the impalement metaphor, see Brana Crncevic in "Istina of Martinovicu," *Politikin Svet,* May 1, 1991; also see M. Jankovic, "Zlocin kao u vreme Turaka," *Ekspres,* January 14, 1991. Also see Vesna Pesic, *Serbian Nationalism and the Origins of the Yugoslav Crisis,* United States Institute of Peace, 1996; and Noel Malcolm, *A Short History of Kosovo,* New York University Press, 1998. For the army barracks shooting incident in Paracin, see Keljmedi Pucao u Jugoslaviju, *Politika,* September 4, 1987; the journalist Slavoljub Djukic's recollection of the incident is in *On, Ona i Mi,* pp. 65–66. The wholesale media attacks on ethnic Albanians are reflected in "Poslednji cas," *Politika,* September 8, 1987; "Zlocin planiran" and "Odgovornost za zlocin," both distributed by the official news agency Tanjug on September 8, 1987; and "Keljmedijevi moraju iz Dusanova," in *Politika,* September 10, 1987. The funeral of Stambolic's daughter is described in Slavoljub Djukic, *Izmedju Slave in Anateme,* Filip Visnjic, Belgrade, 1994, pp. 100–101. Also by Djukic, *Kako se dogodio vodja: borba za vlast u Srbiji posle Josipa Broza,* Filip Visnjic, Belgrade, 1992. Quotations from the *Mountain Wreath* are translated from Petar Petrovic-Njegos, *Gorski Vjenac,* Svjetlost, Sarajevo, 1954. For a detailed study of Njegos, see Milovan Djilas, *Njegos: Poet, Prince, Bishop,* Harcourt Brace Jovanovic, 1966. Quotations of Albanian attitudes toward the Serbs from Edith Durham, *The Burden of the Balkans,* London, 1905. Also see Gramos Pashko, *Albania and Balkan Stability,* United States Institute of Peace, 1996. A history of communism's self-destruction is given in Milovan Djilas, *Fall of the New Class,* Alfred A. Knopf, 1998. A detailed study of Kosovo's ethnic structure appears in Branislav Krstic, *Kosovo: Izmedju Istorijskog i Etnickog Prava,* Kuca Vid, Belgrade, 1994. Also see Tim Judah, *The Serbs,* 1997, and Julie A. Mertus, *Kosovo: How Myths and Truths Started a War,* University of California Press, 1999. For a report on ethnic cleansing in the southern Balkans in 1912 and 1913, see *The Other Balkan Wars,* a 1913 Carnegie Endowment inquiry in retrospect with an introduction and reflections on wars in the former Yugoslavia in the 1990s by George F. Kennan. For a detailed account of Cosic, see Slavoljub Djukic, *Covek U Svom Vremenu: Razgovori sa Dobricom Cosicem,* Filip Visnjic, Belgrade, 1989; and Nebojsa Popov, *Srpski Populizm: Od marginalne do dominantne pojave.* Specijalni dodatak to *Vreme,* No. 135, May 24, 1993.

## 3 In Tito's Long Shadow

The discussion of the origins of Yugoslavia's collapse are based in part on Warren Zimmermann's *Origins of a Catastrophe: Yugoslavia and Its Destroyers,* Times Books, 1996: Misha Glenny, *The Fall of Yugoslavia: The Third Balkan War,* Penguin Books, 1993; see also John R. Lampe, *Yugoslavia as History: Twice There Was a Country,* Cambridge University Press, 1996; Alex N. Dragnich, *Serbs and Croats: The Struggle for Yugoslavia,* Harcourt Brace, 1992; and Robert D. Kaplan, *Balkan Ghosts: A Journey Through History,* St. Martin's Press, 1993. C. L. Sulzberger's quotations from Dusko Doder's *The Yugoslavs.* An example of an anti-Tito campaign encouraged by Milosevic in 1989 was Pero Simic's *Kada, kako i zasto je Tito postavljen za secretara CK KPJ,* Akvarius, Belgrade, 1989. Milosevic's conversations with Borisav Jovic and Defense Minister Veljko Kadijevic are reported in Jovic's *Poslednji dani SFRJ,* Belgrade, November 1995, and in Kadijevic's memoir, *Moje vidjenje raspada: Vojska bez drzave,* Belgrade, 1993. Kadijevic's remark about the transformation of the Yugoslav Army into a Serbian one comes from Tim Judah's *The Serbs.* On Milosevic's electoral shenanigans, see Milorad Savicevic, "Dirigent haosa," *NIN,* November 26, 1993. Tudjman's quotes are taken from Laura Silber and Alan Little, *The Death of Yugoslavia,* Penguin/BBC Books, 1995, pp. 87–94.

## 4 Croatian Intrigues

For a detailed study of Bosnia, see Noel Malcolm, *Bosnia: A Short History,* New York University Press, 1994. The discussion of Bosnian Muslims is based in part on Muhamed Hadzijahic, *Od tradicije do identiteta: Geneza nacionalnog pitanja Bosanskih Muslimana,* Sarajevo, 1974, and Ahmed Murabegovic, *O karakteru i psihi nasih muslimana,* Gajret, Sarajevo, 1926. Also see Muhamed Filipovic's essay "Muslimani—Bosnjaci u uvjetima politickog pluralizma," included in *Bosna i Bosnjastvo,* Sarajevo, 1990.

Borisav Jovic's comments about Milosevic's intentions appear in his *Posljedni dani SFRJ,* Belgrade, 1995; even this was sufficient for Milosevic to push Jovic into political oblivion. For a detailed account of Serbia's involvement in the Croatian war, see Dobrila Gajic-Glisic, *Srpska Vojska,* Litopaper, Cacak, 1995 (500 copies published by Marica and Tomo Spasojevic of Switzerland).

On the problems of Serbs in Croatia and the conditions in Krajina, see Jovan Raskovic, *Luda Zemlja,* Akvarijus, Belgrade, 1990. Also see Marcus Tanner, *Croatia: A Nation Forged in War,* Yale University Press, 1997.

Two excellent travel books provide accounts of the conditions in Yugoslavia in the early 1990s: Mark Thompson, *A Paper House: The Ending of Yugoslavia,* Pantheon Books, 1993, and Brian Hall, *The Impossible Country: A Journey Through the Last Days of Yugoslavia,* David T. Godine, 1994. On Izetbegovic and his main collaborators, see Abid Prguda, *Sarajevski Process: Sudjenje Muslimanskim Intelektualcima 1983 godine,* published by author, Sarajevo, 1990. Also Fahrudin Dapo and Tihomir Loza, *Povratak u Bosnu,* published by the authors, Sarajevo, 1990. Dr.

Mustafa Sehovic's remarks are from an interview with the authors. Lord Carrington's comments on the Milosevic-Tudjman relationship are made in an interview with the BBC and are taken from a five-part BBC series on the death of Yugoslavia. General Slavko Lisica's comments were taken from his interview with the weekly *NIN*, August 1995. Vojislav Seselj's remarks are taken from his interview with the student Radio B92 on July 26, 1994. Other details about direct links between the Milosevic regime and various criminal gangs are taken from an interview a dissident senior police inspector, Dragan Mladenovic, gave to Radio B92 on July 14, 1994 (tapes of both interviews in the possession of the authors). Material about Captain Dragan and General Tomislav Simovic comes from Dobrila Gajic-Glisic, *Srpska Vojska*.

## 5 The Abdication of the West

The discussion of Western policies comes from the authors' interviews with Brent Scowcroft, Lawrence Eagleburger, Warren Zimmermann, David Owen, Rudolph Perina, and a number of other Western officials. George F. Kennan's warning to Zimmermann is taken from Zimmermann's *Origins of a Catastrophe*. For a Serb insider's view of the final days of Yugoslavia, see Predrag Tasic, *Kako je ubijena druga Jugoslavija*, Autorsko Izdanje, Skopje, 1994. Lord Carrington's comments are taken from the five-part BBC series on the collapse of Yugoslavia. Momir Bulatovic's remarks appear in Laura Silber and Allan Little, *The Death of Yugoslavia*. The verse from *The Mountain Wreath* translated by the authors. The war crimes trial of Dusan Vuckovic was reported in the weekly *Vreme* in several issues, including November 14, 1994, and November 28, 1994. Also see *Yugoslavia: Collapse, War, Crimes*, edited by Sonja Biserko, Center for Anti-War Action, Belgrade Circle, 1993. Also see Dobrila Gajic-Glisic, *Srpska Vojska*. For a catalogue of crimes in Bosnia, see Rifat Karic, *Mali Kalendar Velikih Zlocina*, Tuzla, 1996.

## 6 The Summer of Discontent

Remarks about Tomislav reported by Dobrila Gajic-Glisic, *Srpska Vojska*. The incident at the headquarters of Belgrade Radio Television is reported by Djukic in *On, Ona i Mi*. Koljevic's approach to the United States is described in Warren Zimmermann's *Origins of a Catastrophe*. The text of Milosevic's conversation with opposition politicians on June 28, 1992, was made available to the authors by a participant. Dobrica Cosic's remarks about his meetings with Milosevic come from interviews with the authors; also see Slavoljub Djukic, *On, Ona i Mi*. Comments of Dusan Mitevic, Milosevic's confidant, made in interviews with the authors; also the authors interviews with Milan Panic and John Scanlan.

## 7 The Unquiet American

The discussion of Milan Panic's prime ministership is largely based on interviews the authors conducted with Panic, Dobrica Cosic, John Scanlan, Dusan Mitevic,

Sveta Babic, David Owen, William Montgomery, Robert Rachmales, Birch Bayh, Doug Shoen, Lawrence Eagleburger, Brent Scowcroft, Ljubisa Rakic, Ilija Djukic, Ted Olic, David Calef, Marcia O'Hagan, Bill Press, and scores of others. The views of Vance and Owen on Milosevic are cited from the *Financial Times,* February 1, 1993. For details about the 1992 Serbian elections, see Douglas E. Shoen, "How Milosevic Stole the Elections: In Serbia, a veteran of American political wars discovers the shock of real political warfare," *The New York Times Sunday Magazine,* February 14, 1993. For a Serb insider's account, see Svetozar Stojanovic, *Propast komunizma i razbijanje Jugoslavije,* Filip Visnjic, Belgrade, 1994 (Stojanovic was a foreign policy adviser to Dobrica Cosic).

## 8 A Question of Loyalty

Karadzic's approach to Dershowitz was revealed in the *Sunday Times* (London) on April 4, 1993. Seselj's public humiliation of Cosic reported by the authors, including interviews with Seselj and with Cosic's two key assistants, Svetozar Stojanovic and Dragoslav Rancic. Owen's account of Cosic's apparent ignorance about the activities of the Yugoslav Army in Bosnia is taken from Owen's *Balkan Odyssey,* Harcourt, Brace & Company, 1995, p. 139. Owen's account of his negotiations with Milosevic based on the authors' interview with Owen and on his *Balkan Odyssey,* pp. 143–144. The text of Milosevic's letter to the Bosnian Serb Assembly was published in *Politika,* April 26, 1993. The death of Risto Djogo is described in Laura Silber and Allan Little, *The Death of Yugoslavia,* p. 322. Karadzic's comments were made in an interview with the authors. Milosevic's phone conversation with Owen is taken from *Balkan Odyssey,* p. 155; Owen's assessments of the Clinton administration's opposition to the Vance-Owen plan, p. 169. Draskovic's account of his imprisonment is taken from his interview with the authors. Ivan Stambolic's comments about his fall from power and Mira's role were made in an interview with the authors. The interview of Marko Milosevic and Radio Boom 93, of Pozarevac, was reproduced in full in *Vreme,* January 25, 1993. On Marko Milosevic's theme park, see Blaine Harden, *A Milosevic Field of Dreams, The New York Times,* July 6, 1999. For Marija Milosevic as foreign correspondent, see *Vreme,* March 7, 1994. The comments by Mira's brother-in-law, Momcilo Selic, are reported by Slavoljub Djukic, in *On, Ona i Mi.* Quotations of Mira's writing comes from her books *Answer* and *Night and Day.* Mira's face-lift and the attack on her by Mihajlo Popovic is taken from Slavoljub Djukic, *On, Ona i Mi.*

## 9 The Most Expensive Cease-fire in History

On Bosnia's internal conditions and the causes of the internecine war, see Chuck Sudetic, *Blood and Vengeance,* W. W. Norton, 1998, and David Rohde, *Endgame. The Betrayal and Fall of Srebrenica: Europe's Worst Massacre Since World War II,* Farrar, Straus & Giroux, 1997. See also Susan L. Woodward's, "Bosnia After Dayton: Transforming a Compromise into a State," in Robert L. Rothstein, ed., *After the Peace,* Lynne Rienner Publishers, Boulder, 1999. For a detailed account of diplomatic maneuvering before and after Dayton, see Susan L. Woodward, *Balkan Tragedy: Chaos and Dissolution After the Cold War,* Brookings Institution, Washington, 1995. Robert Frasure's comments on his talks with Milosevic were made in an interview with the authors. For details about Madeleine Albright's attitude and policies toward Milosevic and Serbia, see Michael Dobbs, *Madeleine Albright: A Twentieth Century Odyssey,* Henry Holt, 1999; also see Jane Perlez, "An Embattled Albright Tries to Fend Off Her Critics," in *The New York Times,* April 9, 1999. Vice President Gore's remarks reported by Bob Woodward, *The Choice,* Simon & Schuster, 1996, p. 262. Kontic's reaction to the fall of Krajina are taking from Slavoljub Djukic, *On, Ona i Mi.* Details of diplomatic dealings and military moves leading up to the Dayton peace conference are described by Richard Holbrooke, *To End a War,* Random House, 1998, pp. 73, 106, 149–150. Borisav Jovic's comments in personnel changes appeared in *NIN,* November 17, 1995. Kosta Cavoski's remarks to student demonstrators in Novi Sad are taken from Djukic's *On, Ona i Mi.* Milosevic's election as president of Yugoslavia, the *Baltimore Sun,* July 16, 1997.

## 10 The High Priest of Chaos

On the election of Milan Milutinovic as Serbia's president, see Tracy Wilkinson, in the *Los Angeles Times,* December 23, 1997. On the general situation in the former Yugoslavia, see *Unfinished Peace,* a report of the International Commission on the Balkans, Aspen Institute/Carnegie Endowment for International Peace, 1996. Sali Berisha's remarks were reported by Reuter news agency from Tirana on December 27, 1966. General Wesley Clark's conversation with Milosevic is taken from R. Jeffrey Smith, *The Washington Post,* March 24, 1999. Also see Roger Cohen, "Milosevic's Vision of Glory Unleashed Decade of Ruin," *The New York Times,* July 2, 1999; and see Georgie Anne Geyer, "Center Stage Syndrome," in the *Washington Times,* June 6, 1999. On the show of Western air power, see the *Boston Globe,* June 12, 1998; for Albright's comments on the role of the United Nations in Kosovo, see the *Boston Globe,* June 14, 1998. For Milosevic's visit to Moscow, the *Boston Globe,* June 17, 1998. Rugova's appeal to NATO in the *Boston Globe,* June 20, 1998. Rugova's talks with Milosevic were mediated by Monsignor Paglia of the Sant'Edigo community, the Vatican diplomat. For details about internal disputes within the Kosovo Liberation Army's leadership, see Adem Demaqi's interview in *Vreme,* June 26, 1999. General Momcilo Perisic's comments are taken from *NIN,* July 21, 1999. For a more detailed study of the Albanian problem in Macedonia and a 1992 unilateral ethnic Albanian referendum for the autonomy of the western part of Macedonia, which they called Illyrida, see Sabrina Petra Ramet, "All Quiet on the Southern Front: Macedonia Between the Hammer and the Anvil," *Problems of Post-Communism,* November–December 1995.

## 11 The End of the Caravan of Dreams

On the public attitude in Serbia toward the bombing, see Michael Dobbs, "Sympathy to Yugoslav Chief," in the *Washington Post,* March 30, 1999: also see Michael Dobbs, "The War of the Airwaves," in the *Washington Post,* April 19, 1999. Draskovic's statements are reported in *The New York Times,* April 29, 1999. On the situation in Kosovo during the war, see Michael Dobbs, "Serbs Rule Kosovo Vacant Villages," in the *Washington Post,* April 17, 1999. Rugova's departure for Italy was reported by the Yugoslav agency Beta from Rome, May 6, 1999. Arnaud de Borchgrave's interview with Milosevic is in the *Washington Times,* May 1, 1999. On high Yugoslav officials conceding miscalculations, see Arnaud de Borchgrave in the *Washington Times,* June 11, 1999. On Chernomyrdin's dealings with U.S. officials, see *The New York Times,* June 6, 1999; also Blaine Harden, *The New York Times,* May 9, 1999. For details about an Anglo-British plan for a massive ground invasion of Kosovo, see Patrick Wintour, "U.S., Britain Planned Invasion," in the London *Observer,* July 18, 1999. Also see David R. Sands, "Russia in Line for More Aid from IMF," in the *Washington Times,* July 19, 1999.

The text of the Kosovo peace plan was reported by the Associated Press on June 3, 1999. Yugoslav reactions are reflected in *Politika,* June 4, 1999. Michael Dobbs and Daniel Williams, "Milosevic Still Angling for Last Minute Concessions," in the *Washington Post,* June 8, 1999. On limited damage NATO bombings inflicted on Milosevic's forces, see Steven Lee Myers, "Damage to Serb Military Less Than Expected," *The New York Times,* June 28, 1999. General Momcilo Perisic's remarks are taken from *VIP,* Belgrade, July 22, 1999. On the maneuverings of the Serbian opposition, see Steven Erlanger, "Foe Suggests Giving Milosevic Immunity to Get Him to Quit," in *The New York Times,* July 18, 1999; also "Serb Opposition Leader Criticized NATO Force in Kosovo," in *The New York Times,* July 25, 1999. Aleksa Djilas's remarks were taken from "Belgrade Targets Find Unity 'From Heaven,'" in *The New York Times,* March 30, 1999. Aleksandar Tijanic, "Deset Krvavih Godina," a pamphlet circulating in Belgrade.

# INDEX